The Wild Wild West Cookbook

Cuisine from the Land of Cactus and Cowboys

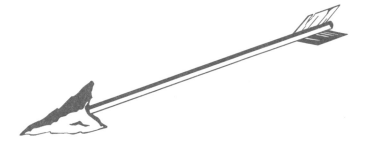

Published by The Junior League of Odessa, Inc.
Odessa, Texas

The purpose of the Junior League is exclusively educational and charitable and is to promote volunteerism; to develop the potential of its members for voluntary participation in community affairs; and to demonstrate the effectiveness of trained volunteers.

Money raised by the sale of THE WILD WILD WEST Cookbook furthers the purpose and projects of the Junior League of Odessa, Inc.

For additional copies, use the order forms at the back of this book or send a check for $19.95 plus $3.50 shipping and handling (Texas residents add $1.65 sales tax) to:

THE WILD WILD WEST COOKBOOK
The Junior League of Odessa, Inc.
2707 Kermit Highway
Odessa, Texas 79764
915/332-0095
1-800-299-WILD

Original Illustrations by Tim O'Reilly
Layout and Design by Womack-Kleypas Advertising Network, Odessa, Texas

Library of Congress catalog card number 90-63827

ISBN 0-9612508-1-X

First Edition
First Printing: 10,000 copies June 1991
Second Printing: 20,000 copies August 1991
Third Printing: 20,000 copies 1994

Favorite Recipes® Press
P.O. Box 305142
Nashville, Tennessee 37230
1-800-358-0560

Introduction

The Cowboy . . .
He is bigger than life; a living legend; the restless mascot of the West. He has rustled cattle, tamed mustangs and settled the Plains. He has romanced the hearts of all Americans for over two centuries.

The cowboy story began out of necessity as Christopher Columbus brought over the first small herd of cattle and horses. His adventures became entertainment as he pioneered his way through America. Cowboy stories, true and untrue, have been told and retold. Tales that began around a campfire over a hot pot of strong coffee soon came to life on the silver screen.

People from the East to the West were able to experience life on the Western frontier at the picture show. They saw tough buck-a-roos dressed in ten gallon hats, pointed boots and silver spurs whooping it up in everything from rodeos to shoot-outs. At night, cowboys gathered under the starry sky around a warm campfire. They would eat a hearty meal and share their day's experiences with family and friends. The movies portrayed the cowboy's days as an endless adventure and their nights as beautifully romantic. This popular image of the cowboy has become a part of Western heritage.

The cowboy legend has been celebrated in many ways since it began at the box office. The still life, of a cowboy in motion, may be found on lunch boxes, fabrics, lamp shades, wall paper, etc. Most of these products, antique or not, have become collector's items.

Westerners, proud of their heritage, still have some good ol' hoe-downs. There is nothing like putttin' on a pair of boots, meetin' friends and eatin' some good food.

THE WILD WILD WEST continues to celebrate the legendary cowboy through food, fun and art.

Enjoy the Adventure of THE WILD WILD WEST!

Cookbook Committee

Cookbook Chairs Melinda Powell Betsy Triplett	*Editors* Dayna Hayes Betsy Triplett	*Creative Director* Melinda Powell

Writing Team Dayna Hayes Melinda Powell Betsy Triplett	*Research Team* Janet Anderson Kim Barcena Belinda Brock Katy Graves Dayna Hayes Melinda Powell Betsy Triplett	*Marketing/Publicity Team* Katy Graves Ann Kennedy Sharon Michie

Secretary Belinda Brock	*Treasurers* Kim Barcena Susan Luskey Suzie Sims	*Shift Coordinator* Glenda Schneider

Section Coordinators

Appetizers/Brunch — Dayna Hayes Soups — Katy Graves
Salads — Glenda Schneider Main Dishes — Kim Barcena
Breads/Beverages — Betsy Triplett Cakes/Cookies/Muffins — Melinda Powell
Side Dishes— Sharon Michie Candy/Pies/Ice Cream — Belinda Brock

Advisors

Janie Howell
Gerri Lu McAdams
Cindi Wiehle

Special Thanks

The Cookbook Committee gives thanks to the following special people for their support:
Andy Anderson, Edward Barcena, Michael Brock, Martin Graves, Tony Hayes,
Glenn Kennedy, Earl Michie, Brad Powell and Robert Schneider.

The Foreword

The Junior League of Odessa, Inc. is a group of volunteers who have accomplished many wonderful things for our community. Through the years, The League has begun or helped with Teen Court, Hospice of Odessa, Odessa Abused Children's Shelter, Ronald McDonald House, LitterBuster's Time Machine Recycling Center, as well as the multifaceted Child's Play, Children's Symphony Concerts, Odessa Day Nursery, Salvation Army Toy Tea and many other projects.

The Cookbook Committee of the Junior League of Odessa is a Ways and Means Committee charged with raising money to be used on various projects. The practical purpose of this book is to raise money. To produce this cookbook, the Committee gathered over 1,100 recipes from West Texas cooks, categorized and organized the testing of each recipe, selected the highest rated recipes, then put them into what you will use. But after working on it for two years, the Cookbook Committee has more than financial aspirations connected with THE WILD WILD WEST.

This book means many different things to each Committee Member: Katy hopes that we have produced a fun book that you will have fun reading while cooking. For Belinda, testing recipes and working on the book was another family project that she, her husband and son enjoyed doing. She hopes your family will cook these recipes together, too. Ann hopes it conveys to you a taste of West Texas and West Texans. Dayna found serving as co-editor to be very time consuming, but extremely rewarding. As a transplanted Texan, she believes the cookbook portrays the true spirit of the Wild West and wishes everyone 'bon appetít from the land of mesquite'. Melinda hopes you will enjoy reading the book and will find what will become your favorite recipes. She believes each cookbook has its own personality. Betsy enjoyed learning about the personalities of the League members who submitted and tested recipes by reading the personal comments written about each one.

After reading and editing each recipe, the Committee found the one ingredient that is not listed, but obviously is in each recipe, is Love. The Love of family, cooking and sharing is expressed so many times in so many ways. And that is what makes all of these recipes so special. It is the sincere wish of THE WILD WILD WEST Cookbook Committee that you enjoy using this book as much as we enjoyed making it for you.

Sincerely,
The Cookbook Committee

Table of Contents

LONE STAR FONDUE
A bread pot filled with ham and cheese fondue.

1	round, firm loaf of bread (1 ½ pounds, 8-10 inches in diameter)	1	8 ounce package cream cheese, softened
2	tablespoons vegetable oil	1	cup ham, diced & cooked (3 ounces)
1	tablespoon butter, melted	½	cup green onions, chopped
1 ½	cups sour cream	1	4 ounce can green chilies, drained & chopped
8	ounces sharp Cheddar cheese, grated	1	teaspoon Worcestershire sauce

Slice off the top of the bread and set aside. Hollow out the insides with a small paring knife, leaving a half inch shell. Cut removed bread into 1 inch cubes. You should have about 4 cups. In a large skillet, combine oil and butter. Add the bread cubes and stir until thoroughly coated. Place on a cookie sheet.

Bake in a preheated 350° oven for 10-15 minutes turning occasionally, until golden brown. Remove from oven and reserve to serve with fondue.

To prepare fondue: In a large bowl, combine sour cream, Cheddar and cream cheeses. Stir in ham, green onions, chilies, and Worcestershire sauce. Spoon cheese into hollowed bread, filling it. Replace the top of bread. Wrap loaf of filled bread with several layers of heavy-duty aluminum foil. Set loaf on a cookie sheet. Bake in a preheated 350° oven for 1 hour and 10 minutes or until cheese filling is melted and heated through. When bread is done remove the wrap and place on a serving dish with the bread cubes placed around it for dipping.

Prep. Time: 1 hour.

STERLING SPINACH DIP

1	10 ounce package frozen spinach, thawed & chopped , drained by squeezing with your hands	1	package dry onion soup
1	8 ounce carton sour cream	1	8 ounce can water chestnuts, drained & chopped

In a medium bowl, mix all the above ingredients until well mixed. Refrigerate overnight (or at least a couple hours). Serve with crackers or chips.

Prep. Time: 15 minutes.
Refrigerating Time: 2 to 12 hours.

Hint: *For a variation add 1 package dry vegetable soup (omit the dry onion soup) and 1 cup mayonnaise.*

BLACK-EYED PEAS DIP

Brings good luck on New Year's Day.

4	16 ounce cans black-eyed peas, cooked & drained	1	4 ounce can green chilies, chopped
5	pickled jalapeños, chopped	1	clove garlic, finely minced
1	tablespoon pickled jalapeño juice	½	pound sharp Cheddar cheese, grated
½	medium onion, chopped	½	pound butter

B lend the first six ingredients in a blender. Heat cheese and butter in the microwave (or a double broiler) until melted. Stir in black-eyed pea mixture and pour into a chafing dish. Serve hot with corn chips for dipping. *Makes 16-20 servings.*

Prep. Time: 15 minutes.

BACON CHEDDAR DIP

4	ounces cream cheese, softened	⅛	teaspoon chili powder
½	cup Cheddar cheese, grated	2	tablespoons bacon pieces

I n a small bowl, combine first three ingredients and mix well. Stir in bacon pieces. Serve with vegetables or chips for dipping.

Prep. Time: 15 minutes.

VEGETABLE DIP

2	8 ounce packages cream cheese, softened	¾	cup green pepper, chopped
1	cup mayonnaise (not salad dressing)	¾	cup red onion, chopped
1	8 ounce carton sour cream	1	4 ounce can green chilies, chopped
1	3 ounce jar real bacon bits	1	4 ounce can black olives, chopped
			lemon juice to taste

I n a medium bowl, combine cream cheese, mayonnaise, and sour cream. Add remaining ingredients and mix well. Refrigerate until needed. Serve with a variety of vegetables for dipping.

Prep. Time: 15 minutes.

QUICK SHOT FRUIT DIP

1	8 ounce package cream cheese, softened	1	7 ounce jar marshmallow cream

In a small bowl, combine cream cheese and marshmallow cream until thoroughly mixed. Refrigerate until needed. Serve with fresh fruit and cookies for dipping.

Prep. Time: 10 minutes.

Hint: For a variation add 1 tablespoon fresh grated orange rind and ½ teaspoon ginger.

TEXAS TUMBLEWEED DIP
A hot broccoli dip.

1	10 ounce package broccoli, chopped	½	cup celery, chopped
3	tablespoons butter	1	can cream of mushroom soup
½	cup fresh mushrooms, chopped	1	6 ounce roll garlic cheese
½	cup yellow onion, chopped		

In the microwave, in a 1 quart casserole dish, cook broccoli. Spread it out on a paper towel to drain. In same casserole dish, place butter, mushrooms, onion and celery. Microwave until vegetables are tender. Stir in broccoli, soup and cheese. Continue to microwave, stirring occasionally, until cheese is melted and hot. Pour into a chafing dish and serve with chips for dipping.

Prep. Time: 15 minutes.

HOT ARTICHOKE DIP
Wonderful on a cold snowy night.

1	cup Parmesan cheese	1	cup mayonnaise
1	cup artichoke hearts, quartered & drained		paprika

In a medium bowl, combine the first three ingredients and pour into a 1 quart casserole dish. Sprinkle paprika on top. In a preheated 350° oven, bake for 1 hour. Serve with crackers for dipping.

Prep. Time: 10 minutes.

CUCUMBER CHIVE DIP

½	small cucumber	1	tablespoon chives, finely minced
4	ounces cream cheese, softened		dash of garlic powder

Peel cucumber and cut in half lengthwise. Remove seeds, then shred it. Add all other ingredients and mix well. Garnish with chive stems or dill if desired. Refrigerate until needed. Serve with assorted vegetables and crackers for dipping.

Prep. Time: 15 minutes.

CREAMY CACTUS DIP

A dilly of a dip.

8	ounces cream cheese, softened	1-2	tablespoons dill weed
8	ounces sour cream	1-2	tablespoons onion, finely minced
1	cup mayonnaise		

Combine all the above ingredients mixing well. Cover and place in the refrigerator for 4 hours to allow the flavors to blend. Serve with chips or vegetables for dipping.

Prep. Time: 10 minutes.
Refrigerating Time: 4 hours.

GREEN ONION DIP

6	ounces cream cheese, softened	2	teaspoons salt
1	cup mayonnaise	½	teaspoon garlic powder
1	cup sour cream	½	cup green onion stems, finely chopped
2	tablespoons lemon juice	⅔	cup fresh parsley, finely chopped
4	tablespoons tarragon vinegar		

In medium bowl, combine all ingredients, mixing well. Cover bowl and place in refrigerator for 3 hours to allow flavors to blend. Serve with vegetables or chips for dipping.

Prep. Time: 10 minutes.
Refrigerating Time: 3 hours.

COLD CHEESE AND OLIVE DIP

You don't have to worry about keeping this dip hot.

1	pound processed cheese	1	cup pecans, chopped
1	12 ounce can evaporated milk	1	cup mayonnaise (not salad dressing)
½-1	cup green olives, chopped	1	small onion, chopped

In a double broiler, heat cheese and milk until cheese is melted. Cool to room temperature. Add remaining ingredients, stirring well. Refrigerate until chilled. Can be frozen until needed. Serve with tortilla chips or vegetables for dipping. *Makes 3 pints.*

Prep. Time: 1 hour.

SHRIMP DIP

¾	cup margarine, softened	1	tablespoon onion, dehydrated & minced
4	tablespoons mayonnaise	4	tablespoons lemon juice
8	ounces cream cheese, softened	2	4.5 ounce cans shrimp, drained

Mix all ingredients except shrimp. Do not worry if it is lumpy. Stir in shrimp. Refrigerate for at least 24 hours. Serve with whole-wheat crackers. *Makes 12 servings.*

Prep. Time: 15 minutes.
Refrigerating Time: 24 hours.

CURRIED SHRIMP DIP

2	4.5 ounce cans shrimp, drained & chopped	½	teaspoon Worcestershire sauce
¾	cup celery, chopped	½	teaspoon salt
½	cup mayonnaise	¼	teaspoon curry powder
1	tablespoon lemon juice	¾	teaspoon onion, minced

In a medium bowl, mix all the above ingredients. Refrigerate overnight. Serve with crackers.

Prep. Time: 20 minutes.
Refrigerating Time: Overnight.

CLAM DIP

1	can clams, minced	2	teaspoons onion, finely chopped
3	ounces cream cheese, softened	1	teaspoon Worcestershire sauce
2	tablespoons mayonnaise		dash of Tabasco sauce

Drain the clams reserving 2 teaspoons of liquid. With a mixer, blend the clams, 2 teaspoons of clam juice, cream cheese and mayonnaise. Stir in all remaining ingredients. Cover and refrigerate overnight to allow flavors to blend. Serve with chips for dipping.

Prep. Time: 10 minutes.
Refrigerating Time: Overnight.

HOT CRAB DIP
A microwave is a must to make this easy dip.

1	8 ounce package cream cheese, softened	1	clove garlic, finely minced
1	6 ounce can flaked crabmeat, drained	¼	cup mayonnaise
		1	teaspoon prepared mustard

Combine all ingredients in a medium microwave safe bowl. Cover with a paper towel because the cheese tends to "spit". Microwave on high for 2 minutes and stir. Microwave on high for 2 more minutes and stir again. Serve with crackers.

Prep. Time: 5 minutes.

WARM CHIP BEEF DIP

1	8 ounce package cream cheese, softened	½	teaspoon garlic powder
2	tablespoons milk	½	cup pecans, chopped
5	ounces dried wafer thin beef, chopped	2	tablespoons margarine, melted

In a medium bowl, combine cream cheese, milk, beef and garlic powder. Pour this into a 9 inch pie pan. In another bowl, combine the remaining ingredients and pour this on top of beef mixture. Bake in a preheated 350° oven for 20 minutes. Serve with corn chips for dipping.

Prep. Time: 10 minutes.

CATTLE RUSTLER'S DIP
A deviled ham dip.

1	4.5 ounce can deviled ham	2	tablespoons salad dressing or mayonnaise
1	5 ounce jar pimento cheese		Worcestershire sauce, to taste

Combine all above ingredients. Cover and refrigerate for 2 hours. Serve with corn chips for dipping.

Prep. Time: 10 minutes.
Refrigerating Time: 2 hours.

MEXICAN CHIHUAHUA DIP

4-5	large tomatoes, chopped	2	fresh jalapeños, seeded & finely chopped
1 ½	bunch green onions, chopped with tops	1 ½	tablespoons olive oil
1	4 ounce can mushrooms, drained & chopped		juice of one lime
1	4 ounce can black olives, drained & chopped		salt, to taste

In a large bowl, combine all the above ingredients and mix well. Cover and refrigerate overnight. Serve with tortillas or chips for dipping.

Prep. Time: 20 minutes.
Refrigerating Time: Overnight.

HOT BEAN DIP

Hot to touch, not to taste.

½	pound ground beef	1	tablespoon chili
¼	cup onion, chopped		powder
¼	cup green pepper, chopped	1	16 ounce can refried beans
1	8 ounce can tomato sauce	1	8 ounce carton sour cream
1	package dry taco seasoning	½	cup Cheddar cheese, finely grated
1	teaspoon dry mustard		chili powder

In a medium saucepan, brown the ground beef, onion and green pepper. Drain off excess fat. Stir in tomato sauce, taco seasoning, dry mustard, and chili powder mixing well. Carefully stir in refried beans. Heat over a medium heat, stirring constantly, until hot and bubbly. Pour into an 8 inch pie pan. In a small bowl, combine sour cream and Cheddar cheese. Carefully spoon sour cream mixture on top of meat mixture until it is completely covered. Lightly sprinkle chili powder on top. Serve with corn chips for dipping.

Prep. Time: 40 minutes.

TENDERFOOT QUESO (MILD)

2	pounds processed cheese	2	4 ounce cans green chilies, chopped
2-4	cloves garlic, finely minced	3	ripe tomatoes, chopped
2	large yellow onions, chopped		

In a double boiler, melt cheese. Stir in all other ingredients. Heat until thoroughly warmed. Serve warm. Serve with tortilla chips for dipping.

Prep. Time: 30 minutes.

CHILI CON QUESO WITH SAUSAGE

1	pound bulk sausage	1 ½	cups mushrooms, chopped
1	onion, chopped		
1	10 ounce can tomatoes with green chilies, diced	2	pounds processed cheese

In a large skillet, brown sausage and onions. Drain off excess fat. Place in a double boiler and add all other ingredients. Heat until cheese is thoroughly melted. Serve warm with tortilla chips for dipping.

Prep. Time: 30 minutes.

SOUTH OF THE BORDER QUESO

This is good with many Mexican dishes.

1	cup tomatoes, chopped		water
½	cup onion, chopped	1-2	cups Cheddar cheese, grated
1	4 ounce can green chilies, chopped		

In a medium saucepan combine tomatoes, onion, and green chilies. Add enough water to cover tomatoes. Simmer about 1 hour or until onion is translucent, then drain. Add cheese and heat until melted. Pour into a chafing dish and serve with tortilla chips for dipping.

Prep. Time: 1½ hours.

SOMBRERO DIP

A great party dip. Not only does it taste terrific, but it looks terrific too!

1	pound ground beef	2	bunches green onions, chopped
1	small onion, chopped		
	cumin, to taste	2	4.5 ounce cans black olives, drained & chopped
	garlic powder, to taste		
1	14 ounce bottle hot ketchup		sharp Cheddar cheese
1	16 ounce can refried beans		

In a large skillet, brown ground beef and onions. Drain. Stir in cumin and garlic powder. Next add ketchup, stirring well. Finally, add refried beans. Heat until warm. Pour into a chafing dish. In the middle of the beef and beans mixture, place the chopped green onions to form a 3 inch circle. Next to the green onions, place the chopped olive to form a 3 inch ring around the onions. Fill in the rest of the dish with the Cheddar cheese. This should form 3 rings to give the effect of a sombrero. Serve with tortilla chips for dipping.

Prep. Time: 1 hour.

MUY DELICIOSO SALSA

This never stays around the house for long.

3	large fresh tomatoes, chopped & peeled	1	teaspoon salt
1	large red onion, chopped	1	16 ounce or larger jar Pace picante sauce
1	teaspoon fresh garlic, finely minced		

In a large bowl, combine all the above ingredients. Store in a covered container and refrigerate. This can be eaten immediately; however, it is best if stored for 3 days (if you can resist the temptation). Stores for up to 2 weeks in the refrigerator. Serve with tortilla chips for dipping.

Prep. Time: 30 minutes.
Marinating Time: Overnight.

GUACAMOLE DIP

Holy molé, this is good guacamole!

6	ripe avocados	1	tablespoon lemon juice
½	cup picante sauce (more if desired)	1	tomato, chopped & drained (optional)
½	cup sour cream		
½	teaspoon garlic salt		

Mash avocados with a fork. Stir in picante sauce, sour cream, garlic salt and lemon juice. Place mixture in a blender or food processor and purée. Stir in chopped tomatoes by hand. Refrigerate until needed. Serve with tortilla chips for dipping or serve with fajitas (see Main Dishes, page 138).

Prep. Time: 10 minutes.

PICADILLO

2	cups onions, chopped	1	apple, peeled, cored & chopped
2	tablespoons butter or margarine	1	jalapeño pepper, remove seeds & chop
3	pounds ground beef	½	cup chili sauce
2	tablespoons flour	4	stalks celery with leaves, chopped
3	tablespoons chili powder	1	cup raisins
½	teaspoon cardamom seeds, crushed	1	cup seedless grapes, chopped
2	cans beef consommé		
1	green pepper, chopped	salt & pepper, to taste	
1	small can crushed pineapple, drained	1	large potato, peeled & chopped

In a large Dutch oven, combine onions and butter. Cook until the onions are tender. Crumble ground beef into the cooked onions. Cook until beef is lightly browned. Sprinkle flour on top of beef and stir. Continue cooking a little longer. Drain off excess fat. Add remaining ingredients except for potato. Cover and simmer for 1 hour. Add potato. Cover and simmer another hour. Serve with corn or tortilla chips for dipping.

Prep. Time: 2 ½ hours.

MEXICAN LAYERED DIP

2	9 ounce cans bean dip with jalapeños	2	cups lettuce, shredded
1	cup sour cream	3	medium tomatoes, seeded & chopped
½	cup salad dressing	1	cup green onions with tops, chopped
1	package taco seasoning mix	1	4 ounce can black olives, sliced
3	medium avocados	1	cup Cheddar cheese, grated
½	medium lemon, juiced		pickled jalapeños, sliced
⅛	teaspoon salt		
⅛	teaspoon pepper		

S pread bean dip on large platter. Blend sour cream, salad dressing and taco seasoning. Spread on top of bean dip. Mash peeled and seeded avocados with lemon juice, salt and pepper. Spread avocado mixture over sour cream layer. Place lettuce over the avocado layer and sprinkle with tomatoes, green onions and black olives. Cover with grated cheese. Randomly place pickled jalapeños on top of cheese. Chill well and serve with tortilla chips or crackers.

Prep. Time: 10 minutes.
Refrigerating Time: At least 30 minutes.

PICO DE GALLO

Fresh tomato garnish.

4	firm pink tomatoes, chopped	1-2	teaspoons sugar
1	red onion, chopped	1	tablespoon chili powder
3	jalapeño peppers, seeds removed & chopped	½	teaspoon salt (optional)
2	cloves garlic, finely minced	3	tablespoons fresh cilantro, chopped
2	teaspoons wine vinegar		

I n a medium bowl, combine all the above ingredients. Pour into a container with an airtight lid. Refrigerate until needed. Serve with tortilla chips, fajitas (see Main Dishes, page 138), or many other Mexican dishes. *Makes 4 servings.*

Prep. Time: 20 to 30 minutes.

MEXICAN–STYLE CREAM CHEESE DIP

8	ounces cream cheese, softened	¼	cup picante sauce (more if desired)
			juice of ½ lime

P lace all the above ingredients in a food processor. Process until thoroughly blended. Refrigerate until it has hardened. Serve with corn chips for dipping.

Prep. Time: 5 minutes.
Refrigerating Time: 30 minutes.

QUESADILLA

1	burrito-sized flour tortilla	1	teaspoon green chilies, chopped
4	tablespoons Cheddar cheese, grated	1	green onion, including tops, chopped
4	tablespoons Monterey-Jack cheese, grated		

Spread cheeses evenly on half of the flour tortilla. Top with green chilies and green onion. Fold the tortilla in half and place on an ungreased cookie sheet. Bake in a preheated 350° oven, turning once, until both sides of the tortilla are browned and cheese is melted. Cut into wedge shapes and serve with picante sauce, sour cream, and guacamole for dipping. *Makes 1 serving.*

Prep. Time: 15 minutes.

MEXICAN MAGIC

Cheesy nut squares.

| 2 | pounds processed Mexican-style cheese | 5 | tablespoons Tabasco sauce |
| | | 1 | cup nuts, chopped |

In a microwave safe pan, microwave the cheese until melted. Stir in the remaining ingredients. Spray an 8 x 8 inch pan with a non-stick cooking spray. Pour the cheese mixture into the pan. Cover and let harden. Cut into squares.

Prep. Time: 1 hour.

MEXICAN PINWHEELS

It is easy to eat one after another!

3	8 ounce packages cream cheese, softened	1	4 ounce can black olives, drained & chopped
1	8 ounce carton sour cream	½	cup chives, chopped juice of one lime
½	teaspoon garlic powder	¼	cup picante sauce
1	4 ounce can green chilies, chopped	36	taco-sized flour tortillas

In a medium bowl, combine the first eight ingredients. Divide among 36 flour tortillas and spread out. Roll tortillas into logs and refrigerate overnight. (It is best if they are refrigerated overnight; but, if you do not have that long, at least refrigerate them for a few hours to help them hold together better.) To serve, slice logs into bite-sized pieces. These freeze well. Serve with more picante sauce for dipping.

Prep. Time: 30 minutes.
Refrigerating Time: 2 to 12 hours.

TOSTADO CHIPS

12	corn tortillas		salt, to taste (optional)

enough lard to be 1 inch
    deep when melted

Cut the tortillas into fourths. Set aside. Melt the lard so it is hot enough that it is almost smoking. Place 4 tortillas in the skillet at a time. Cook both sides by either turning the tortillas over or submerging them below the surface. Cook for 2 or 3 minutes, until they begin to darken. Drain on paper towels. Sprinkle salt on tostados while they are still hot.

Prep. Time: 15 minutes.

FRIED STUFFED JALAPEÑOS
A snack for the true cowboy.

24	fresh or canned jalapeño peppers	1	12 ounce bottle of a Texas-style beer
½	cup yellow cornmeal		oil for frying
1	cup flour	4	ounces Cheddar or Monterey-Jack cheese, grated
1	teaspoon baking powder		
½	teaspoon salt	½	cup flour
1	tablespoon oil		

Cut each pepper, making a small slit. (If your skin is sensitive to jalapeño oil, wear thin plastic gloves.) Remove the seeds. Carefully wash them keeping the peppers intact. Place on a paper towel to drain. Meanwhile, in a small bowl, combine cornmeal, 1 cup flour, baking powder and salt. Add 8 ounces of beer (the other 4 ounces is for the cook). Mix in 1 tablespoon oil. Let stand for 15 minutes. Pour 3 inches of oil in a large skillet and heat to 350° (a medium heat). Carefully stuff each pepper with cheese. Roll it in the flour and then dip in the batter. Place it in hot oil and fry until brown on all sides, 1 to 2 minutes. Place on a paper towel to drain. *Makes 24 peppers.*

Prep. Time: 30 minutes.

ARTICHOKE CHEESE SQUARES
Serve warm.

1/3	cup onion, chopped	1/4	cup dry bread crumbs
1	clove garlic, finely mashed or 1/8 teaspoon garlic powder	1/2	pound Swiss cheese, grated
2	tablespoons bacon fat	2	tablespoons parsley, minced
4	eggs, beaten until frothy	1/2	teaspoon salt
1	14 ounce jar artichoke hearts, drained & chopped	1/4	teaspoon oregano
		1/8	teaspoon Tabasco sauce

Sauté onion and garlic in bacon fat. Add the remaining ingredients and mix well. Pour into a greased 7 x 11 inch baking dish. Bake in a preheated 325° oven for 25 to 30 minutes. Cut into 1 inch squares. *Makes 77 squares.*

Prep. Time: 20 minutes.

SPICY CHEESE FINGERS
Keep in the freezer for drop-in guests.

3	5 ounce jars Old English cheese, softened	3/4	teaspoon dill weed
1/2	cup margarine or butter, softened	1	teaspoon Worcestershire sauce
1/2	teaspoon Tabasco sauce	1	4 ounce jar green chilies, chopped & drained
1/2	teaspoon onion powder		dash of cayenne pepper (optional)
1/2	teaspoon beau monde powder		thinly sliced white bread

In a medium bowl, combine all ingredients except the bread. Mix well. Spread some of the cheese mixture over three slices of bread. Place the bread in a stack. Repeat this until all the cheese mixture is used. Cut each stack into quarters. Place on a cookie sheet and freeze. Once frozen, these can be moved to a large plastic bag. When ready to use, place on a cookie sheet. Bake in a preheated oven at 300° for 20 minutes. Do not thaw before baking. *Makes 60 squares.*

Prep. Time: 30 minutes.

JALAPEÑO CHEESE BITES

1-2	tablespoons butter	1	pound Cheddar cheese, grated
	jalapeño peppers (at least 8) fresh or in a jar, seeds removed	6	eggs, lightly beaten
		1 1/2	cups cooked rice

Use the butter to grease a 9 x 13 inch baking pan. Chop enough jalapeño peppers to cover the bottom of the pan and set aside. In a medium bowl, place the cheese and add the eggs stirring well. Stir in the cooked rice. Pour over the peppers. In a preheated 250° oven, bake for 1 hour. Allow to cool. Cut into 1 inch squares to serve. *Makes 117 squares.*

Prep. Time: 10 minutes.

Hint: To make a festive Christmas appetizer, add chopped pimento before baking.

CHILE CON QUESO MINI-QUICHE

½	cup tomato, chopped	1	teaspoon chili powder
¼	cup green onion, finely chopped	½	teaspoon cumin, ground
1	clove garlic, minced	⅛	teaspoon cayenne pepper
4	eggs, beaten	1	4 ounce can green chilies, rinsed, drained, & chopped
2	ounces Cheddar cheese, grated		
2	ounces Monterey-Jack cheese with jalapeño peppers, grated		Additional whole green chilies, sliced (optional)

Spray a non-stick skillet with a non-stick cooking spray. Heat over medium-high heat until hot. Add tomato, green onions, garlic and sauté until onions are tender. Combine tomato mixture, eggs and stir well. Add the rest of ingredients except the whole green chilies and mix well. Spray miniature muffin pans with a non-stick cooking spray. Spoon 1 tablespoon of the mixture into the miniature muffin pans. Bake in a 425° preheated oven for 8 to 10 minutes or until centers are set. Remove from oven and let cool in pans for 1 minute. Loosen edges with a knife and remove from pans. Serve warm. Garnish with sliced chilies if desired. *Makes 30 mini-bites.*

Prep. Time: 20 to 30 minutes.

PEPPER PICK-UPS

6	ounces cream cheese	1 ½	teaspoons dried minced onions
8	ounces Cheddar cheese, grated	9	drops Tabasco sauce
3	tablespoons green chilies, chopped	2	8 ounce cans crescent rolls
2	tablespoons black olives, chopped		

Combine the first six ingredients mixing well. Open the crescent roll cans. Instead of tearing the crescent rolls apart in 16 triangles, press the middle seam together to form 8 squares. Divide the cheese mixture evenly among the crescent rolls. Spread the mixture out evenly on the rolls. Roll the crescent rolls up like logs so that the crescent roll is on the outside. Cut them in ½ inch slices. Place on a cookie sheet that has been sprayed with a non-stick cooking spray. Bake in a preheated 400° oven for 15 minutes or until the crescent rolls are brown. Serve warm. *Makes 80 rolls.*

Prep. Time: 15 minutes.

TEXAS TOASTIES

½	cup margarine	12	ounces Monterey-
1	4 ounce can green		Jack cheese, grated
	chilies, chopped		mayonnaise
1	large clove garlic,		(not salad dressing)
	finely minced (or		French bread, thinly sliced
	dried garlic)		

In a small bowl, combine margarine, green chilies and garlic. Mix well and set aside. In another bowl combine cheese and just enough mayonnaise to hold cheese together. On each slice of bread, spread a thin layer of the green chili mixture. On top of this, spread a thin layer of cheese and mayonnaise mixture. Place on an ungreased cookie sheet. Bake in a preheated 400° oven until lightly browned or toasty.

Prep. Time: 30 minutes.

For a variation, substitute:

8	ounces of fresh or	*Leave out:*	
	imitation crabmeat,	1	4 ounce can green
	finely minced		chilies, chopped
½	teaspoon curry	1	large clove garlic
	powder	12	ounces Monterey-
12	ounces Cheddar		Jack cheese, grated
	cheese, grated		
½	onion, finely grated		

On each slice of bread, spread a thin layer of margarine. In a food processor, combine the crab, curry powder, Cheddar cheese, onion and mayonnaise. Process until the crab mixture is spreadable. Spread this on the buttered bread. Place on a cookie sheet and bake in a preheated 400° oven until thoroughly browned and toasty.

SPINACH ROLLS

2	10 ounce packages	6	eggs, beaten
	frozen spinach,	¾	cup butter or
	cooked & drained		margarine, melted
2	8 ounce packages		salt & pepper, to taste
	plain stuffing mix		
1	cup Parmesan cheese,		
	grated		

In a large bowl, combine all ingredients mixing well. Break off pieces and roll them into 1 inch balls. Place in the freezer until needed. To serve, thaw out the desired portion needed. Place them on a cookie sheet. Bake in a preheated 350° oven for 12 to 15 minutes. *Makes 15 to 16 dozen.*

Prep. Time: 20 minutes.

PRAIRIE DOG FOOD

1	12 ounce package	½	cup margarine
	chocolate chips	1	13.3 ounce box
	(semi-sweet or sweet)		Crispix cereal
1	cup creamy or		powdered sugar
	crunchy peanut		
	butter		

In a double boiler combine the chocolate chips, peanut butter and margarine. Heat until melted. Pour over cereal and stir until totally coated. Place a few cupfuls at a time in a paper sack. Add powdered sugar and shake until coated. Repeat.

Prep. Time: 20 minutes.

PICKLED OKRA

8	cups vinegar	2	jalapeño peppers,
8	cups water		seeded &
1	cup salt		finely minced
1	teaspoon dill seed		fresh okra
2	cloves garlic,	10	pint jars
	finely minced		

I n a large saucepan, combine the vinegar, water and salt. Over a medium-high heat, bring to a boil and boil for 10 minutes. While boiling, wash the okra and remove the stems. Divide them among the 10 pint jars. Divide the dill, garlic and jalapeños among the 10 jars. Pour the hot mixture over the okra until totally covered. Seal. Store in a dark place for 3 weeks to allow to pickle. Chill before serving.

Prep. Time: 20 minutes
Pickling Time: 3 weeks.

DEVILED EGGS

2	dozen eggs,	¾	cup sandwich &
	hard-boiled		salad sauce
1	tablespoon mustard	½-1	cup salad dressing
½	teaspoon salt		paprika

S lice eggs in half. Place yolks in a blender. Add other ingredients except the salad dressing and blend. Slowly add salad dressing and blend until smooth and creamy. Be careful not to make this too thin. Spoon the yolk mixture back into the egg whites. Sprinkle paprika on top.

Prep. Time: 30 minutes.

PRAIRIE TOAST

Herb mix:		½	teaspoon onion
2	teaspoons salt		powder
2	teaspoons MSG		
2	teaspoons parsley		*Margarine mix:*
	flakes, dehydrated	½	cup margarine,
1	teaspoon garlic		melted
	powder	1-2	tablespoons herb mix
1	teaspoon black pepper		bread slices

M ix all the herb mix ingredients in a jar. Cover. Shake well to mix. Combine margarine with herb mix. With a pastry brush, spread margarine mixture over one side of bread slices. Stack slices and cut into strips. Place on ungreased cookie sheet. Bake in a preheated 150° oven for several hours (overnight) until dry and crisp. Goes great with dips, salads or soups.

Prep. Time: 20 minutes.

GOLDEN NUGGET VEGGIES

your favorite vegetables
2 *eggs, beaten*
1 *teaspoon salt*
½ *teaspoon black or cayenne pepper (optional)*
¼ *teaspoon garlic powder (optional)*
½ *cup milk*
1 *cup all-purpose flour*
1 *tablespoon shortening, melted*

Slice vegetables and place in refrigerator to chill. In a medium bowl, combine the remaining ingredients in the order they appear, mixing in between each until batter is smooth. When convenient, chill batter before using. Dip raw vegetables into batter, draining excess. Place in preheated oil, 1 piece at a time. Fry until golden brown. Remove from oil onto a paper towel to drain.

Prep. Time: 1 hour 15 minutes if batter is chilled, 15 minutes if not.

Note: For a variation, substitute ¼ cup flat beer for ¼ cup of the milk.

PHYLLO TRIANGLES

1 ¼ *pound Feta cheese, crumbled*
3 *ounces cream cheese, softened*
1 *egg*
dash of nutmeg
dash of white pepper
30 *pieces phyllo dough melted butter, not margarine*

Combine the first five ingredients. Mix until it forms a smooth paste. Cut phyllo dough into strips, 8 x 3 inches. Keep phyllo covered while not using to keep it from drying out. Brush a strip with butter. Fold in half lengthwise. Brush with butter again. Spoon ½ teaspoon of the cheese mixture on a corner. Fold the other corner over to form a triangle. Continue folding the corners over until you have a bite-sized triangle. Place on a cookie sheet, brush with butter, and chill for 30 minutes in the refrigerator. Place in a preheated 350° oven for 30 minutes or until lightly browned.

Prep. Time: 1½ hours.

WAGON WHEELS

Salty Texas-style pretzels.

1	¼ ounce package dry yeast	1	teaspoon sugar	
1 ½	cups lukewarm water (105 to 115°)	4	cups unbleached flour	
1	teaspoon salt	1	egg, beaten	
			margarita salt	

In a large mixing bowl, dissolve yeast in warm water. Stir in salt, sugar and 2 cups flour. Mix until smooth. Stir in remaining 2 cups flour to make dough easy to handle. Place dough on a lightly floured board and knead until dough is elastic and smooth. Place dough in a bowl that has been lightly greased and roll dough completely over to coat. Set in a warm place and allow dough to rise until double in size. Grease 2 cookie sheets. Punch dough down. Cut dough into 16 equal parts. Roll into 18 inch ropes. Form ropes into the shape of pretzels on the cookie sheets. Brush the pretzels with beaten eggs (cover them well because this is what will give them the brown shiny appearance). Sprinkle generously with margarita salt. Bake in a preheated 425° oven for 15 to 20 minutes or until golden brown. Serve with melted cheese for dipping. *Makes 16 pretzels.*

Prep. Time: 30 minutes,
           plus 1 to 2 hours for dough to rise.

BAKED BRIE

Easy and very elegant – a real winner!

12	celery leaves	1	round whole Brie or Camembert cheese (5 to 7 inches in diameter)	
1	cup boiling water			
1	frozen puffed pastry sheet, thawed	1	egg, slightly beaten	
			string	

Pour the boiling water over the celery leaves and allow to stand for 2 minutes. Drain and pat the celery dry. Roll the pastry out to ⅛ inch thick. Make sure it is large enough to wrap completely around the cheese. Place half of celery leaves in the middle of the pastry. Place the cheese on top of celery leaves. Top with remaining celery leaves. Pull the edges of the pastry up around the cheese. Secure the middle tightly with string. Drape edges over string to form a flower. Brush completely with beaten egg. Place on an ungreased cookie sheet. Bake in a preheated 400° oven until the pastry is golden brown, about 20 minutes. Remove from heat and let stand 15 minutes. Remove the string before serving. Cut into small wedges. *Makes 6 to 10 servings.*

Prep. Time: 25 minutes.

SUGAR–N–SPICED PECANS
Sugar 'n spice 'n everything nice.

1	cup brown sugar	1/4	cup water
1/8	teaspoon cream	1	teaspoon vanilla
	of tartar	2	cups pecans
1/2	teaspoon cinnamon		

In a saucepan, combine first four ingredients and heat to 250°. Let stand for 3 minutes. Stir in the vanilla and pecans. Spread out on wax paper and allow to dry.

Prep. Time: 30 minutes.

OVEN CARAMEL CORN

15	cups popped popcorn	1/4	cup light corn syrup
1	cup brown sugar, packed	1/2	teaspoon salt
1/2	cup margarine or butter	1/2	teaspoon baking soda

Divide the popcorn between two 9 x 13 x 2 inch pans. In a saucepan over a medium-high heat, combine the brown sugar, margarine, corn syrup and salt. Stirring constantly, heat until simmering. Cook an additional 5 minutes, stirring occasionally. Remove from heat and stir in the baking soda. Pour over the popcorn. Stir well until thoroughly coated. Bake in a preheated 200° oven for 1 hour, stirring every 15 minutes.

Prep. Time: 2 hours.

Hint: For a variation you may add 1 1/2 cups of walnuts, pecans or almonds to each pan. Just decrease the amount of popcorn to 12 cups.

MICROWAVE CARAMEL CORN
"Shake, rattle and pop."

1/4	cup light corn syrup	3	quarts popped
1/2	cup margarine		popcorn
1	cup brown sugar, packed		nuts, if desired
1/2	teaspoon baking soda		

Pop popcorn in microwave or hot air popper (no oil works best). Mix corn syrup, margarine (not butter), and brown sugar in a large bowl. In the microwave, bring to a boil, stir. Microwave 2 minutes on high power. Stir in baking soda. A large bowl is needed because if mixture boils over, it is a real mess!!! In a large paper bag, spray inside with a non-stick cooking spray. Pour in popcorn, nuts and caramel. Roll folded top down to seal. Shake hard. Microwave 1 1/2 minutes on high and shake. Again, microwave 1 1/2 minutes on high and shake. Microwave 30 seconds on high and shake. Microwave 20 seconds on high and shake. Pour onto a cookie sheet and cool.

Prep. Time: 10 minutes.

MARINATED CHEESE

1	16 ounce package Mozzarella cheese	1	tablespoon dried oregano, crushed
2	cups olive oil	1	tablespoon green peppercorns, crushed
1	medium bell pepper, seeds removed & cut in strips	1	teaspoon thyme, dried & crushed
¼	cup wine vinegar	2	cloves garlic, halved
1	tablespoon cayenne pepper		

Cut block of cheese into half inch cubes. Using a fork, randomly prick cheese to allow marinade to penetrate. Place cheese in a 1 quart container with a tight-fitting lid and set aside. In a small saucepan stir together the rest of the above ingredients. Cook and stir until thoroughly heated. Remove from heat and allow to cool. Pour mixture over cheese. Cover and shake gently. Store in the refrigerator, about 2 weeks. Using a slotted spoon, divide cheese and pepper strips among 3 decorative 1 cup containers. Pour marinade over cheese and peppers to cover. Cover, seal and label. Store in refrigerator 2 weeks before using. To serve, let stand at room temperature for 1 hour allowing the oil in the marinade to soften. Serve in salads, antipasto or on relish trays. Stores for up to 6 weeks in the refrigerator.

Prep. Time: 20 minutes.
Marinating Time: 4 weeks.

FANCY COCKTAIL TOMATOES

A beautiful dish for special occasions.

cherry tomatoes

Filling, one of the following:
guacamole
Roquefort cheese mixed with cognac & butter
yogurt mixed with grated cucumber & dill
smoked salmon mixed with cream cheese, Worcestershire sauce & chives
Ricotta cheese mixed with Italian dressing & chives
Cheddar cheese mixed with pimentos & mayonnaise
tuna or chicken mixed with cream cheese, chopped celery & onions

Hollow the tomatoes. Stuff them with one of the above fillings. Place on a platter and chill until ready to serve.

Prep. Time: 30 minutes.

STUFFED MUSHROOMS
Quick, fast and sinful.

24	large fresh mushrooms	4	ounces Mozzarella cheese, grated
2	tablespoons margarine	1/4	cup Parmesan cheese, grated
2	cloves garlic, finely minced	2	tablespoons fresh parsley, finely minced
8	ounces bulk hot sausage	1/4	cup margarine, melted
1/4	teaspoon thyme	2	tablespoons white wine or vermouth
1/4	teaspoon basil		fresh parsley
1/4	teaspoon savory		
1/4	teaspoon salt		
1/8	teaspoon cayenne pepper		
2	tablespoons seasoned bread crumbs		

Clean mushrooms and remove stems. Finely chop stems. Microwave, in a 4 cup bowl, margarine on high for about 30 seconds. Stir in chopped mushroom stems, garlic, and sausage and cover with waxed paper. Microwave on high for 5 minutes or until sausage is fully cooked, stir well. Drain off fat. Stir in thyme, basil, savory, salt, cayenne pepper, bread crumbs, cheeses and parsley. Spoon into mushroom caps. Place filled mushroom caps on 2 large glass plates with larger caps on the outer edge of plate. Brush each with the 1/4 cup melted margarine. Pour 1 tablespoon wine in center of each dish. Cover with plastic wrap and microwave each dish on high 2 minutes, rotating once. Serve warm and garnish with fresh parsley.

Prep. Time: 20 minutes.

EMPANADAS

1/2	pound ground beef	2	teaspoons chili powder
1/2	yellow onion, chopped	1/4	teaspoon Tabasco sauce
6	ounces Cheddar cheese	4	9 inch pie crusts
1/4	cup ketchup		

In a large skillet combine beef and onion. Over a medium-high heat cook until meat is brown. Drain off excess fat. Reduce heat. Stir in remaining ingredients and cook until cheese is melted. Roll out pastries. Cut round circles out of dough with a 2 1/2 inch cookie cutter. Spoon 1 heaping teaspoon of filling in center of each circle. Fold in half and seal the edges. Bake in a preheated 450° oven 10 to 12 minutes or until lightly brown turning once. *Makes 4 dozen empanadas.*

Prep. Time: 30 minutes.

ARMADILLO EGGS

This will leave your mouth a blazin'.

½	pound Monterey-Jack cheese, grated	15	fresh or canned jalapeño peppers (up to 20, if desired)
½	pound Cheddar cheese, grated	1	egg, beaten slightly
½	pound bulk hot sausage	1	package Shake N Bake for pork
1 ½	cups Bisquick		

In a large bowl, combine ¼ pound of Monterey-Jack cheese, ¼ pound Cheddar cheese, sausage and Bisquick. Mix well. Carefully, slit jalapeños and remove the seeds and stems. Do not rinse. Stuff each pepper with remaining cheeses. Pinch off a piece of sausage dough mixture and pat out ¼ inch flat. Place jalapeño in center of this dough. Roll with your hands to form an egg shape. Roll armadillo egg in beaten egg and then coat with Shake N Bake mix. Place on a cookie sheet. Bake in a preheated 325° oven for 20 minutes or until lightly browned.

Prep. Time: 30 minutes.

WRANGLER MEATBALLS

3	pounds lean ground round	2	tablespoons sugar
1	cup soy sauce	3	tablespoons rum, bourbon or red wine
1	teaspoon ground ginger		prepared horseradish sauce, chili sauce or picante sauce for dipping
2	cloves garlic, finely minced		
½	cup water		

Form 1 inch balls with ground round and place them in a large baking dish. Combine soy sauce, ginger, garlic, water, sugar and rum. Pour mixture over balls. Bake in a preheated 275° oven for 1 hour, gently turning balls several times to make sure they are thoroughly coated. Remove from pan and place on a serving tray with one of the sauces listed above for dipping.

Prep. Time: 20 minutes.

HOT CRAB CANAPES

1	6.5 ounce can of crabmeat, drained	1	teaspoon Worcestershire sauce
1	5 ounce jar sharp Cheddar cheese	¼	teaspoon pepper
2	tablespoons mayonnaise	¼	teaspoon Tabasco sauce
1	teaspoon onion juice	1	package round rye bread, thinly sliced

Combine all the ingredients except the rye bread. Mix well. Spread mixture on rye bread. Place on a cookie sheet. Bake in a preheated 400° oven for 12 to 15 minutes. Serve immediately.

Prep. Time: 15 minutes.

BUFFALO WINGS

Great for tailgate parties.

½	teaspoon salt	½	cup Parmesan cheese,
½	teaspoon celery seeds		grated
⅛	teaspoon black	2	teaspoons chives,
	pepper		finely minced
⅛	teaspoon cayenne	½	cup butter or
	pepper		margarine, melted
½	cup cracker crumbs	24	chicken wings

In a bowl, combine salt, celery seeds, peppers, cracker crumbs, cheese and chives. Dip chicken wings in melted butter. Roll in the cracker mixture to thoroughly coat. Place on a flat baking pan. Drizzle remaining butter over wings. Bake in a preheated 375° oven for 30 to 45 minutes or until golden brown and thoroughly cooked.

Prep. Time: 15 minutes.

SCAMPI ON A STICK

1	pound fresh or frozen	½	cup butter, melted
	uncooked shrimp	1	tablespoon parsley,
1	20 ounce can		chopped
	pineapple chunks	½	teaspoon garlic salt
24	large pitted		
	black olives		

Shell shrimp leaving tail shell on. Drain pineapple, reserving ¼ cup juice. Assemble shrimp, pineapple and olives on skewers. In a small bowl, combine butter, pineapple juice, parsley, and garlic salt. Brush over skewers. Broil in the oven until the shrimp is thoroughly cooked. Use remaining marinade for dip. *Makes 24 appetizers.*

Prep. Time: 15 minutes.

SALAMI

2 ½	pounds ground chuck	1 ½	teaspoons poultry seasoning
2 ½	pounds ground hamburger	2	teaspoons liquid smoke
2 ½	teaspoons garlic salt	3	tablespoons hot peppers, crushed
2 ½	teaspoons coarse black pepper, ground		
1 ½	teaspoons onion powder		
5	heaping teaspoons tender quick salt (for curing-not table salt or rock salt)		

I n a large bowl, combine all the above ingredients. Mix well. Cover tightly and refrigerate 24 hours. Remove from refrigerator and knead mixture thoroughly. Cover and refrigerate for 24 hours. Remove from refrigerator and roll into 5 rolls, 1 pound each, 1½ inches thick. Place on a broiler pan. Bake in a preheated 150° oven for 10 hours. Turn rolls once after 5 hours of baking. Cool and wrap tightly for storage. Serve with crackers and cheese.

Prep. Time: 15 minutes.
Seasoning Time: 2 days.
Cooking Time: 10 hours.

Hint: For a variation, substitute 2 ½ pounds of ground venison for the ground chuck or ground hamburger meat.

DEVILED HAM CORNUCOPIAS

Great for a holiday party!

20 slices white bread, thinly sliced mayonnaise	Filling:

3	tablespoons mayonnaise
1	4.5 ounce can deviled ham
2	eggs, hard-boiled & grated
1	tablespoon mustard

C ut each slice of bread with a 2 ½ inch diameter round cookie cutter, discarding the crusts. With a rolling pin, flatten each slice of bread. Spread a thin layer of mayonnaise on each side of the bread. Roll into a cone to form a cornucopia. Secure with toothpicks. Place on a cookie sheet and bake in a preheated 350° oven for 12 to 15 minutes or until lightly brown. Remove toothpicks.

For filling: Combine all filling ingredients. Fill each cornucopia with 1 heaping teaspoon.

Prep. Time: 30 minutes.

TERIYAKI BITES

These lasted only 15 minutes at a Sunday School social!

2	pounds top round steak		green olives
1	20 ounce can pineapple chunks		green bell peppers (optional)
1	cup teriyaki sauce		fresh mushrooms (optional)
2	tablespoons honey		zucchini chunks (optional)
1/2	teaspoon ground ginger		sesame seeds
12	green onions, cut in 2 inch lengths	24	cherry tomatoes

Cut steak into 1 inch chunks. Drain pineapple, reserving 1/2 cup of juice. In a small bowl, combine pineapple juice, teriyaki sauce, honey and ginger. Marinate steak in mixture over night. Assemble steak, pineapple chunks, onions, olives and other optional items on skewers. Brush with marinade. Broil in the oven, or cook on a charcoal grill, until the meat is cooked to your desire. Sprinkle with sesame seeds and add a cherry tomato. *Makes 24 appetizers.*

Prep. Time: 30 minutes.
Marinating Time: 24 hours.

TEX-MEX MUNCHIES

2	cups chicken, cooked & shredded	1/4	cup green onion tops, finely chopped
1	teaspoon (or to taste) chili powder	1/3	cup Monterey-Jack cheese, grated
Tabasco sauce to taste			
1	4 ounce can green chilies, chopped	1	pound package wonton wrappers
1	4 ounce can black olives, chopped & drained		vegetable oil for frying salsa for dipping

In a medium bowl, toss the first seven ingredients together mixing well. Place about 1 teaspoon of chicken mixture in the center of each wonton wrapper. Fold one corner over filling. Then fold in sides with points overlapping, as if you were making an envelope. Wet edges slightly to seal. Fold the final corner down sealing edge. Drop in preheated vegetable oil and fry until brown and crisp. Remove from oil. Place on a paper towel to drain. Serve with salsa for dipping. *Makes 12 servings.*

Prep. Time: 30 minutes.

PARTY PIZZAS

1	pound hot bulk sausage	2	14 ounce jars pizza quick sauce
1	pound ground beef	1 ½	tablespoons onion, finely chopped
1	pound processed cheese	1	teaspoon oregano, crushed
1 ½	tablespoons Worcestershire sauce	1	loaf of party rye bread

I n a large saucepan, brown sausage and ground beef. Drain thoroughly. Place back on stove and turn heat down to low. Add cheese and heat until melted. Stir in pizza quick sauce. Stir in Worcestershire sauce, onions and oregano. Spread on rye bread and place on a cookie sheet. In a preheated 350° oven, bake for 10 minutes.

Prep. Time: 30 minutes.

SWEET AND SOUR MEATBALLS

Meatballs:		Sauce:	
1 ½	pounds ground beef	2	12 ounce bottles chili sauce
½	onion, chopped	1	12 ounce jar mint apple jelly
⅔	cup Italian flavored bread crumbs		
1	egg		

M ix all the meatball ingredients in a large mixing bowl. Roll into 1 inch meatballs. Fry in a frying pan until cooked through. Place on a paper towel and allow to drain.

To prepare sauce: In a saucepan, mix the chili sauce and the mint apple jelly. Heat until jelly melts. Add the meatballs and heat until they are well heated. Serve in a Crockpot or chafing dish to keep warm. This freezes well.

Prep. Time: 1 hour.

HAM-FILLED CREAM PUFFS

Puff:		Filling:	
½	cup water	¼	cup sweet pickles, chopped
½	cup all-purpose flour	¼	cup onion, chopped
¼	cup butter or margarine	2	tablespoons pimento, finely chopped
¼	teaspoon salt	2	cups ham, chopped
2	eggs	¼	cup mayonnaise

I n a medium saucepan, bring water and butter or margarine to a boil. Add flour and salt. Stir vigorously over a low heat until mixture forms a ball. Remove from heat. Add eggs one at a time, beating well after each until mixture is smooth. Drop half teaspoonfuls of batter onto ungreased cookie sheet. Bake in a preheated 400° oven 10 to 15 minutes or until brown. Cool thoroughly, then cut tops off of each puff.

For filling: In a medium bowl, combine all the filling ingredients. Mix well. Fill each puff with ham mixture. Replace tops and serve. These freeze well. *Makes 48 appetizers.*

Prep. Time: 20 minutes.

SUPER SEAFOOD SPREAD

1	7 ounce can shrimp, crab or tuna, drained	2	teaspoons lemon juice
12	ounces sour cream	1	hard-boiled egg, finely chopped
1/3	cup picante sauce		
1	package dry Italian salad dressing mix	1/4	cup black olives, drained & sliced

I n a medium bowl, place seafood of your choice. Crumble this into very small pieces. Stir in all remaining ingredients except the black olives. Place in refrigerator and chill. When ready to serve, garnish with black olives and extra picante sauce (optional). Serve with chips, crackers, or vegetables for spreading. *Makes 2 1/2 cups of seafood spread.*

Prep. Time: 15 minutes.
Refrigerating Time: 2 hours.

CAVIAR SPREAD

This makes a beautiful dish for a special party.

1	8 ounce package cream cheese, softened	1	teaspoon lemon juice dash of Tabasco sauce
1/2	cup sour cream	3-4	ounces caviar
1/2	teaspoon onion, grated		

C ombine all ingredients except the caviar. Spread onto a serving dish. Place in refrigerator until chilled. Spread caviar on top of cream cheese mixture. Serve with round crackers.

Prep. Time: 10 minutes.
Refrigerating Time: 1 hour.

PIZZA–TYPE SHRIMP SPREAD

Even people who don't like shrimp love this!

1	8 ounce package cream cheese, softened	3	green onions, chopped
1	3 ounce package cream cheese, softened	1	4 ounce can mushrooms, drained & sliced
1	12 ounce bottle chili sauce	1	4 ounce can black olives, drained & chopped
1	4.5 ounce can shrimp, drained	1	8 ounce package Mozzarella cheese, grated
1/2	green pepper, chopped		

I n small bowl, combine cream cheese. On a platter, flatten out the cream cheese so it looks like a large round pizza. Line a bowl with a paper towel. Pour chili sauce into bowl to drain off excess liquid. Spread the drained chili sauce onto the cream cheese. Then layer the shrimp, green pepper, onions, mushrooms, black olives, and the Mozzarella. This should look like a large pizza and makes a beautiful dish. Serve with crackers. *Makes 20 servings.*

Prep. Time: 30 minutes.

SMOKY SALMON SPREAD

1	7.5 ounce can salmon	3	drops Liquid Smoke flavoring
1	8 ounce package cream cheese, softened	3	tablespoons green onion, chopped

Drain salmon, reserving 2 tablespoons salmon liquid. Combine cream cheese, Liquid Smoke and salmon liquid. Blend thoroughly. Stir in green onion. Fold in salmon. Refrigerate at least 2 hours or overnight. Serve with crackers.

Prep. Time: 10 minutes.
Refrigerating Time: 2 to 12 hours.

Hint: For a variation, substitute chicken, tuna or turkey for the salmon. Use as a sandwich spread. Shape into a log or ball and roll in chopped nuts.

CHEESY FRUIT AND NUT SPREAD

1	8 ounce package light Neufchatel cheese, softened	½	cup dried apple chunks, chopped
3	tablespoons honey	¼	cup pecans, chopped & toasted
1	tablespoon apple flavored brandy		

Place cheese in a medium mixing bowl. Gradually mix in honey and brandy. Stir in apples and pecans. Cover and place in refrigerator until chilled. Serve with apple and pear slices for dipping, assorted crackers, or muffins for spreading.

Prep. Time: 15 minutes.
Refrigerating Time: 2 hours.

Hint: For a variation, substitute orange juice for the brandy.

EDAM CHEESE SPREAD

1 ½	pounds of Edam cheese (up to 2 ½ pounds if needed) mayonnaise	¼	teaspoon Worcestershire sauce
1 ½	tablespoons fresh parsley, chopped	¼	teaspoon cayenne pepper
1	tablespoon dry white wine		dash of onion powder
1 ½	teaspoons dry mustard		dash of garlic powder
			dash of paprika

Cut a small lid from top of cheese. Scoop out cheese, leaving a thin but sturdy wall ¼ inch thick. Grate cheese that was scooped out. Add enough mayonnaise to make a thick, but spreadable consistency. Add remaining ingredients and mix well. Spoon into shell. Cover with lid and chill. Remove from refrigerator for 1 hour before serving. Serve with crackers.

Prep. Time: 15 minutes.

CHILI POWDER CHEESE LOG

1	pound longhorn Cheddar cheese, grated	⅛	teaspoon garlic powder, or to taste
½	cup pecans, finely chopped	1	tablespoon Worcestershire sauce, or to taste
1	8 ounce package cream cheese	½	cup chili powder

Either in a food processor or a large bowl, mix the first five ingredients until thoroughly mixed. Form into 2 logs each 1½ inches in diameter. Sprinkle chili powder on a piece of waxed paper. Roll logs in the chili powder until totally covered. Wrap in plastic wrap until needed. This does not freeze well. It tends to crumble after thawed. Serve with crackers.

Prep. Time: 20 minutes.

CHUTNEY CHEESE BALL

Not a bite was left after a party!

1	8 ounce package cream cheese, softened	½	cup green onions, chopped
2	tablespoons sour cream	½	cup golden raisins
2	tablespoons curry powder	½	cup dry roasted peanuts, coarsely chopped
		1	cup chutney

In a medium bowl, combine cream cheese and sour cream. Blend in curry powder. Add onions, raisins, and peanuts. Form into a ball. This can be made 4 days in advance, but the flavors will intensify. To serve, pour chutney over the cheese balls and serve with crackers for spreading on.

Prep. Time: 15 minutes.

CHICKEN LIVER PÂTÉ

Very easy and wonderful.

⅓	cup onions, finely minced	¼	teaspoon thyme
3	tablespoons butter	¼	teaspoon salt
¾	pound chicken livers	⅓	cup cognac brandy
¼	teaspoon allspice	½	cup butter, soften
¼	teaspoon mace	4	ounces cream cheese, softened
¼	teaspoon white pepper		

Sauté onions in butter over a very low heat about 10 to 15 minutes or until they are tender yet not brown. Add livers and spices. Toss over a high heat for 2 to 3 minutes. Livers should still be pink on the inside. Add cognac and heat to bubbling. Flame with a lighted match for 1 minute until the flames extinguish. Purée mixture in a food processor (best) or blender. Beat in softened butter and cream cheese until well mixed. Pour into a covered pâté crock (or a mold or a bowl). Refrigerate for several hours until thoroughly chilled. Garnish with parsley. Serve with crackers.

Prep. Time: 20 minutes.

CREAM CHEESE BALL

1	8 ounce package cream cheese	4	green onions, finely chopped
1	2 ½ ounce package wafer thin beef, finely chopped	2	green onion tops, finely chopped
6	radishes, finely chopped		

In a medium bowl, mix all the above ingredients and form into a ball. Refrigerate until needed. Serve with crackers.

Prep. Time: 30 minutes.

Note: *Variation #1 - Substitute garlic salt, pepper, and pecans to taste for the radishes, green onions and green onion tops.*

Variation #2 - Substitute 2 teaspoons Accent and 2 teaspoons of Worcestershire sauce for the radishes.

CREAMY CUCUMBER SPREAD

1	medium cucumber, peeled		dash of cayenne pepper or pepper sauce (optional)
1	medium onion		
1	8 ounce package cream cheese	1	tablespoon mayonnaise
1	medium onion	1	drop green food coloring
1	teaspoon salt		

Grind cucumber pulp and place on a cheese cloth. Squeeze out juice. Repeat for onion. Blend all ingredients, except food coloring, well. This should be in a spreadable consistency. Add green food coloring to make color more eye appealing. Refrigerate until thoroughly chilled. Serve on crackers or as a canapé filling.

Prep. Time: 10 minutes.

STUFFED GOUDA CHEESE

Very Gooda!

| 1 | 7 ounce Gouda cheese | 2-3 | tablespoons dry sherry |

With a sharp knife, cut ¼ inch off the top of the cheese and remove the top circle of wax. Scoop out inside cheese leaving ¼ inch on the bottom and sides. Remove wax cover. Place scooped-out cheese in a blender or food processor and add the sherry. Blend until light and fluffy. Pile cheese back into the gouda shell, mounding it with a spatula. Serve with crackers.

Prep. Time: 15 minutes.

FRUIT AND CHEESE LOG

½	cup dried apricots	½	teaspoon seasoned
1	cup water		salt
1	pound Monterey-Jack cheese, grated	⅓	cup golden seedless raisins
1	8 ounce package cream cheese, softened	⅛	cup pitted dates, snipped
⅓	cup milk	¾	cup walnuts or pecans, finely
1	teaspoon poppy seeds		chopped

Soak apricots in water for 2 hours. Drain and chop into fine pieces. In a large bowl, combine Monterey-Jack and cream cheeses. Add milk, poppy seeds and salt, mixing well. Fold in fruits. Divide among 2 pieces of foil. Shape into 2 logs each 1½ inches in diameter. Place in refrigerator and thoroughly chill. When ready to serve, remove from refrigerator and roll in nuts. Serve with poppy or plain crackers.

Prep. Time: 30 minutes, plus 2 hours to soak apricots.

CEREAL AND FRUIT TOSS

2	cups toasted round oat cereal	½	cup butter
2	cups Rice Chex cereal	1½	teaspoons cinnamon
2	cups chow mein noodles	½	teaspoon nutmeg
1	cup peanuts	1	cup mixed dried fruit, chopped

In a large bowl, combine the cereals, noodles and peanuts. In a large skillet over low heat, melt the butter. Stir in the cinnamon and nutmeg. Add cereal mixture and stir until well coated. Cook for 1 minute. Stir in dried fruit. Transfer mixture to a paper towel and cool. Store in an airtight container. *Makes 8 cups.*

Prep. Time: 10 minutes.

RODEO MUNCHIES

Some Western fare for your next party!

8	cups popped popcorn	6	tablespoons butter, melted
4	cups corn tortilla chips, slightly broken	1	package taco seasoning

In a large bowl, mix popcorn and chips. In a medium pan, mix butter and taco seasoning, stirring until well blended. Pour over popcorn and chip mixture, stir until thoroughly coated. Store in an airtight container.

Prep. Time: 10 minutes.

BUNK HOUSE CRACKER MIX

1	10 ounce package oyster crackers	1	teaspoon dill weed
1	11 ounce box Cheese Tidbits	½	teaspoon garlic salt
1	7.5 ounce box original Quackers	¼	teaspoon garlic powder
1 ½	cups oil	1	package original ranch salad dressing mix

In a large bowl, mix the 3 packages of crackers. In another bowl, mix all remaining ingredients. Once mixed, pour oil mixture over cracker mixture. Stir once every 30 minutes until all liquid is absorbed. This will require 3 hours.

Prep. Time: 3 hours, 10 minutes.

LITTLE BUCKAROO SNACKS

Kids really love this!

2	cups animal crackers or animal shaped graham crackers	1	cup salted peanuts
		½	cup candy-coated chocolate candies or jelly beans
		½	cup raisins

In a medium bowl, mix all the above ingredients. Store in an airtight container. *Makes 3 ½ cups.*

Prep. Time: 5 minutes.

TEXAS TRASH

Spicier than most cereal mixes.

1-2	12 ounce packages pretzels	1	pound margarine
1	13.3 ounce box Crispix cereal	2	ounces Accent
1	12 ounce box Rice Chex cereal	3-4	tablespoons Worcestershire sauce
1	16 ounce box Wheat Chex cereal	2 ½	tablespoons garlic powder
1	12 ounce box Corn Chex cereal	2 ½	tablespoons allspice
3-4	pounds mixed nuts	1	teaspoon celery salt
		1	cup oil

Mix first six ingredients in 2 very large roasting pans. Heat the next 7 ingredients over a medium heat until margarine is melted and all ingredients are thoroughly mixed. Pour over cereal mixture and stir well. Place in a preheated 200° oven for 2 hours stirring every 30 minutes. This recipe freezes well.

Prep. Time: 15 minutes.

CAMPFIRE OMELET

Great on camp outs. Make it in a cast iron Dutch oven over hot coals.

$\frac{1}{4}$	cup butter	4	green onions,
18	eggs		finely sliced
1	cup sour cream	1	2 ounce jar
1	cup milk		pimentos, diced &
salt & pepper, to taste			drained
$\frac{1}{4}$	teaspoon basil leaves,	4	slices bacon, cooked
	dried & crushed		crisp & crumbled
8	ounces Monterey-Jack	4	green onion tops
	cheese, grated		($\frac{1}{4}$ cup), finely
8	ounces American		sliced
	cheese, grated		
1	4 ounce can		
	mushrooms, sliced &		
	drained		

In a preheated 325° oven, melt butter in a 9 x 13 inch baking dish. Tilt dish to thoroughly coat the bottom and sides of the dish. In a large bowl, beat eggs, sour cream, milk, salt, pepper and basil until well blended. Stir in cheeses, mushrooms, green onions and pimentos. Pour into the buttered baking dish. Bake uncovered 40 to 45 minutes or until omelet is set but still moist. Cut into squares and garnish with bacon and green onion tops. If you need to make this recipe in advance, pour the mixture into the buttered pan, cover and refrigerate no longer than 24 hours. Bake in a 325° preheated oven for 50 to 55 minutes.

Prep. Time: 40 minutes.

FRONTIER BREAKFAST

At a Junior League meeting it received rave reviews. This is a "must try."

2	pie crusts	1	cup Monterey-Jack
1	pound bulk sausage,		cheese, grated
	browned, drained &		(you can use 2 cups
	crumbled		of Monterey if
$\frac{1}{4}$	cup green onions,		desired instead of
	chopped		the Cheddar)
$\frac{1}{2}$	cup picante sauce	$\frac{1}{4}$	cup canned green
10	eggs (or 12 if needed)		chilies, chopped
$\frac{1}{2}$	cup milk	$\frac{1}{4}$	cup canned black
1	cup Cheddar cheese,		olives, drained &
	grated		sliced

Lightly grease a 9 x 13 x 2 inch pan. Line the bottom of the pan with the 2 pie crusts. In a large skillet, brown sausage and onions. Drain excess fat. Pour the sausage mixture in the pan on top of the pie crusts. Pour the picante sauce over this. In another bowl beat eggs until frothy. Add milk and beat again. Stir in cheeses, chilies and olives mixing well. Pour mixture over the sausage on top of the pie crusts. Bake in a preheated 350° degree oven for 1 hour or until the center is set.

Prep. Time: 30 minutes.

CHEESY BACON AND EGG CASSEROLE

1	6 ounce box seasoned croutons	1	pound bacon, cooked & crumbled
1 ½	cups Cheddar cheese, grated	1	pint half-and-half cream
1	cup baby Swiss cheese, grated	10	eggs
		½	cup milk
1	cup Monterey-Jack cheese, grated	¾	teaspoon salt
		¾	teaspoon pepper

Spray a 9 x 13 inch baking pan with a non-stick cooking spray. Spread croutons on the bottom of pan. Spread the 3 cheeses on top of croutons. Spread bacon on top of cheeses. In a large bowl, combine cream, eggs, milk, salt, and pepper and mix well. Pour this evenly on top of contents in pan. Cover and refrigerate overnight. Uncover and bake in a preheated 350° oven for 30 to 45 minutes or until hot and bubbly. This can be heated a little in microwave to speed up the cooking process. However, it does need to be placed in oven for a little while to brown the cheese. *Makes 8 servings.*

Prep. Time: 30 minutes.
Refrigerating Time: Overnight.

LONE STAR BREAKFAST CRUNCH CASSEROLE

This will feed the whole bunch of ya'll.

2	cups toasted croutons	1	4 ounce can green chilies, chopped
1	pound bulk sausage, cooked & drained	8	eggs, beaten
1 ½	cups Monterey -Jack cheese, grated	1	teaspoon dry mustard
½	cup Cheddar cheese, grated	1	teaspoon salt
		2	cups milk
¼	cup fresh mushrooms, sliced		

Combine the first six ingredients and pour into a greased 9 x 13 inch casserole dish. In a medium bowl, combine the remaining ingredients mixing well. Pour over sausage mixture in casserole dish. Cover and refrigerate at least 12 hours. Uncover and bake in a preheated 325° oven for 35 to 40 minutes until hot. *Makes 10 servings.*

Prep. Time: 30 minutes.

CHILI CHEESE CASSEROLE

2	4 ounce cans green chilies, chopped	4	eggs
1	pound Monterey-Jack cheese, grated	²/₃	cup evaporated milk
1	pound Cheddar cheese, grated	1	tablespoon flour
		½	teaspoon salt
		¼	teaspoon pepper
			sliced tomatoes

Butter a 9 x 13 inch glass pan. In a large bowl, combine green chilies and cheeses. Place on bottom of the glass pan. Separate egg whites from yolks. Beat egg whites until stiff. Add flour and evaporated milk to yolks and mix well. Fold in egg whites. Spread this mixture over cheese mixture in glass pan. In a 325˚ preheated oven, bake for 30 minutes. Place tomato slices on top and continue baking for 30 more minutes. Serve warm. *Makes 8 servings.*

Prep. Time: 15 minutes.

CHEESY MUSHROOM CREPES

Basic Crepe:
1 ½ cups flour
3 eggs
1 ¼ cups milk
2 tablespoons margarine, melted
pinch of salt

Filling:
fresh mushrooms, chopped
green onions, chopped
Monterey-Jack cheese, sliced
sour cream, or low-fat cottage cheese
salt, to taste
pepper, to taste

Place all crepe ingredients in a blender and blend until smooth. Let stand at room temperature at least 1 hour. Using a crepe pan that has been sprayed with a non-stick cooking spray, cook crepes until lightly browned.

In the center of each crepe, place a row of mushrooms. Next, place a row of green onions. Then, top with sliced cheese. Spread a little sour cream or low-fat cottage cheese on top of cheese. Sprinkle with salt and pepper to season. Roll crepes up and secure with a toothpick. Place on a cookie sheet that has been sprayed with a non-stick cooking spray. Bake in a preheated 325˚ oven for 10 to 15 minutes or until thoroughly heated. Serve immediately. *Makes 8 servings, 2 crepes each.*

Prep. Time: 30 minutes.

CREPES A LA CRAB

8	prepared crepes	3	tablespoons flour
1	6 ounce package	1 ⅓	cups milk
	frozen crabmeat	⅓	cup Swiss cheese,
¼	cup butter or		grated
	margarine	¼	teaspoon salt
⅓	cup green onions,	⅛	teaspoon pepper
	chopped		dash of nutmeg
1	cup celery,		Parmesan cheese
	thinly sliced		
1	cup fresh		
	mushrooms,		
	chopped		

Thaw crabmeat; retain liquid and separate into chunks. In saucepan, sauté onions, celery and mushrooms in butter for 2 to 3 minutes. Remove with slotted spoon and set aside. Stir flour into fat until smooth. Add milk and crab liquid; cook until thickened. Stir in cheese, salt, pepper, and nutmeg. In small bowl, toss together crab, onions, celery, mushrooms and half cup of sauce. Spread equal amount across center of each crepe and roll up or fold over. Place in shallow baking dish and pour remaining sauce over. Sprinkle with Parmesan cheese. Bake in a preheated 350° oven for 10 to 15 minutes. *Makes 4 servings, 2 crepes each.*

Prep. Time: 20 minutes.

Hint: *See Cheesy Mushroom Crepe recipe for a good basic crepe recipe, page 35.*

CHICKEN DIVAN CREPES

¼	cup butter	2	10 ounce packages
¼	cup flour		frozen broccoli
2	cups chicken broth		spears or 1 ½
2	teaspoons		pounds fresh
	Worcestershire sauce		broccoli, cooked &
3	cups Cheddar cheese,		drained
	grated	2	cups chicken,
2	cups sour cream		cooked & cut in
12	prepared crepes		bite-sized pieces

Over medium heat, melt butter in small saucepan. Stir in flour and cook until bubbly. Add broth and Worcestershire sauce; cook, stirring until thickened. Add 2 cups cheese. Set aside. Empty sour cream into medium bowl; gradually add hot cheese sauce, stirring constantly. Assemble crepes by placing some broccoli and chicken on each crepe. Spoon 1 tablespoon sauce over each. Fold crepes over and place in shallow baking pan. Pour remaining sauce over crepes. Sprinkle with remaining cup of cheese. Cover and bake at 350° for 20 to 30 minutes. *Makes 6 servings, 2 crepes each.*

Prep. Time: 20 minutes.

CHEESE SOUFFLÉ

1	6 ounce package cheese flavored croutons	1	teaspoon onion salt
		½	teaspoon dry mustard
1 ¾	cups milk	¼	teaspoon cayenne pepper
1 ½	cups Cheddar cheese, grated	4	eggs, separated

In a medium saucepan, combine the first six ingredients. Over a medium heat, cook until cheese is melted. Remove from heat. Slightly beat egg yolks. Stir in slowly so that they do not cook. In a metal bowl, beat egg whites until stiff. Fold into cheese mixture. Pour into a 1 ½ quart casserole dish. Bake in a preheated 325° oven for 45 minutes or until brown and center is set. *Makes 6 to 8 servings.*

Prep. Time: 15 minutes.

SAUSAGE CASSEROLE

1	pound bulk sausage	1	teaspoon salt
6	eggs, beaten	1	cup sharp Cheddar cheese, grated
2	cups milk		
6	slices bread, cubed		dash of oregano
1	teaspoon dry mustard		

Brown and drain sausage. Mix all ingredients together, and place in a 9 x 13 inch casserole dish. Cover and refrigerate overnight. Bake in a preheated 350° oven for 30 to 45 minutes or until mixture sets good and browns around the edge. *Makes 10 servings.*

Prep. Time: 20 minutes.
Refrigerating Time: Overnight.

ADAPT-A-QUICHE
Wonderful because it is so versatile!

1	9 inch pie shell	¼	cup mayonnaise
2	tablespoons onions, leeks, shallots or scallions, chopped	½	teaspoon salt (more if desired)
		¼	teaspoon pepper
2	tablespoons butter	¼	teaspoon herbs or spice (nutmeg, curry, basil, thyme, dill, etc.)
½	cup vegetables or meat, cooked & chopped (spinach, broccoli, ham, chicken, shrimp, etc.)		
		3	large eggs
		1 ¼	cups half-and-half cream or milk
¼	cup (more if desired) cheese (Cheddar, Swiss, Monterey-Jack, Parmesan, etc.), grated		additional cheese if desired

Sauté onions in butter, in a small skillet, until tender. Place in a partially-cooked pie shell. Next add cooked meat or vegetables. Top with cheese. In a medium bowl, combine mayonnaise, salt, pepper, herbs, eggs and cream. Pour over contents in the pie shell. Sprinkle additional cheese on top if desired. Bake in a preheated 350° oven for 45 minutes or until center is set. It should be medium brown. It will begin shrinking immediately when removed from oven. *Makes 6 servings.*

Prep. Time: 10 minutes.

SPINACH QUICHE

1	3 ounce package cream cheese	1	4 ounce jar mushrooms, drained & chopped
1	cup light cream (half-and-half)	1	large onion, finely chopped
½	cup soft bread crumbs	4	tablespoons margarine
¼	cup Parmesan cheese	1	teaspoon tarragon
2	eggs	¾	teaspoon salt
1	10 ounce package frozen spinach, cooked, drained & chopped	1	9 inch unbaked pie shell

In a large bowl, mix cream cheese and cream. Stir in bread crumbs, cheese, and eggs mixing well. Stir in spinach. In a small skillet, sauté mushrooms and onion in margarine until tender. Add tarragon and salt to taste. Add this mixture to cheese and spinach mixture and mix well. Pour into the pie shell. Bake in a preheated 400° oven for 25 minutes or until center is set and crust is browned. Remove from oven and allow to stand for 10 minutes before serving. *Makes 6 servings.*

Prep. Time: 20 minutes.

QUICHE LORRAINE

Pastry:

½	cup butter (not margarine), softened	½	cup mushrooms (optional)
1	egg yolk	2	tablespoons margarine
1	teaspoon salt	6	slices bacon, fried & drained
½	teaspoon dry mustard	1	cup Swiss cheese, grated
1	teaspoon paprika	4	eggs
1 ¼	cups all-purpose flour, sifted	1 ½	cups evaporated milk
1	tablespoon ice water	½	teaspoon salt
		½	teaspoon dry mustard

Filling:

¼	cup green onions (optional)		dash of nutmeg
			dash of pepper

In a medium bowl, combine first five ingredients and mix into a paste. Work in flour. Sprinkle water in and toss with fork. Form into a ball and chill 10 minutes. Roll out on a board between two pieces of plastic wrap. Remove plastic wrap and transfer to a quiche pan. Bake in a preheated 450° oven for 5 to 10 minutes. Remove from oven and allow to cool while making filling.

To prepare filling: In a small skillet, sauté onions and mushrooms in margarine until tender, drain. Place in pastry. Next place bacon, and Swiss cheese on top of mushrooms and onions. In a large bowl, beat eggs, evaporated milk, salt, mustard, nutmeg and pepper well. Pour over bacon and cheese. Bake in a preheated 350° oven for 35 to 40 minutes or until the center is set. If you are making this in advance, cover unbaked quiche with plastic wrap and refrigerate. To bake, uncover and bake as instructed above.

Prep. Time: 1 hour.

TOMATO QUICHE

1	pie crust (either homemade or bought)	1	medium onion, finely chopped
3	large tomatoes, peeled, seeded & chopped (must be the yummy ones from your garden or the farmer's market-- don't bother to make the quiche with the supermarket variety)	3	tablespoons butter
		1	teaspoon salt
		1/4	teaspoon thyme
		1/2	pound Swiss cheese, grated
		3	eggs, well beaten
		1	cup light cream (half-and-half)

Combine the tomatoes, onion, butter, salt and thyme in saucepan and cook over medium heat until reduced by half. Place cheese on pie crust. Pour tomato mixture over cheese. Beat eggs and cream together and pour over tomato mixture. Bake for 10 minutes in a preheated 425° oven, then reduce to 375° for 35 minutes. Let quiche set 10 minutes before cutting.

Prep. Time: 1 1/2 hours.

MUSHROOM ARTICHOKE QUICHE

6	petite whole artichokes	2	cups Monterey-Jack cheese, grated
1/2	pound fresh mushrooms, coarsely chopped	1	cup small curd cottage cheese
6	tablespoons butter	3	eggs
10	tablespoons salted crackers, crushed	1/4	cup light cream (half-and-half)
1/4 - 3/4	cup green onion, chopped	1/4	teaspoon cayenne pepper
1	tablespoon butter	1/4	teaspoon paprika

Over a medium-high heat, boil artichokes for 6 minutes or until fork tender. Drain and cool. In a medium saucepan, sauté mushrooms in 6 tablespoons butter. Stir in crushed crackers. Press into a lightly buttered 9 inch pie pan to make crust. Chill until butter hardens. Sauté green onions in 1 tablespoon of butter. Spread over mushroom crust. Coarsely chop artichokes and place on top of green onions. Next sprinkle cheese on top. Place cottage cheese, eggs, cream, cayenne pepper and paprika into a blender and blend until smooth. Pour over other ingredients in crust. Bake in a preheated 350° oven for 25 to 30 minutes or until set in center. Remove from oven and let stand for 10 minutes before cutting into wedges. *Makes 6 servings.*

Prep. Time: 35 minutes.

SAUSAGE AND CHEDDAR QUICHE

1	prepared 9 inch pie shell	½	teaspoon whole basil leaves, crushed
1	pound hot bulk sausage	dash of garlic powder	
¼	cup green pepper, chopped	1 ½	cups Cheddar cheese, grated
½	cup onion, chopped	2	eggs
1	4 ounce can sliced mushrooms, drained	1	cup milk
1	teaspoon parsley minced, (optional)	paprika	

Prick the prepared pie shell several times with a fork. In a preheated 400° oven, bake pie shell for 12 to 15 minutes, or until lightly browned. Remove from heat and allow to cool a little. In a large skillet, cook sausage, green pepper, and onion until sausage is brown. Drain excess fat. Stir in mushrooms, parsley, basil, and garlic powder. Spoon into pie shell. Top with grated Cheddar cheese. In another bowl, combine the eggs and milk. Beat until foamy. Pour evenly over quiche. Sprinkle paprika on top. Bake in a preheated 325° oven for 50 minutes or until the cheese is lightly browned and center of quiche is set.

Prep. Time: 30 minutes.

CHEESE AND BACON QUICHE

1	prepared 9 inch pie shell, unbaked	4	eggs
10	slices bacon, fried until crisp & crumbled	2	cups light cream (half-and-half)
1 ¼	cups Swiss cheese, grated	½	teaspoon salt
		⅛	teaspoon nutmeg
		pinch of cayenne pepper	

Sprinkle crumbled bacon in bottom of pie dish. Sprinkle Swiss cheese on top of bacon. In a large bowl, combine eggs, cream, salt, nutmeg and cayenne pepper and stir well. Gently ladle egg mixture over bacon and cheese. Bake in a preheated 350° oven for 30 minutes or until center is set. *Makes 6 servings.*

Prep. Time: 10 minutes.

SPICED HONEY BUTTER

½	cup butter or margarine, softened	¼	teaspoon cinnamon
		dash of nutmeg	
¼	cup honey	½	teaspoon vanilla

Beat all ingredients until thoroughly mixed. Cover tightly and refrigerate. Use on waffles, pancakes, toast or hot biscuits. *Makes ¾ cup.*

Prep. Time: 10 minutes.

BITTY BISCUITS

6	cups flour	1	teaspoon salt
2 ½	cups butter	1	cup poppy seeds
2 ½	cups cream cheese		

Blend all above ingredients thoroughly. Form into a ball. Wrap in plastic wrap and refrigerate until thoroughly chilled. Roll out to ⅓ inch thick. Cut with a 1 inch round cutter. Place on an ungreased cookie sheet. Bake in a 400° preheated oven for 15 minutes. Serve cool or warm. Dough can be made 2 weeks ahead and kept in the refrigerator. *Makes 31 dozen.*

Prep. Time: 15 minutes.

MINI-BACON AND CHEDDAR QUICHE

Excellent for any party. Always the first to disappear. Make ahead and freeze until needed.

2	10 ounce cans of biscuits	½	teaspoon basil leaves, crushed
1	pound bacon, cooked & crumbled	⅛	teaspoon salt
1	4 ounce jar of mushrooms, drained & chopped	⅛	teaspoon garlic powder
½	cup onion, finely chopped	1 ½	cups Cheddar cheese, grated
¼	cup green bell pepper, finely chopped	1	cup milk
1	teaspoon parsley, minced	2	eggs
			paprika

Spray mini-muffin pans with a non-stick cooking spray. Cut each biscuit into quarters. Press each quarter into one of the mini-muffin tins. Combine the next 11 ingredients mixing well. Fill each muffin to top. Do not over fill. Sprinkle with paprika. Bake in a preheated 325° oven for 25 minutes or until lightly browned. Allow to stand for 10 minutes and then remove from pans. These freeze well.

Prep. Time: 1 ½ hours.

PUMPKIN PANCAKES

Great to serve to guests during the holidays!

2	cups Bisquick mix	½	cup solid pack canned pumpkin
2	tablespoons brown sugar, packed	2	tablespoons vegetable oil
2	teaspoons cinnamon		
1	teaspoon allspice	2	eggs (egg beaters equal to 2 eggs may be substituted)
1	teaspoon vanilla		
1	12 ounce can evaporated milk (light may be used)		

In a large mixing bowl with a mixer combine all the above ingredients and mix well. Lightly grease a non-stick griddle and heat to a medium heat. Pour ¼ to ½ cupfuls of pancake mix onto griddle. Cook until top surface is bubbly and edges are lightly browned. Turn and cook until other side is lightly browned. Remove from griddle and serve warm with maple syrup.

Prep. Time: 30 minutes.

GERMAN PUFF PANCAKES

This is a wonderful low calorie breakfast.

2	tablespoons butter or margarine	¼	cup flour
1	egg	¼	teaspoon salt
¼	cup milk		powdered sugar
			lemon juice

Preheat the oven to 425°. Melt butter or margarine in a 5 inch skillet. Place skillet in the oven and preheat. In a small bowl mix remaining ingredients well. Pour into the preheated skillet. Bake at 425° for 15 minutes. Remove from oven and cut into wedges to serve. Top with powdered sugar and lemon juice, or syrup, whichever, is preferred. *Makes 2 to 4 servings.*

Prep. Time: 15 minutes.

CINNAMON PULL-A-PART PASTRY

3	10 ounce cans biscuits	1	tablespoon cinnamon
1	cup butter or margarine	¾	cup pecans, chopped
1 ½	cups brown sugar, packed	¼	cup pecans, chopped

Separate biscuits and cut each into quarters. In a small saucepan, melt butter or margarine. Stir in brown sugar, cinnamon and ¾ cup pecans. Place biscuit quarters in a bundt pan. Pour sugar mixture over biscuit quarters. Top with remaining nuts. Bake in a preheated 450° oven for 25 minutes. Allow to cool for 10 to 15 minutes. Turn onto a plate and serve.

Prep. Time: 25 minutes.

SOUTH OF THE BORDER BREAKFAST

Why don't you rustle some up for breakfast today!

½	pound ham or bulk sausage, finely chopped	5	eggs
¼	cup onions, chopped	¼	cup milk
¼	cup green bell pepper, chopped	½	teaspoon salt
3	tablespoons margarine, melted	¼	teaspoon pepper
½	inch thick slice of processed cheese		Cheddar cheese, grated
			taco-sized flour tortillas
			picante sauce
			sour cream

Sauté ham (sausage), onions and bell peppers in margarine until thoroughly cooked. If sausage is used, drain well. Add cheese and cook over a low heat until melted. Mix well. In another bowl, combine eggs, milk, salt, and pepper. Mix well. Pour this mixture in with ham and cheese mixture and stir well. Cook over a medium heat stirring constantly until eggs are scrambled. Transfer to a serving bowl. Take a flour tortilla and place some of the egg mixture in the middle. Top with picante sauce, sour cream, and Cheddar cheese or chili con queso with sausage (see Appetizers, page 7). Roll it up to eat and enjoy.

Prep. Time: 20 minutes.

SOUR CREAM CINNAMON TWISTS

Great and very easy to make. Kids love them!

1	$\frac{1}{4}$ ounce package yeast	1	large egg
$\frac{1}{4}$	cup warm water	3	cups flour
$\frac{3}{4}$	cup sour cream at room temperature	2	tablespoons margarine, softened
3	tablespoons sugar	$\frac{1}{3}$	cup light brown sugar, packed
$\frac{1}{8}$	teaspoon baking soda	1	teaspoon cinnamon
1	teaspoon salt		

D issolve yeast in water. Add the next six ingredients and stir well. Turn dough onto a lightly floured board. Roll out dough until it measures 24 x 6 inches. Spread soft margarine over the dough. Sprinkle brown sugar and cinnamon over the dough. Fold dough in half so that it now measures 24 x 3 inches. Cut into 1 x 3 inch strips. Twist and place on a greased cookie sheet. Cover and let rise until double in size. Bake in a preheated 375° oven for 12 to 15 minutes. *Makes 24 twists.*

Prep. Time: 10 minutes,
            plus time for dough to rise.

HOT STUFFED AVOCADOS

2	tablespoons butter or margarine, melted	2	cups chicken, cooked & cubed
2	tablespoons flour	3	ripe avocados, peeled & sliced in half
1	cup light cream (half-and-half)		
$\frac{1}{2}$	teaspoon Worcestershire sauce	$\frac{1}{2}$	cup Cheddar cheese, grated
2	tablespoons onion, finely minced	water	
2	tablespoons celery, finely minced		

P lace the melted butter, and flour in a saucepan. Cook over a high heat for 1 minute to lightly brown, stirring constantly.   Stir in the cream. Continue cooking, stirring constantly, until thick. Turn the heat down and add the Worcestershire sauce, onion, celery and chicken.   Heat thoroughly but, do not boil.   Place the avocado halves in a baking dish. Fill with chicken mixture. Sprinkle cheese on top. Pour $\frac{1}{4}$ inch of water in bottom of baking dish. Bake in a preheated 350° oven for 15 to 20 minutes or until the avocados are hot and the cheese is melted. *Makes 6 servings.*

Prep. Time: 20 minutes.

CANUCK CAESARS

This is a **must try** recipe! It is a Canadian drink that is so much better than the American Bloody Mary. Everytime it has been served to Americans they have loved it, even those who don't care for Bloody Marys.

lime juice
margarita salt
1   ounce vodka or
       dry gin
5   ounces clamato juice
1   teaspoon
       Worcestershire sauce
4   drops Tabasco
       sauce, or to taste
¼   teaspoon seasoned
       pepper, or to taste
¼   teaspoon seasoned
       salt, or to taste

½   teaspoon fresh
       lemon juice
½   teaspoon fresh
       lime juice
⅓   stalk celery
       (substitute ¼
       teaspoon celery salt
       & leave out the
       seasoned salt if you
       desire; however, it is
       worth your effort to
       use the celery stalk)

Dip the rim of a 10 ounce double old-fashion glass in lime juice and then in margarita salt. Pour the first eight ingredients into the glass. Stir. Using the finest grater possible, grate the celery (juice and pulp included) into the glass. Stir well. Garnish with celery stalk tops.

HOT SPICED APPLE CIDER
The civilized Cowboy's Christmas Toddy!

1   gallon apple cider
       or apple juice
1   9 ounce bag of
       cinnamon red
       hot candies
½   cup sugar
5   cinnamon sticks
20   whole cloves (up to
       25 can be added if
       desired)

1   cup prepared
       cranberry juice (if
       you have it)
1   cup prepared orange
       juice (if you have it)
1   fifth of rum
       (optional)
butter

In a large pot, combine all the ingredients except the rum and butter. Over a medium heat, bring to a boil. Stir this frequently until the sugar and candies are dissolved. Reduce heat and simmer for 1 hour. Add the rum and continue to cook a few minutes until it is simmering again. Before serving, place a small pat (¼ to ½ teaspoon) of butter in each mug. Pour the apple cider on top of this. Garnish with a cinnamon stick for each mug.

Prep. Time: 1 hour.

BEST LITTLE MARGARITA IN TEXAS

That's a margarita!

extra lime juice	*1½ ounces light tequila*
margarita salt	*ice cubes*
½ ounce triple sec	
1 ounce fresh squeezed	
lime juice	

D ip rim of glass in lime juice and then salt. Place triple sec, 1 ounce lime juice, tequila and ice cubes in a shaker. Shake. Strain into glass. Don't include ice, or the drink will be too watery.

RIO GRANDE SANGRIA

juice of 2 Texas ruby red	*1 lemon, sliced thin*
grapefruits	*1 750 ml bottle Texas*
juice of 2 oranges	*white wine*
1 cup sugar	*1 quart club soda,*
1 orange, sliced thin	*chilled*
1 lime, sliced thin	

I n a large sangria pitcher, combine the juice and sugar mixing well. Add the fruit slices and give it a quick stir. Add the wine and refrigerate for one hour. Stir in the club soda. Serve in chilled wine glasses. Garnish glasses with extra lime or lemon slices.

Prep. Time: 10 minutes,
plus 1 hour refrigeration time.

CHRISTMAS EGGNOG

12	*eggs*	*1*	*pint whipping*
2	*cups sugar*		*cream*
1	*quart bourbon*		*nutmeg*
1	*pint brandy*	*1*	*quart vanilla*
2	*quarts milk*		*ice cream*

S eparate the egg yolks from the whites. Place yolks in a large mixing bowl. Add sugar and mix on high until thoroughly mixed. Add bourbon, brandy, milk and whipping cream mixing well. Pour this mixture into a large punch bowl. Place the egg whites in the mixing bowl and beat until stiff. Slowly fold this into the mixture in the punch bowl. Add nutmeg to taste. Spoon the ice cream by the spoonful into this mixture. It will still be hard. Place in the refrigerator and chill for 1 hour. This will allow the ice cream to melt and the egg whites to soften a little. When ready to serve, remove from the refrigerator and give it a quick stir. Garnish with nutmeg on top.

Prep. Time: 20 minutes,
plus 1 hour refrigeration time.

WASSAIL

6	cups apple cider or apple juice	1	18 ounce can prepared pineapple
1	stick cinnamon		juice (not
1/4	teaspoon nutmeg		concentrate)
1/4	cup fresh lemon juice	1/4	cup honey

In a large saucepan, combine the apple cider and cinnamon stick. Over a medium high heat, bring to a boil. Reduce the heat, cover the pan and simmer for 5 minutes. Uncover the pan and stir in the remaining ingredients. Simmer for an additional 5 minutes. Remove the cinnamon stick and serve. Garnish each glass with a cinnamon stick for stirring.

Prep. Time: 15 minutes.

COFFEE PUNCH

1	quart coffee, already brewed	1/4	teaspoon almond or vanilla extract
1	gallon chocolate ice cream	1/2	pint whipping cream nutmeg

Chill coffee and pour in punch bowl. Add half of the chocolate ice cream. Stir. Add almond or vanilla extract to whipping cream and whip. Place whipped cream and rest of ice cream alternately on top of coffee. Sprinkle with nutmeg. *Makes 12 to 15 servings.*

Prep. Time: 5 minutes.

HOT SPICED CRANBERRY DRINK

This drink makes you look forward to winter.

2	cups cranberry juice	2	tablespoons whole cloves
2 1/2	cups unsweetened pineapple juice	1/2	tablespoon allspice
1 3/4	cups water	1/4	teaspoon salt
2	sticks cinnamon, broken	1/2	cup brown sugar, loosely packed

Make this recipe in a percolator coffee maker. If you do not have one, then make it in a saucepan on the stove. Pour the cranberry juice, pineapple juice, and water into the percolator. Place the remaining spices in the filter section of the percolator. Plug the percolator in and let it perk until hot. *Makes 6 to 8 servings.*

Prep. Time: 5 minutes.

CATTLE RUSTLER'S SANGRIA

1/2	cup brandy	1	750 ml bottle Texas red wine
1/4	cup sugar		
1	lemon, sliced thin		juice of one lime
1	lime, sliced thin	1	quart club soda, chilled
1	orange, sliced thin		

In a large sangria pitcher, combine brandy and sugar. Mix until sugar is dissolved. Add fruit slices and give it a quick stir. Let stand at room temperature for 1 hour. Add wine and lime juice, stir and refrigerate for 1 hour. Add the club soda and stir again. Serve in large chilled wine glasses. Garnish glasses with additional lime or lemon slices.

Prep. Time: 2 hours and 10 minutes.

INDIAN TEA

Use instead of punch for showers, luncheons, etc.

2	cups sugar	1	tablespoon almond
4	cups water		extract
juice of 4 lemons		1	cup boiling water
1	tablespoon vanilla	2	small tea bags
	extract	1	quart ginger ale

Heat to boil first three ingredients. Next add vanilla and almond extracts. Steep 2 small tea bags in 1 cup boiling water. Add this to above mixture, removing tea bags. Add 1 quart ginger ale and serve. *Makes 3 quarts.*

Prep. Time: 20 minutes.

SPICED TEA MIX

Makes enough to give to a friend.

2	cups Tang	2	6 ounce packages
1	cup powdered		orange/pineapple
	instant tea		gelatin
1	cup apple cider mix	2	teaspoons apple pie
1/2	cup sugar		spice
2	6 ounce packages	2	teaspoons cinnamon
	lemon gelatin		

Mix all ingredients together. Add 3 heaping teaspoons to a large cup. Pour hot water into cup. Stir until mixture is dissolved. Store mix in airtight container. *Makes 50 servings.*

Prep. Time: 10 minutes.

FROZEN STRAWBERRY PUNCH

This recipe is wonderful. It has been taken to dinner parties, showers and birthday parties and there has never been any left over.

1	large package strawberry gelatin	juice from two lemons	
6	cups boiling water	5	bananas, liquified
1	12 ounce can unsweetened orange juice, thawed	1	8 ounce can pineapple, liquified (optional)
1	12 ounce can unsweetened pineapple juice, thawed	3	cups sugar
		4	1 liter bottles ginger ale

Dissolve the gelatin in the boiling water. Add all the remaining ingredients except for the ginger ale. Pour into 2 one-gallon inner-lock plastic bags and freeze until needed. 1½ hours before needed, thaw slightly. Work the mixture with your hands into a fine ice. Pour into a punch bowl and add the ginger ale. Stir.

Prep. Time: 15 minutes.

MAGNOLIAS

4	cups orange juice	½	cup Grand Marnier
1	24.5 ounce bottle champagne		orange slices marachino cherries

Combine orange juice, champagne and Grand Marnier. Serve over crushed ice in tulip glasses. Garnish with orange slice and cherry. *Makes 7 ½ cups.*

Prep. Time: 10 minutes.

MOCK CHAMPAGNE PUNCH

Great for baby showers.

1	2 liter bottle ginger ale	1	large can frozen apple juice, thawed (no water added)

Mix together and pour over crushed ice or ice ring. *Makes 20 servings.*

Prep. Time: 5 minutes.

PEACH SPIKE

2	10 ounce packages frozen peach slices, partially thawed	1 ⅓	cups vodka (optional)
2	6 ounce cans frozen concentrated lemonade, partially thawed	24	ice cubes marachino cherries lemon wedges

In blender combine 1 package peaches, 1 can concentrated lemonade, and half the vodka. Cover and blend. Add 12 ice cubes, 1 at a time, blending on low until slushy. Pour into punch bowl. Repeat blending with remaining ingredients. Garnish with marachino cherries and lemon wedges. *Makes 8 cups.*

Prep. Time: 10 minutes.

WHITE WINE PUNCH

1 ½	gallons white wine	2	quarts ginger ale
2	quarts 7-Up ®		whole strawberries
2	quarts soda water		sliced oranges

Combine ingredients and pour in a punch bowl. Garnish with floating whole strawberries and sliced oranges.

Prep. Time: 5 minutes.

Breads & Sandwiches

DUTCH OVEN BISCUITS

This is an authentic ranch recipe still used today for special events.

6	cups flour	1	tablespoon salt
2	tablespoons baking powder	1 ½	cups shortening
		3 ¾	cups buttermilk
1 ½	teaspoons soda	1	bottle vegetable oil

Materials:
2   cast iron Dutch ovens
1   Chuck Wagon Cook
1   Wrangler, usually the Horse Wrangler, to
     gather wood
1   pair leather gloves
1   heavy-duty hook to lift Dutch oven lids
1   shovel
1   rick of firewood, preferably mesquite

Mix dry ingredients. Cut in shortening. Stir in buttermilk. Roll out on floured board. Cut with a biscuit cutter or metal coffee cup. Build a raging fire. When the fire begins to die, preheat Dutch ovens and lids by placing them separately on the coals.

Take hot ovens from fire, leaving the lids. Pour in enough vegetable oil to generously coat the bottom. Dip biscuits in the oven and cover with hot lid. Use shovel to separate out enough coals to cover the perimeter of each Dutch oven. Place Dutch oven on coals. Place more coals on top of lid. Cooking time varies, but it could be as little as 5 minutes. Use hook to carefully lift lid to check the biscuits. Biscuits should be brown on top and bottom. *Makes about 3 dozen biscuits.*

Note: Now that you've mastered this, all of the other bread recipes should be easy.

GRANDMOTHER'S FAVORITE ROLLS

Sweeter than usual rolls.

1	package dry yeast	½	cup sugar
1	cup plus 3 tablespoons very warm water	2	eggs, beaten
		1	teaspoon salt
		4-6	cups sifted flour
1	pinch of sugar		
½	cup melted shortening in 1 cup hot water		

Dissolve yeast in water. Add sugar to yeast mixture to activate yeast. Set aside. In a large bowl, mix melted shortening, sugar, eggs and salt. Add all of the flour you can. Let rise until double in size. Punch down. You can now pinch off dough for dinner rolls, etc., or you can cover the dough and place in the refrigerator to save for when needed. Dough can be rolled to ¼ inch thickness and cut out with biscuit cutter. Allow dough to rise 2 to 3 hours before baking. Bake at 375° for 10 to 15 minutes.

Prep time: 20 minutes to mix dough,
              plus 2 to 3 hours for dough to rise.

Hint: This bread can be used as a loaf bread, rolls, hot dog buns or hamburger buns.

MOTHER'S CINNAMON ROLLS

Mother made these like other people made coffee; and they'd be gone just as fast!

1	package dry yeast	⅛	cup butter, melted
¼	cup warm water	¼	cup brown sugar
1	pinch of sugar		cinnamon, to taste
1	cup milk		
¾	cup sugar		*Icing:*
¼	teaspoon salt	1	cup powdered sugar, sifted
2	eggs		A few tablespoons of cream
¼	cup butter, melted		
3 ½	cups flour		

Dissolve yeast in warm water with pinch of sugar. Scald milk. Add sugar, ¼ cup butter and salt. Let cool. Add scalded milk to yeast mixture. Stir in eggs and flour. Dough will be very soft and moist. Cover and let rise in a warm place until double the size. Roll out into 2 rectangles. Brush rectangles with melted ⅛ cup butter. Spread brown sugar and cinnamon over the melted butter. Roll up the rectangle. To make cinnamon rolls, cut slices about 1 inch thick. To make a cinnamon ring, place around outside of a pie plate. With kitchen shears, cut dough at even intervals. Let either dough rise until double. Bake at 400° for 25 to 30 minutes.

Drizzle with powdered sugar icing by combining both ingredients. *Makes 2 rings or 40 rolls.*

Prep time: 20 minutes,
plus 2 hours for dough to rise.

YOUR MODERN FRENCH BREAD

Easy bread, the food processor way.

1	package dry yeast	½	teaspoon salt
1	teaspoon sugar	1	cup unbleached all-purpose flour
1	cup plus 2 tablespoons warm water; 105° to 115°	2	cups bread flour
1	large egg	1	teaspoon salt

Combine the yeast and sugar in the warm water in a small bowl. Let stand for 10 minutes or until it is foamy. Meanwhile, with a metal blade, process the egg and ½ teaspoon salt for 2 seconds and reserve. Do not clean the work bowl. Put the flours and remaining salt in the work bowl. With metal blade, turn on the machine and add the yeast mixture through the feed tube. Process the mixture for 45 seconds, or until the dough is uniformly moist. Add more flour if the mixture is too wet. Place dough in an oiled bowl, turning the dough to coat the surface with oil. Cover the bowl with a towel.

Warm the oven at the lowest setting for 2 minutes. Turn off. Place dough in oven. Let it rise for 1 hour, or until it has doubled in bulk. Heavily flour a working area. Knead the dough with additional flour until it is no longer sticky. Divide the dough in half. Roll each half into a rectangle. Then roll the rectangle into an oblong loaf. Place the loaves into an oiled French bread pan. Return loaves to the warm oven, allowing them to rise another 45 minutes. Remove from oven. Preheat the oven to 425°. Brush the loaves with the egg mixture. Bake for 30 minutes. *Makes 2 loaves.*

Prep time: 15 minutes,
plus 2 hours for dough to rise.

SOUR CREAM CRESCENTS

2	packages of dry yeast	2	eggs, beaten
1	teaspoon sugar	1/3	cup sugar
1/2	cup lukewarm water	1	teaspoon salt
1	cup sour cream	4	cups unbleached
1	cup butter, softened		flour

Proof yeast and sugar in water. Heat sour cream in small pan over low heat to 105° (scald the sour cream). Combine the sour cream, butter, eggs, sugar and salt in a large bowl. Stir in the yeast mixture and mix thoroughly. Gradually add the flour. Place the dough in a greased bowl and turn to grease the top. Cover and place in the refrigerator for at least 6 hours. (May rise for up to 24 hours. It does not double when rising). Divide the dough into 4 parts. Roll each part into a 12 inch circle on a floured surface. Cut into 12 pie shaped wedges and roll up each wedge tightly. Place on a greased baking sheet and curve into crescents. Cover and let rise in a warm place for 30 minutes. Bake at 375° for 12 minutes. *Makes 4 dozen.*

Prep time: 20 minutes,
        plus 6 hours for dough to rise.

HARVEST MOON BREAD

1	cup oats (old-fashioned or quick cooking)	1/2	teaspoon sugar
1/2	cup yellow cornmeal	1/2	cup honey or 1/3 cup molasses
1 1/2	teaspoons salt	3 1/4	cups unbleached flour
2	cups water, boiling		
1/2	cup (1 stick) margarine	2 1/2	cups whole-wheat flour
1	package dry yeast		
1/2	cup warm water		

In large bowl, combine oats, cornmeal and salt. Stir in boiling water and blend. Add margarine and stir until melted. Let stand until lukewarm. In small bowl, put dry yeast and add the 1/2 cup warm water and sugar (to proof). Stir until yeast dissolves. To oats mixture, add yeast mixture and honey or molasses. Stir in flour which has been measured beginning with 2 cups of unbleached flour. Gradually add the whole wheat flour to make a soft dough. All of the flours may not be needed. Turn dough onto a well floured surface and knead until smooth and elastic. Continue to knead in the remainder of the flour as long as dough is sticky to the touch. Shape into a ball and place in a greased bowl, turning to grease top. Let rise in a warm place until doubled, about 1 1/2 hours. Punch down. Take out dough and divide into 3 parts. With rolling pin, roll out 8 x 10 inches long. Fold the 2 long sides to the middle and pinch together. Pinch dough together at the ends and place into greased loaf pans. Let rise again until doubled (from 40 minutes to 1 hour). Preheat oven to 350°. Bake 40 to 45 minutes until browned and loaves sound hollow when thumped. Remove from pans and cool on a rack. Do not set loaves directly on a counter or board or the bottoms will become soggy. When cool, wrap in foil. *Makes 3 medium loaves or 3 dozen rolls.*

Prep time: 30 minutes,
        plus 2 1/2 hours for dough to rise.

Note: *Start 3 hours before serving if using regular yeast; time can be shortened if using double action yeast.*

TEXAS TWISTERS

Hot Roll Mix:
5   pounds all-purpose
     flour
1 ¼ cups sugar
4   teaspoons salt
1   cup instant non-fat
     dry milk

Pretzels:
1   tablespoon active
     dry yeast
1 ½ cups lukewarm water
2   eggs, beaten
½   cup vegetable oil (or
     melted margarine)
5-6 cups hot roll mix
1   egg, beaten
2   tablespoons coarse
     salt

I n a large bowl, combine the flour, sugar, salt and instant milk. Stir together to distribute evenly. Store in a dry place in an airtight container.

In a large mixing bowl, dissolve the yeast in the lukewarm water. Stir in the eggs and oil. Add 5 cups of the hot roll mix. Stir well. Add more of the hot roll mix to make a soft, but not sticky, dough. Turn the dough onto a lightly floured surface and knead for 5 minutes. Roll pieces of the dough into ½ inch thick, 18 to 24 inch long ropes. Form into pretzels and place on 2 lightly greased cookie sheets. Brush the tops of them with the remaining beaten egg. Sprinkle the salt on top. Bake in a preheated 425° oven for 12 to 15 minutes or until the pretzels are lightly browned. *Makes 12 to 15 pretzels.*

Prep. Time: 30 minutes

*Hint: Use hot roll mix within 6 to 8 months.
          Makes 22 cups of mix.*

FOOD PROCESSOR PIZZA DOUGH

3   cups all-purpose flour
1   package dry yeast
1   teaspoon salt
1   tablespoon honey
2   tablespoons olive oil
¾   cup warm water

P lace flour and yeast in food processor bowl. Mix briefly. In separate small bowl, mix salt, honey, olive oil and warm water. With the motor running, slowly pour the liquid into the processor. Process until the dough forms into a ball. If the mixture seems too dry, add up to another ¼ cup warm water. To make this dough by hand, sprinkle the yeast into the warm water. Add the honey and allow mixture to foam. Mix in the oil, salt and flour. Proceed to the next step. Remove dough to a lightly floured surface and knead, adding more flour to prevent sticking. Knead for 5 minutes until dough is smooth and satiny. Place dough in lightly oiled bowl, turning to oil the surface of the dough. Cover with a damp towel. Let rise in a warm place until doubled in size, about 1 hour. Turn the dough out onto a slightly floured surface. Cut into 5 or 6 pieces and roll each into a ball. Place them on a baking sheet, cover with a damp towel. This can be refrigerated up to 3 hours before baking. Return dough to room temperature. Flatten each ball into a 6 inch circle, then stretch into an 8 inch circle. Brush each pizza lightly with olive oil. Top each pizza with your favorite pizza mixture. Place on lightly greased cookie sheet. Bake in a preheated oven at 475° until crisp and browned.

Prep. Time: 20 minutes,
            plus 1 hour for dough to rise.

PICKIN' AND GRINNIN' BREAD

1	cup mashed potatoes	2	packages dry yeast
½	cup shortening	2	eggs, beaten
1	cup boiling water	6-7	cups flour
½-¾	cup sugar or honey	2	sticks butter or
2	teaspoons salt		margarine
1	cup cold water		

In a large bowl, mix the potatoes, shortening and boiling water well. Next add the sugar or honey, salt, cold water, yeast, eggs and flour. More flour may be added. Knead until the lumps are out and the dough is well mixed (smooth and elastic).   Let the dough rise until doubled. Punch dough down in the middle. Cover and let it rest for 10 minutes. On a large floured board, roll out half of the dough to ¼ inch thickness.   Cut into various shapes or roll into balls. Melt the butter or margarine. Dip the various shapes in the melted butter and layer in a tube pan.   Fill pan half full.   Repeat for the other half of the dough and layer in another tube pan. Let rise until doubled. Bake at 350° for 30 to 40 minutes.

Prep. Time: 20 minutes,
                  plus 2 hours for dough to rise.

Hint: Let dinner guests pull this bread apart.

BREADSTICKS

2	packages dry yeast	1	teaspoon salt
2	teaspoons sugar	3	cups all-purpose flour
1	cup lukewarm water		or half all-purpose
2	tablespoons vegetable		flour & half
	oil		whole-wheat flour

Combine the yeast, sugar and water in a large bowl. Let stand for 10 minutes. Mix in the oil and salt, then slowly mix in the flour. Add enough flour so the dough can be easily kneaded. Knead for 5 minutes. Roll into long sticks, about ½ inch thick and 8 inches long. Place the sticks on a lightly oiled baking sheet. Bake at 375° on the high rack of the oven for 15 minutes, or until golden brown. *Makes 2 dozen sticks.*

Prep. Time: 30 minutes.

ROUND UP SOURDOUGH ROLLS

1	package dry yeast	3	cups flour
½	cup warm water	2	teaspoons baking
3	tablespoons sugar		powder
1	cup buttermilk	¼	teaspoon baking soda
½	cup corn oil	1	teaspoon salt

Dissolve yeast in warm water with sugar. Mix dry ingredients, then add liquid. Place in covered bowl in refrigerator. No need to rise. Roll out to ½ inch thickness. Cut out with biscuit cutter or pinch off bits of dough and roll into balls. Bake at 350° until light brown, 15 to 20 minutes.

Prep time: 15 minutes

WHOLE–WHEAT BANANA BREAD

1	stick butter, softened	1 ½	cups whole-wheat
½	cup brown sugar,		flour
	firmly packed	½	teaspoon baking soda
2	eggs, lightly beaten	½	teaspoon nutmeg
1	cup bananas, mashed	½	teaspoon salt
1	teaspoon vanilla	½	cup half-and-half
		½	cup pecans, chopped

Cream butter and sugar until light and fluffy. Add eggs, bananas and vanilla, blending well. Combine dry ingredients. Stir into banana mixture. Add half-and-half and pecans. Spoon into greased 5 x 9 x 2 inch loaf pan. Bake at 350° for 60 to 70 minutes.

Prep. Time: 20 minutes.

BUBBA'S BREW BREAD

This makes a great bread for toast.

1	extra large egg	1	12 ounce bottle dark
	or 2 large eggs		beer (only dark beer
¼	cup molasses		will work)
2 ½	cups self-rising flour		

Grease a 5 x 9 inch loaf pan. Mix egg and molasses in large bowl. Stir in flour. Slowly stir in beer. Mix with wooden spoon until blended. Pour into pan. Bake in a preheated oven at 350° on middle shelf for 45 to 50 minutes or until bread sounds hollow when thumped.

Prep. Time: 20 minutes.

WHOLE–WHEAT BREAD, THE MODERN WAY

1	egg	1	cup stone-ground
½	teaspoon salt		whole-wheat flour
1	package dry yeast	1 ¾	cups bread flour
1	tablespoon sugar	1 ½	teaspoons salt
1	cup plus 2		
	tablespoons		
	warm water		

With a metal blade, process the egg and salt for 2 seconds in food processor. Set aside. Do not clean the work bowl. In a small bowl, proof the yeast and sugar. Let stand for approximately 10 minutes or until foamy. Put the flours and remaining salt in the work bowl. With the food processor running, add the yeast mixture through the feed tube. Process the mixture until it forms a ball, then continue processing another 40 seconds. The dough should be moist and elastic. Add flour, 1 tablespoon at a time, if the dough is too moist. Transfer the dough to an oiled bowl and rotate the dough to cover it with oil. Cover the bowl with a damp towel and place in a slightly warmed oven. Let the dough rise for 1 hour or until it has doubled in bulk. Roll the dough out onto a lightly floured board, shaping into a rectangle. Beginning with the short end, roll up the dough. Tightly pinch the ends and seam. Place the dough, seam side down, into a greased loaf pan. Brush the top of the bread with the reserved egg. Let rise in a slightly warmed oven for another hour or until doubled. Bake in a preheated oven at 350° for 35 minutes.

Prep. Time: 2½ hours.

Hint: *1 cup sunflower seeds or pumpkin seeds can be kneaded into the dough after the first rising.*

ZUCCHINI BREAD

4	eggs	1 ½	teaspoons salt
1	cup brown sugar	1	tablespoon cinnamon
1	cup granulated sugar	2	cups grated zucchini
1	cup vegetable oil	1	cup pecans, chopped
3 ½	cups all-purpose flour	2	teaspoons vanilla
1 ½	teaspoons baking soda	½	teaspoon nutmeg
1	teaspoon baking powder		

Beat eggs well. Gradually beat in sugars, then oil. Combine flour, baking soda, baking powder, salt and cinnamon. Add to egg mixture alternating the dry ingredients with zucchini. Add pecans, vanilla and nutmeg. Spoon batter into two 9 x 5 inch greased and floured bread pans. Bake at 350° on the lowest rack for approximately 1 hour.

Prep. Time: 20 minutes.

HOMEMADE CROUTONS

4	slices whole-grain bread	¼	teaspoon oregano
1	tablespoon margarine or butter	¼	teaspoon onion powder
1	teaspoon basil, finely chopped	¼	teaspoon thyme
1	teaspoon parsley, finely chopped	¼	teaspoon garlic powder

Cut the bread into ½ inch cubes. In a skillet, melt the margarine or butter, then add the seasonings. Stir in the bread cubes. Sauté until crisp.

Prep. Time: 10 minutes.

Hint: Other herbs and spices may be used to your taste.

ZU-NANA BREAD

Zucchini and bananas never tasted so good!

3	cups all-purpose flour	1	tablespoon vanilla
1	teaspoon baking soda	1	teaspoon imitation banana extract
1	teaspoon salt		
1	teaspoon ground cinnamon	2	cups bananas, mashed
½	teaspoon baking powder	2	cups unpeeled zucchini, shredded
1	cup vegetable oil	1	cup pecans or walnuts, chopped
3	eggs		
2	cups sugar		

Combine flour, soda, salt, cinnamon and baking powder in a mixing bowl. Set aside. Combine oil, eggs, sugar and flavorings in a large bowl. Beat well. Stir in bananas and zucchini. Add flour mixture, stirring until moistened. Stir in nuts. Pour batter into 2 greased and floured 4½ x 8 ½ x 3 inch loaf pans. Bake at 350° for 1 hour. Cool in pans 10 minutes. Remove from pans and cool completely on wire racks. *Makes 2 loaves.*

Prep. Time: 20 to 30 minutes.

FESTIVE PUMPKIN BREAD

3 ½	cups sifted flour	1	cup salad oil
2	teaspoons baking soda	2	cups pumpkin, either canned or fresh
3	cups sugar	4	eggs
1	teaspoon salt	²/₃	cup water
1	teaspoon nutmeg	1	cup raisins
2	teaspoons cinnamon	1	cup nuts

S ift together first six ingredients. Make a well. Pour in next 6 ingredients. Mix together. Grease four 1-pound cans or 1 bundt pan. Pour batter into baking dish. Bake 1 hour at 350°. Cool slightly before removing from baking dish.

Prep. Time: 30 minutes.

LEMON BREAD

4	eggs	1	package pound cake mix
½	cup cooking oil		
¾	cup apricot nectar	1	small package lemon gelatin
1	teaspoon lemon extract		
1	teaspoon butter flavoring	2	tablespoons poppy seeds; 3 tablespoons if needed

B lend together the first five ingredients. Add the next 3 ingredients. Blend all well. Bake in 2 loaf pans at 350° for 35 to 40 minutes.

Prep. Time: 15 minutes.

FRESH JALAPEÑO CORNBREAD

¼	stick butter	1	cup yellow cornmeal
2	eggs, beaten	1	cup grated cheese
1	cup milk	1	teaspoon salt
1	can cream-style corn	½	teaspoon baking soda
½	cup fresh or frozen whole kernel corn	5	tablespoons flour (optional)
3	jalapeño peppers (remove seeds, chop) or ½ cup green chilies, chopped		
1	cup yellow onions		

M elt the butter in a pan to thoroughly coat the pan. In a bowl, mix all of the remaining ingredients, adding any excess melted butter. Pour batter into pan. Bake at 375° for 50 minutes or until golden brown. *Makes 8 servings.*

Prep. Time: 20 minutes.

Hint: Use a heavy cast iron skillet for best results.

OPEN AND DUMP CORNBREAD THAT'S SO GOOD

Ingredients for 1 recipe cornbread (from scratch or mix)   *Ingredients for 1 yellow cake mix*

In separate bowls, mix cornbread using all the liquid and egg as stated. Mix ingredients for cake using all the liquid and egg as stated. Combine both batters in a large bowl. Beat with a hand-mixer until smooth. Pour into a 9 x 13 inch pan that has been sprayed with a non-stick spray. Preheat oven to 375˚. However, bake at 350˚ for 40 to 45 minutes or until lightly browned.

Prep. Time: 20 minutes.

HAPPY HEART CORNBREAD

¼	cup vegetable oil	4 teaspoons baking powder
1	cup yellow cornmeal	
1	cup all-purpose flour	1 cup skim milk
2-4	tablespoons sugar	2 egg whites

Spray non-stick cooking spray in 8 inch pie plate. Combine all ingredients. Bake in a preheated oven at 400˚ for 20 minutes until lightly brown.

Prep. Time: 20 minutes.

BUTTERMILK APPLE MUFFINS

⅓	cup sugar	1 teaspoon baking soda
1	tablespoon butter, room temperature	1 teaspoon salt
		1 teaspoon vanilla
¾	cup firmly packed brown sugar	1 ½ cups flour
		1 ½ cups peeled apples in ¼ inch pieces
⅔	cup vegetable oil	
1	egg	½ cup pecans, chopped
1	cup buttermilk	

Grease and flour muffin tins. Combine ⅓ cup sugar and butter in a small bowl. Mix until crumbly. Set aside. Combine brown sugar, oil and egg in a large bowl. In another bowl, combine buttermilk, soda, salt and vanilla. Blend flour into brown sugar mixture, alternating with buttermilk mixture. Stir until ingredients are combined. Do not overmix. Fold in apples and pecans. Divide batter among pans. Sprinkle tops with sugar and butter mixture. Bake in a preheated oven at 325˚ for 30 minutes.

Prep. Time: 30 minutes.

CRIOLLO MUFFINS

Colorful muffins and good tasting.

2	eggs	¾	cup Cheddar cheese, grated
1 ½	cups milk		
¾	cup butter, melted	2 ½	cups flour
2	tablespoons bell pepper, chopped	1	teaspoon salt
2	tablespoons onion, chopped	2	tablespoons baking powder
2	tablespoons pimentos, chopped	5	tablespoons sugar
		5	tablespoons yellow cornmeal

Put milk, eggs and butter in bowl. Whisk and set aside. Toss pepper, onion, pimentos and cheese with all of the dry ingredients. Add to egg-butter-milk mixture. Stir lightly until moistened. Do not overmix. Fill greased muffin tins almost three-fourths full. Bake at 400° about 30 minutes.

Prep. Time: 20 minutes.

FRESH APPLE MUFFINS

Your friends will rave.

2	cups flour	1	cup sugar
2	teaspoons cinnamon	1	teaspoon vanilla
1	teaspoon baking soda	4	cups tart apples, unpeeled & chopped
½	teaspoon salt		
2	eggs	1	cup walnuts, chopped
1	cup oil		

In small bowl, stir together flour, cinnamon, baking soda and salt. In large bowl beat eggs until foamy. Beat in oil, sugar and vanilla. Stir into flour mixture until blended. Stir apples and nuts into flour mixture. Spoon into muffin tins lined with baking cups. Bake in a preheated oven at 350° for 15 to 20 minutes. Remove from pan and cool.

Prep. Time: 20 minutes.

MUFFINS FOR CHOLESTEROL-CONSCIOUS COWBOYS & COWGIRLS

2 ¼	cups oat bran cereal	1 ¼	cups skim milk or evaporated skim milk
1	tablespoon baking powder		
		2	egg whites
¼	cup brown sugar	2	tablespoons corn syrup
½	cup dried fruits		

Mix the dry ingredients in a large bowl. Mix the milk, egg whites and corn syrup together. Blend with dry ingredients. Line muffin pans with paper baking cups. Fill with batter equally divided. Bake in a preheated oven at 425° for about 15 minutes.

Prep. Time: 25 minutes.

COCONUT CHEESE MUFFINS

2	cups sugar	½	cup Parmesan
½	cup water		cheese, grated
6	eggs, slightly beaten	1 ½	cups coconut,
1	cup whole-wheat flour		freshly grated
3	tablespoons butter		

Over high heat, boil sugar and water to soft-ball, stirring frequently. Do not overcook; 240° on a candy thermometer. Remove from heat and beat syrup slowly into eggs with electric hand mixer at low speed. Slowly add flour, butter, cheese, coconut and mix well. Spoon batter into well greased Madeleine pans or 1½ inch muffin tins. Bake at 350° for 20 minutes. Serve warm or cold with fruit salads or desserts. *Makes 4 dozen.*

Prep. Time: 20 minutes.

VERY MOIST SQUASH MUFFINS

2	pounds yellow squash	1	teaspoon salt
2	eggs, beaten	1	tablespoon plus
1	cup butter, melted		2 teaspoons
1	cup sugar		baking powder
3	cups flour	½	teaspoon cinnamon

Cook squash until tender, drain and mash. Measure 2 cups of squash. Add eggs and butter then set aside. Combine dry ingredients. Stir in squash mixture until moistened. Spoon into greased muffin tins. Bake at 375° for 30 minutes.

Prep. Time: 20 to 30 minutes.

DISAPPEARING BLUEBERRY MUFFINS

½	cup milk	1	teaspoon salt
¼	cup fresh lemon juice	¾	cup pecans, chopped
¾	cup margarine	2	teaspoons lemon
	(1 ½ sticks)		rind, grated
1 ¼	cups sugar	1	cup blueberries
3	eggs	½	cup butter, melted
2	cups all-purpose flour	¼	cup sugar
2	teaspoons baking powder		

Mix milk with lemon juice. Set aside. Cream together the margarine and sugar in a large bowl. Add eggs to margarine and sugar. Combine dry ingredients. Add to the creamed mixture, alternating with the milk. Stir in pecans, lemon rind and blueberries. Bake in greased muffin tins or tins lined with baking cups. Bake at 350° for 30 to 40 minutes. When done, dip tops in melted butter, then in sugar.

Prep. Time: 15 minutes.

GOOD GINGERBREAD MUFFINS

1 ½	cups unbleached white flour	¾	cup walnuts, chopped
¾	cup sugar	1	egg, beaten
1	teaspoon dried ginger, ground	3	tablespoons molasses
		¾	cup buttermilk
1	teaspoon cinnamon	1	teaspoon baking soda
½	cup butter or margarine	¾	teaspoon salt
		½	cup raisins

Combine flour, sugar, ginger, cinnamon. Cut in butter or margarine. Set aside a quarter of the mixture, tossing with walnuts. To the remaining flour mixture, add the egg and molasses. Dissolve the baking soda and salt in the buttermilk. Stir the buttermilk mixture quickly into the batter. Do not overmix. Add the raisins. Spoon the batter into greased muffin tins. Fill only half full. Sprinkle with the nut topping. Bake at 350° for 20 minutes.

Prep. Time: 20 minutes.

NOT HEAVY OAT BRAN MUFFINS

2	cups oat bran	1	cup brown sugar
2	cups buttermilk	2	egg whites
2	cups whole-wheat flour	½	cup orange juice
2	teaspoons baking powder	1	cup pecans, chopped (optional)
1	teaspoon baking soda	½	cup raisins (optional)
1	teaspoon salt	1	tablespoon cinnamon (optional)
⅔	cup margarine, melted	2	ripe bananas, mashed (optional)

Mix all until well blended. Add any of the options to your taste. Bake at 350° for 20 to 25 minutes. *Makes 36 small muffins.*

Prep. Time: 30 minutes.

HAPPY TRAILS MUFFINS

¾	cup toasted oat bran	¼	teaspoon salt
¾	cup flour	2	large egg whites, lightly beaten
½	cup whole-wheat flour	1	cup applesauce
2	teaspoons baking powder	½	cup plain low fat yogurt
½	teaspoon baking soda	3	tablespoons vegetable oil
½	teaspoon cinnamon	3	tablespoons honey
¼	teaspoon nutmeg	1	cup apples, chopped
		½	cup pecans, chopped (optional)

Coat 12 muffin cups with non-stick cooking spray. Combine first eight ingredients in large bowl. Combine egg whites, applesauce, yogurt, oil and honey in another bowl. Add to flour mixture. Stir until moistened. Fold in apples and pecans. Pour batter in muffin cups. Bake in a preheated oven at 400° for 30 minutes. *Makes 12 muffins.*

Prep. Time: 20 minutes.

SOMETHING DIFFERENT, FOR A CHANGE TOAST

¾	cup Parmesan cheese (3 ounces), freshly grated	½	teaspoon white pepper, ground
½	cup mayonnaise	24	slices white sandwich bread

In a small bowl, combine the cheese, mayonnaise, and white pepper. Lay the bread on a work surface and cut with a cookie cutter. (If you do not want to use a cookie cutter, cut off the bread crust and quarter each slice.) Spread 2 teaspoons of the mixture evenly onto each bread slice. Arrange the slices on a large baking sheet. Bake in a preheated oven at 400° for 5 to 7 minutes, until golden and bubbly. Serve immediately.

Prep. Time: 20 minutes.

FRENCH BREAD SPREAD

Even if you don't like chives, you'll like this bread.

½	cup butter	1	small can black olives, sliced
½	cup mayonnaise		
½	cup Cheddar cheese, shredded	½	teaspoon garlic salt
		½	teaspoon black pepper
¼	cup chives, chopped	1	loaf French bread

Except for the bread, mix all of the ingredients. Slice the loaf of bread into 10 to 12 pieces. Spread the mixture thickly onto each slice. Lay slices "spread up" on a cookie sheet. Broil only until the edges are brown.

Prep. Time: 15 minutes.

HEARTBURN, BUT GOOD, SANDWICH

1	pound mild sausage, casing removed & sliced	¼	cup water
		¼	teaspoon garlic salt
½	pound ground beef	¼	teaspoon oregano leaves, crushed
1	cup onion, chopped	¼	teaspoon rosemary, crushed
½	cup green pepper, chopped	¼	cup Parmesan cheese, grated
1	2.5 ounce can mushrooms, sliced & drained	6	ounces Mozzarella cheese, grated
1	6 ounce can tomato paste	1	loaf Vienna bread
1	8 ounce can tomato sauce		

In a large saucepan, brown the sausage and the ground beef. Drain off the excess fat. Stir in the onion, pepper and mushrooms. Cook for 5 minutes. Stir in the tomato paste, tomato sauce, water, garlic salt, oregano, rosemary and Parmesan cheese. Simmer for 10 minutes, stirring constantly. Cut the top of the bread off and hollow it out to form a shell. Place 3 ounces of Mozzarella cheese in the bottom of the bread. Pour the meat mixture on top of this. Top with the remaining 3 ounces of Mozzarella cheese. Place the top slice of the bread on loaf. Wrap in foil. Bake in a preheated 400° oven for 6 to 8 minutes. Cut into pie shaped sandwiches. *Makes 8 servings.*

Prep. Time: 30 minutes.

HOT POPPY HAM SANDWICHES

½	cup margarine, melted	¼	cup prepared mustard
1	tablespoon poppy seeds	12	split buns
1	tablespoon dried onion flakes	¾	pound ham, sliced very thin
		12	slices of Swiss cheese

In a small bowl, combine the margarine, poppy seeds, onion flakes and mustard. Spread this mixture on bottom piece of the buns. Set the tops of the buns aside. Divide the ham evenly among the 12 bun bottoms. Top with a slice of Swiss cheese. Place the top of the bun on the sandwich. Wrap in aluminum foil. Place in a preheated 350° oven and bake 15 minutes until warm.

Prep. Time: 15 minutes.

WEST TEXAS HOT SANDWICH

Fast, good and different.

4-6	tablespoons butter	8	slices trimmed bread, toasted
3-4	tablespoons flour		chicken, poached & sliced (enough to cover 8 slices of bread)
	salt, to taste		
	cayenne pepper, to taste		
2-3	cups milk		
2	egg yolks	8	slices bacon, slightly cooked
	Tabasco sauce, to taste		
1½	cups mild Cheddar cheese, shredded	8	slices tomato
½	cup Parmesan cheese, grated		

Melt butter. Add flour, salt and cayenne. Stir constantly until smooth and bubbly. Remove from heat. Add however much milk is needed, stirring until smooth. Return to heat and cook slowly until thickened. Beat in egg yolks and Tabasco sauce. Stir in cheeses until melted. Place toast on baking dish. Cover with chicken. Cover completely with sauce. Place bacon and tomatoes on each slice of covered toast. Broil until bacon is cooked, well done, and the sauce is slightly browned.

Prep. Time: 30 minutes.

MONTE CRISTO SANDWICH
Takes time to prepare, but is worth it.

Batter:		*Sandwich:*	
¾	*cup water*	2	*slices white bread*
1	*egg*	1	*ounce turkey, sliced*
½	*teaspoon salt*	1	*ounce Swiss cheese,*
½	*cup all-purpose flour*		*sliced*
dash of pepper		1	*ounce ham, sliced*
1 ¾	*teaspoons baking*	*powdered sugar*	
	powder	*jam or fruit compote*	
2	*drops yellow food*		
	coloring		

Combine water, egg, salt, flour and pepper. Mix with a mixer or wire whisk until thoroughly mixed. Stir in the baking powder and food coloring. Mix until the batter is smooth. Place in the refrigerator and chill. This must be used the same day as prepared.

To assemble the sandwich, place the cheese between the ham and turkey and then place this between the two slices of bread. Cut into fourths. Secure each piece with a toothpick. Dip the sandwich in the batter.

In a deep frying pan, pour in the oil until it is about 6 inches deep. Place the sandwiches in hot oil. Fry until each side is lightly browned, turning the sandwiches once. Remove from the oil and place on a paper towel to allow to drain. Remove the toothpicks. Sprinkle powdered sugar on top and serve with jam or fruit compote.

Prep. Time: 20 to 30 minutes.

VEGGIE SANDWICH
Not the cowboy way to eat.

Dressing:		*Sandwich:*	
½	*cup sunflower seeds*	2-4	*leaves fresh spinach,*
1	*clove garlic*		*washed*
1	*tablespoon fresh*	¼	*cup bean sprouts*
	parsley	¼	*cup mushrooms,*
1	*tablespoon fresh*		*sliced*
	cilantro	1-2	*slices tomato*
2	*tablespoons lemon*	¼	*cup red cabbage,*
	juice		*shredded*
1	*cup plain yogurt*	¼	*cup carrots, grated*
salt & pepper, to taste		¼	*cup pecans, walnuts*
			or almonds
		¼	*cup raisins*
		2	*slices whole-wheat*
			bread

Grind sunflower seeds in a blender or food processor. Add garlic and herbs and continue to process. Blend in lemon juice and yogurt. Process until smooth. Cover a slice of bread with dressing, then spinach. Add remaining ingredients.

Prep. Time: 10 minutes.

Hint: *Other herbs may be used.*

HOT CHICKEN SANDWICHES

16	slices of very thin white bread	3	hard-boiled eggs, chopped
½	cup butter or margarine	⅓	cup black olives, drained & sliced
¼	pound fresh mushrooms, sliced	¾	cup mayonnaise, not salad dressing
2	tablespoons onions, finely minced	1	10.75 ounce can cream of chicken soup
2	tablespoons butter or margarine	1	cup sour cream
2	cups cooked chicken cut into bite-sized pieces	2	tablespoons cream sherry
			paprika

Cut the crust off the bread. Spread the ½ cup of butter on both sides of each slice of bread. Place 8 of the 16 slices of bread in a 9 x 13 inch baking dish that has been sprayed with a non-stick cooking spray. In a large saucepan, sauté the mushrooms and onions in the remaining butter until the mushrooms are lightly browned. Remove from heat. Stir in the chicken, eggs, olives and mayonnaise, mixing well. Spread on top of the bread in the baking dish. Top with the remaining 8 slices of bread. In a medium bowl, combine the soup, sour cream, cream sherry and paprika. Pour over the chicken sandwiches in the baking dish. Bake in a preheated 325° oven for 30 minutes or until thoroughly heated. *Makes 8 servings.*

Prep. Time: 30 minutes.

TURKEY DELIGHT

Dressing:

1	cup mayonnaise
1	tablespoon chili sauce
3-5	sweet pickles
1-2	tender celery stalks (or peeled)
1	medium onion
½	green bell pepper

Sandwich:

2	slices bread, toasted
	turkey breast, sliced & cooked
1	egg, hard-boiled & sliced
1	lettuce curl
2	cherry tomatoes
2	olives
2	broccoli florets that have been blanched for 2 minutes in salted boiling water

Place all of the dressing ingredients in the food processor. Using a pulsing action, process until smooth, but still slightly lumpy.

Place the turkey on 1 slice of the bread. Cover with the dressing. Top with the sliced hard-boiled eggs. Place the second slice of bread on top. Serve with the lettuce curl, tomatoes, olives and broccoli florets on the side.

Prep. Time: 30 minutes.

Soups & Salads

CHUCK WAGON SOUP

1	pound sirloin	6	cups beef bouillon
½	pound ground beef	½	teaspoon celery salt
3	tablespoons butter	½	teaspoon garlic salt
	or margarine	2	teaspoons seasoned
1 ½	cups onions		salt
1 ½	cups celery	1	teaspoon black
1 ½	cups tomato		pepper
4	tablespoons oil	¼	teaspoon red pepper
6	tablespoons flour	2	teaspoons browning
			sauce

Brown sirloin and ground beef. Sauté vegetables in butter. Add meat to vegetables. Set aside. Make a roux in skillet with the oil and flour. Add bouillon, stirring until smooth. Pour over meat and vegetable mixture. Add remaining ingredients. Bring to a boil. Cover and reduce heat. Simmer for 2 hours. *Makes 4 to 6 servings.*

Prep. Time: 30 minutes.

SAVORY STEAK SOUP

12	cans beef broth	1	cup fresh parsley,
1	cup carrots, sliced		chopped
1	teaspoon	1	clove garlic, crushed
	Worcestershire sauce	1	green pepper,
1	teaspoon garlic salt		chopped
¼	teaspoon marjoram	1	stick butter or
¼	teaspoon rosemary		margarine
½	cup red vermouth	1	sirloin steak
1	teaspoon salt	1	12 ounce package
1	onion, coarsely		whole wheat
	chopped		noodles
1	onion, finely chopped		sharp Cheddar cheese,
1	pound fresh		grated
	mushrooms, sliced		green onion, chopped

In a large pot, simmer the first nine ingredients until the vegetables are tender. Sauté the onion, mushrooms, parsley, garlic and green pepper in the butter until tender. Add to broth and let sit until just before serving. Thirty minutes before serving, cook the steak very rare and cut into bite-sized pieces. (It will finish cooking in the soup.) Bring broth to a boil and add noodles. Cook 10 to 15 minutes or until tender. When noodles are cooked, add steak and cook a minute or two longer. Ladle into oven-proof bowls and top with chopped green onions and cheese. Bake in a preheated 350° oven for 10 to 15 minutes or until bubbly around the edges. *Makes 10 servings.*

Prep. Time: 1 hour.

CHILI SOUP

3	tablespoons cooking oil	1	16 ounce can whole tomatoes, cut up
1	medium onion, chopped	1	13.5 ounce can tomato juice
1 ½	pounds hamburger	2	cans water
1	15 ounce can ranch-style beans	⅔	10 ounce package macaroni

In a large stew pot, sauté onion in oil until tender and hamburger is brown. Drain. Add all the rest of the ingredients. Bring to a boil for 5 minutes. Cover and simmer for 30 to 45 minutes (until macaroni is tender). If it gets too thick, add water. Should be a thick soup consistency.

Prep. Time: 15 minutes.

SAUSAGE VEGETABLE SOUP

1	pound smoked sausage, cut into ½ inch pieces	1	cup carrots, sliced
		1	tablespoon chicken bouillon
¾	cup celery, sliced	4	cups water
⅓	cup onion, chopped	½	teaspoon thyme
1	cup potatoes, peeled and cubed	1	cup frozen cut green beans

In a large pot, brown sausage. Remove from pot. In drippings, cook celery and onions until tender. Add remaining ingredients, except beans. Bring to a boil, then reduce heat. Simmer covered 15 minutes. Add beans, cover and simmer 15 minutes longer or until vegetables are tender. *Makes 4 servings.*

Prep. Time: 1 hour.

THICK BEEF STEW

1 ½	pounds stew meat		dash of pepper
1	cup carrots, sliced	1	can cream of mushroom soup
1	onion, chopped		
3	large potatoes, peeled & cubed	½	soup can filled with water
1	cup celery, chopped (optional)	1	bay leaf
1 ½	teaspoons salt	½	cup burgundy (optional)

Combine first ten ingredients in a covered casserole dish. Bake at 275° for 5 hours. During last half hour of cooking, add burgundy. Can be cooked in Crockpot for 10 hours on low. May need to thicken gravy. *Makes 4 to 6 servings.*

Prep. Time: 20 minutes.

TORTILLA SOUP
A South of the border treat.

1	onion, chopped	1	teaspoon chili powder
2	cloves garlic, mashed	1	teaspoon salt
2	tablespoons oil	1	teaspoon pepper
2	1 pound cans stewed tomatoes	2	teaspoons Worcestershire sauce
1	10.75 ounce can chicken broth		several dashes hot sauce
1	chicken broth can filled with water	1	10 ounce can chilies & tomatoes
1	teaspoon cumin powder	8	corn tortillas, cut in strips
1	10.75 ounce can beef bouillon		Monterey-Jack cheese, shredded
			fresh cilantro, chopped

Combine first four ingredients and sauté in large pot. Add the next 10 ingredients and simmer for 1 hour. Add tortillas to soup and simmer for 10 minutes. Serve in bowls and garnish with cheese and cilantro. *Makes 6 to 8 servings.*

Prep. Time: 10 minutes.

Hint: Broth can be cooked and frozen in advance.
Wait to add tortillas until serving.
Tortillas can also be fried before adding to broth,
for a crunchy taste.

CALDILLO (MEXICAN STEW)

1	pork chop, cubed	2	tablespoons garlic powder
3	pounds cubed beef	2	teaspoons cumin
1 ½	cups onions, diced	1	tablespoon chili powder
3	cups tomatoes, diced	2	pounds potatoes, cubed
3	cups green chili strips		water
1	cup beef stock		flour tortillas
1	cup chicken stock		
2	tablespoons salt		
1	tablespoon black pepper		

Sauté pork, beef and onions until meat is brown and onions are clear. Add the rest of the ingredients. Add enough water to make soupy. Cook for 3 hours on medium heat. Serve with warmed and buttered flour tortillas.

Prep. Time: 20 minutes.

VERSATILE MEXICAN SOUP

1	onion, chopped	1	15 ounce can ranch-style beans
1	tablespoon butter	1	4 ounce can green chilies
1	pound hamburger meat, browned & drained		cheese (optional)
1	17 ounce can corn		sour cream (optional)

Sauté onions in butter. Put all ingredients in Crockpot and heat until warm. Serve with tortilla chips. Top with cheese or sour cream. *Makes 6 servings.*

Prep. Time: 30 minutes.

Hint: To make "Frito Pie", spoon soup over a bowl
of corn chips.
To make a "Soup Burrito", spoon soup into a
flour tortilla, add cheese and roll it up.

MEXICAN POTATO SOUP

Great on a cold day!

3	slices bacon, diced	1 ½	teaspoons salt
3	large potatoes, peeled & cubed	1	10 ounce can green chilies, chopped
5	cups water	½	pound sharp cheese, grated
1	cup tomato sauce		
¼	cup onion, chopped		

Brown bacon. Add potatoes and stir to coat. Add water, tomato sauce, onion and salt. Reduce heat to simmer and cook 1 hour. Place chilies and cheese in bowls. Spoon hot soup over chilies and cheese to serve. *Makes 6 servings.*

Prep. Time: 10 minutes.

SWISS–STYLE POTATO SOUP

4	small potatoes (6 if needed)	1	cup Swiss cheese, cubed
1	tablespoon butter	1	13 ounce can evaporated milk
4	fresh green onions, sliced	¼	teaspoon salt

Boil potatoes until tender. Drain, reserving one-half cup water. Peel and cube. Sauté onions in butter. Combine potatoes, onions, cheese, milk, water and salt. Microwave on high for 8 minutes. *Makes 4 servings.*

Prep. Time: 45 minutes.

CALICO CHEESE SOUP

1	cup carrots, chopped	salt, to taste	
1	cup celery, sliced	¼	teaspoon cayenne pepper
1	cup potatoes, cubed	1	pound American cheese, cubed
4	cups water		
½	cup butter	1	10 ounce package frozen peas, defrosted
½	cup onion, minced		
6	tablespoons flour		
4	cups milk, heated		

Cook carrots, celery and potatoes in water 20 minutes until tender. In another heavy pan, cook butter and onions until onions are soft and transparent. Sprinkle flour over onions, stirring frequently until flour is cooked. Gradually add hot milk, stirring constantly. Add salt and pepper. Cook until bubbly and thickened. Remove from heat and add cheese. Stir in cooked vegetables and uncooked peas. Serve hot. Flavor mellows if allowed to sit awhile. *Makes 6 servings.*

Prep. Time: 45 minutes.

GREEN CHILIES, RICE AND CHEDDAR SOUP

1	tablespoon butter	5	cans chicken broth
1	large yellow onion, chopped	2	cups cooked rice
1	8 ounce package cream cheese, room temperature	2	4 ounce cans green chilies, chopped
2	packages spreadable sharp Cheddar cheese	1	teaspoon garlic salt
		2	13 ounce cans evaporated milk

Sauté butter and onions until onions are soft. Add cream cheese and Cheddar cheese and begin melting it. Use a wire whisk. Add the chicken broth a little at a time. Add rice, green chilies and garlic salt. Reduce heat and add milk. Do not boil, cheese and milk will curdle.

Prep. Time: 30 minutes.

CHEESE SOUP

¼	cup onions, chopped	⅔	cup warm beer
½	cup butter	2	cups sharp Cheddar cheese
¼	cup flour		
2 ½	cups milk	⅛	teaspoon salt
1	package leek soup		popcorn
1	can cream of celery soup		

Cook chopped onions in butter. Blend in flour. Stir in milk, leek soup, celery soup and beer. Add cheese and salt. Do not boil. Sprinkle a handful of popcorn on top of each serving. *Makes 4 servings.*

Prep. Time: 30 minutes.

CANADIAN CHEESE SOUP

2	cups chicken stock	8	ounces Cheddar cheese, shredded
1	cup carrots, diced		
1 ½	cups celery, diced		fresh parsley, chopped (optional)
8	ounces butter		
¼	cup onion, minced		bacon, cooked & crumbled (optional)
½	cup flour, sifted		
6	cups milk		
8	ounces American cheese, shredded		

Heat chicken stock. Add celery and carrots. Cook until vegetables are tender. Set aside. Heat butter in saucepan, add onions and sauté lightly. Add flour and stir with wire whisk. Cook 2 to 4 minutes making sure flour and butter are well blended. Add vegetable broth and milk. Stir with whisk and bring to a boil. Turn heat to low as it thickens. Add cheeses and stir over low heat until cheese is melted. Serve hot. Garnish with fresh chopped parsley or bacon. *Makes 8 servings.*

Prep. Time: 20 to 30 minutes.

RED PEPPER SOUP

1	tablespoon olive oil	1	clove garlic, crushed
4	tablespoons unsalted butter	1	pear, peeled & quartered
6	red peppers, thinly sliced	1	quart chicken broth
3	carrots, peeled & sliced	1	tablespoon crushed dried red pepper
1	medium onion, chopped		cayenne pepper, to taste
			salt & pepper, to taste
			fresh tarragon, to taste

Heat the oil and butter in a large skillet. Sauté the vegetables and pear over medium low heat until tender for 8 to 10 minutes. Add the broth, dried red pepper, cayenne pepper, salt and pepper. Bring to a boil, then simmer covered for 25 to 30 minutes. Purée the soup in a food processor or blender. Pour the puréed soup back into the skillet. Reheat. Garnish with tarragon.

Prep. Time: 20 minutes.

LEMON BLACK BEAN SOUP

Low calorie and delicious.

30	ounces canned black beans	1	teaspoon dried oregano
2	cups chicken stock	1	teaspoon cumin
2	cups water	1/8	teaspoon cayenne pepper
1	carrot, grated	1	bay leaf
1	onion, chopped	1/2	teaspoon paprika
1	potato, grated	1/4	cup lemon juice

Place all ingredients except lemon juice in a 2 quart saucepan. Cook, over medium heat for 25 minutes. Cool. Purée half of mixture in blender or food processor. Add back to saucepan. Reheat to serve. Add lemon juice just before serving.

Prep. Time: 20 minutes.

OKRA SOUP

4	potatoes, peeled & chopped	1	10 ounce package frozen okra or 1 cup fresh, sliced
2	onions		
1/2	cup butter	1/4	teaspoon lemon pepper
2	16 ounce cans tomatoes		salt, to taste

In a large pot, boil potatoes, onions and butter in just enough water to cover. Simmer until potatoes are tender but not mushy. Add tomatoes and okra. Add lemon pepper and salt to taste. Cook until okra is tender. *Makes 4 to 6 servings.*

Prep. Time: 15 minutes.

INSPIRATION SOUP

1   can mixed Chinese vegetables, drained & rinsed (use juice on remaining ingredients)
1   4 ounce can mushrooms
1   15.5 ounce can French-style green beans
3   cups tomato juice
2   cups water
1/4 cup onion flakes or 1/2 onion, chopped
1 1/2 cups carrots, sliced
2   stalks celery, chopped
4   beef bouillon cubes
4   packages unflavored gelatin softened in 2 cups of water
    dash of celery salt
    dash of oregano
    dash of garlic
    dash of salt & pepper
    dash of thyme
    dash of Worcestershire sauce
    dash of Tabasco sauce

P lace all ingredients, except for the softened gelatin, in a large pot. Bring to a boil. Add the softened gelatin. Lower the heat and simmer for 20 minutes. Add more water if needed. *Makes 8 to 10 servings.*

Prep. Time: 20 minutes.

Hint: *After the soup has been chilled, it can be used as a congealed salad.*

BROCCOLI-MUSHROOM CHOWDER

1   pound fresh broccoli, cut into 1/2 inch pieces
1/2 cup water
8   ounces butter
1   cup flour, sifted
1   quart chicken stock (either homemade, canned or 4 bouillon cubes dissolved in water)
8   ounces fresh mushrooms, sliced
1   quart half-and-half (milk can be substituted)
1/4 teaspoon white pepper
2   teaspoons salt
1/4 teaspoon fresh tarragon leaves, crushed

S team broccoli in one-half cup water until tender. Do not drain. Set aside. Melt butter in saucepan over medium heat. Add flour to make a roux. Cook for 2 to 4 minutes. Add chicken stock, stirring with a wire whisk. Bring to a boil. Turn heat to low. Add broccoli, mushrooms, half-and-half and spices. Heat, but do not boil.

Prep. Time: 15 minutes.

SEA SHELL MACARONI SOUP

1	tablespoon olive oil	3	teaspoons chicken bouillon
6	ounces sea shell macaroni	42	ounces water
1	onion, chopped	½	cup white wine
1	clove garlic, minced	½	teaspoon prepared mustard
1	16 ounce can stewed tomatoes		

Fry shell macaroni in oil until brown. Remove macaroni. Set aside. Cook onion and garlic in oil until clear. Return macaroni to soup pot. Add tomatoes, water and bouillon. Cook until macaroni is done. Add wine and mustard. Season to taste. *Makes 6 to 8 servings.*

Prep. Time: 1 hour.

ITALIAN TORTELLINI SOUP

1 ½	pounds mild Italian sausage	½	teaspoon basil leaves
1 ½	cups onion, chopped	½	teaspoon oregano leaves
2	cloves garlic, minced	1	8 ounce can tomato sauce
5	cups beef broth	2	medium zucchini, thinly sliced
1 ½	cups dry red wine or water	1	7 ounce box cheese-filled tortellini or fresh tortellini
1	16 ounce can tomatoes, diced		grated Parmesan cheese
1 ½	cups carrots, thinly sliced		

Remove sausage casing and brown in a large stock pot. Remove sausage, drain and reserve two tablespoons of drippings. Sauté onion and garlic until onions are tender. Add broth, wine, tomatoes, carrots, spices, tomato sauce and sausage. Bring to a boil and simmer uncovered for 30 minutes. Stir in zucchini and tortellini. Simmer covered for an additional 20 to 30 minutes or until tortellini is tender. Garnish each bowl of soup with Parmesan. *Makes 10 servings.*

Prep. Time: 30 minutes.

Hint: Can be made in advance, but add tortellini just before serving.

GAZPACHO

½	cup celery, chopped	1	tablespoon Italian salad dressing
½	cup bell pepper, chopped	1	tablespoon garlic wine vinegar
½	cup onion, chopped	¼	teaspoon salt
½	cup cucumber, chopped	⅛	teaspoon black pepper
1	cup tomatoes, chopped		garlic salt, to taste
1	can tomato soup (undiluted)	6	drops Tabasco sauce
1	tomato soup can filled with water	2	drops Worcestershire sauce
1	12 ounce can vegetable juice (hot spicy)		

Mix all of the ingredients well. Refrigerate for at least 4 hours or overnight. Soupy salad—eat with a spoon or drink as a soup.

Prep. Time: 15 minutes,
plus 4 hours to marinate.

BASIC ROUX

¾	cup oil	water or stock
⅔	cup flour	

In a heavy pot (cast iron or aluminum is best), combine the flour and oil, mixing until all lumps are gone. It is very important to heat the water or stock before beginning to cook the roux. Never change the temperature of the roux by adding cold water. The roux could curdle or separate the flour from the oil. This would ruin the roux. A spoiled roux makes for a spoiled soup or gumbo. Turn the heat to a medium to low setting on the oil and flour mixture. With a whisk, stir constantly during cooking to avoid scorching. As the roux is whisked, it will slowly turn a golden brown. Do not try to hurry this process by increasing the heat or the roux could burn. Once the roux has reached a golden to dark brown, remove from the heat immediately. Continue stirring and add hot water or stock. Once the liquid is completely stirred in, place the pot back on the stove and add remaining ingredients for soup, gumbo or jambalaya. Makes enough roux for a stew or gumbo with one hen or two pounds of shrimp.

Prep. Time: 15 to 20 minutes.

A PRETTY GREEN SALAD

Dressing:
¼ cup sugar
¾ teaspoon dry mustard
¾ teaspoon salt
½ teaspoon celery seed
1 ½ tablespoons minced onion
¼ cup wine vinegar
½ cup oil

Salad:
½ pound fresh spinach, washed & dried
½ small head purple cabbage
dried fruit bits
slivered almonds, toasted

Combine all the dressing ingredients, mixing well. Set aside until needed. In a large bowl tear the spinach and cabbage into bite-sized pieces. Add the dried fruit and slivered almonds. Toss to mix. Top with dressing. *Makes 6 servings.*

Prep. Time: 20 minutes.

MANDARIN ORANGE & SPINACH SALAD

Dressing:
½ cup oil
¼ cup vinegar
¼ cup ketchup
¼ cup sugar

Salad:
1 10 ounce package spinach
½ cup toasted walnuts or pecans
1 11 ounce can mandarin oranges, drained
10 fresh mushrooms, sliced (12 if needed)
1 medium red onion, sliced thin in rings

Combine all the dressing ingredients. Mix well. Wash and dry the spinach, removing the stems. Place spinach in a large bowl. Add the remaining ingredients and toss to mix. Pour the dressing on just before serving. *Makes 4 servings.*

Prep. Time: 15 minutes.

LAYERED SALAD

1	10 ounce package fresh spinach		pepper, to taste red onion, sliced & in rings
½	head lettuce	1	16 ounce box frozen English peas
4-5	slices bacon, cooked & crumbled	1	pint sour cream
2	hard-boiled eggs, sliced	1	cup mayonnaise
1	tablespoon sugar	1	cup Mozzarella cheese, grated
	salt, to taste		

Tear the spinach and lettuce into bite-sized pieces and place in a large bowl. Add the bacon, eggs, sugar, salt, pepper and onion slices to the spinach. Toss the ingredients. Pour the box of frozen peas over the spinach mixture. Do not stir. In a small bowl, combine the sour cream and mayonnaise. Pour over the salad and spread covering the top of the salad. Sprinkle the cheese on top. *Makes 10 to 12 servings.*

Prep. Time: 45 minutes.

SPINACH TWIST

1	pound fresh spinach	1	11 ounce can of mandarin oranges, drained
5	small fresh mushrooms, sliced		
3	green onions, chopped	12	slices bacon, cooked & crumbled
1	8 ounce can pineapple chunks, drained		ranch-style dressing slivered almonds
1	14 ounce can artichoke hearts, drained & quartered		

Remove the stems from spinach, wash leaves, pat dry, and tear into bite-size pieces. In a large bowl, place spinach, mushrooms, green onions, pineapple, artichoke hearts and oranges. Sprinkle with bacon pieces and serve with salad dressing. Garnish with almonds.

Prep. Time: 15 to 20 minutes.

MANDARIN ROMAINE SALAD

1	bunch romaine lettuce, washed & torn in bite-sized pieces	*Dressing:*
		Mix equal parts of Italian dressing & any commercial poppy seed dressing.
1	11 ounce can mandarin oranges, drained	
1	purple onion, sliced	
2	handfuls raisins	

Place everything in salad bowl, toss with dressing. *Makes 4 to 6 servings.*

Prep. Time: 20 minutes.

Hint: Substitute fresh grapefruit sections or sliced strawberries in place of mandarin oranges.

MIXED SALAD WITH WARM BACON DRESSING

Salad:
4	cups romaine lettuce
2	cups fresh spinach
4	tablespoons Swiss or Provolone cheese, shredded
4	tablespoons croutons
8	fresh mushrooms (10 if needed), sliced

Dressing:
$\frac{1}{2}$	pound bacon
2	large onions, diced
$\frac{1}{2}$	teaspoon celery seeds
$\frac{1}{2}$	teaspoon basil leaves, crushed
$\frac{1}{2}$	teaspoon poppy seeds
1	pound brown sugar
3	cups cider vinegar
2	cups vegetable oil
$\frac{1}{2}$	teaspoon chives, fresh or dry

In a large bowl, combine all the salad ingredients. Toss to mix. Cut the bacon into 1 inch pieces and fry until crisp. Add the onion to this and continue cooking until the onions are tender. Stir in the celery seeds, basil leaves and poppy seeds. In another bowl, combine the brown sugar and cider vinegar, mixing well. Add to the bacon and onion mixture. Bring to a boil and then turn the heat off. Add the oil and chives. Pour warm mixture over salad greens. *Makes 6 to 8 servings.*

Prep. Time: 20 to 30 minutes.

Hint: Refrigerate the unused dressing. Reheat to use. Dressing recipe can be halved.

BRITTANY SALAD

1	head lettuce, chopped	$\frac{1}{2}$	cup mayonnaise
1	cup celery, diced	$\frac{1}{4}$	cup sugar
1	small red onion, thinly sliced	3	tablespoons vinegar
		1	pound bacon, cooked & crumbled
	Swiss cheese, cubed		
1	cup sour cream		Parmesan cheese

Toss the lettuce, celery, onion and cheese. Place in a serving bowl. Mix together the sour cream, mayonnaise, sugar and vinegar. Spread over salad. Top with bacon and lots of Parmesan cheese. Refrigerate several hours before serving.

Prep. Time: 20 to 30 minutes, plus several hours to chill.

TRADITIONAL SPINACH SALAD WITH CURRY MUSTARD DRESSING

$\frac{3}{4}$	cup oil	$\frac{1}{2}$	teaspoon salt
$\frac{1}{4}$	cup wine vinegar	1	teaspoon sugar
1	teaspoon dry mustard	1	bunch fresh spinach, torn in pieces
$\frac{1}{2}$	teaspoon curry		
1	teaspoon season pepper	3	eggs, hard-boiled
		6	slices bacon, cooked & crumbled
2	tablespoons red vermouth		
2	tablespoons soy sauce	1	medium purple onion, sliced

Mix first nine ingredients in jar to make dressing. Shake well. Pour over spinach and top with sliced hard-boiled eggs, crumbled bacon and sliced onions.

Prep. Time: 30 minutes.

ORANGE AND GREEN SALAD

Dressing:
½	teaspoon salt
⅛	teaspoon pepper, freshly ground
¼	cup olive oil
2	tablespoons fresh parsley, chopped
2	tablespoons sugar
2	tablespoons red wine vinegar
2-4	drops Tabasco sauce

Salad:
3	tablespoons sugar
½	cup slivered almonds for garnish
1	head iceberg lettuce
1	head romaine lettuce
2	celery stalks, thinly sliced
4	scallions, chopped
1	11 ounce can mandarin oranges, drained

In a medium bowl, combine the dressing ingredients, mixing well. Cover and refrigerate at least 1 hour to allow the flavors to blend. In a dry skillet over a medium heat, combine the sugar and almonds. Cook until lightly toasted and sugar just melts. Set aside. Tear the lettuce into bite-sized pieces and place in a large bowl. Add to this, the celery, scallions, and oranges. Pour the dressing over greens and toss well. Garnish with the toasted almonds. *Makes 6 servings.*

Prep. Time: 25 to 30 minutes.
Refrigerating Time: 1 hour.

NINE DAY SLAW

1	medium cabbage, finely shredded	2	cups sugar
2	stalks celery, chopped	1	cup salad oil
1	onion, chopped	1	cup vinegar
1	green pepper, chopped	2	tablespoons sugar
		1	tablespoon salt

In a large bowl, combine the cabbage, celery, onion and green pepper. Stir in the sugar. In a medium saucepan, combine the remaining ingredients. Bring to a boil stirring constantly. Remove from heat and immediately pour dressing mixture over the cabbage mixture. Allow to cool. Cover and chill at least 1 day before serving to allow the flavors to blend. Slaw will stay crisp for 9 days in the refrigerator.

Prep. Time: 20 minutes,
            plus 24 hours to chill.

GARDEN GREEN SALAD

1	head of lettuce, chopped	½	cup oil (¾ cup if needed)
½	medium onion (or to taste), chopped		dash of vinegar
			garlic salt, to taste

In a large bowl, combine the lettuce and onion. In another bowl, combine the oil, vinegar, and garlic salt.   Pour the oil mixture over the salad just before you are ready to serve. *Makes 6 to 8 servings.*

Prep. Time: 10 minutes.

BLACK–EYED PEA SALAD

3	15.8 ounce cans black-eyed peas, drained	¼	cup plus 2 tablespoons sugar
1	2 ounce jar of pimentos, drained	¼	cup plus 2 tablespoons vegetable oil
½	cup red onion, chopped	¾	teaspoon ground red pepper
¼	cup vinegar	¼	teaspoon salt
¼	cup plus 2 tablespoons red wine vinegar		

In a large bowl, combine the first three ingredients and toss gently. In another bowl, combine the remaining ingredients mixing well. Pour this mixture over the pea mixture and toss. Refrigerate at least 3 hours. *Makes 6 to 8 servings.*

Prep. Time: 20 minutes,
                plus 3 hours to chill.

Hint: For a zesty taste, substitute Balsamic vinegar for either vinegar.

OKRA SALAD
A man pleaser.

Dressing:

¼	cup oil	6	slices bacon, cooked & crumbled
¼	cup vinegar	1	green bell pepper, chopped
1	teaspoon sugar	4	green onions, including tops, chopped

Salad:

2	12 ounce packages frozen breaded okra		
	vegetable oil	2	fresh tomatoes, diced

In a small bowl, combine all the dressing ingredients, mixing well. Deep fat fry the okra in oil until golden brown. Remove from the oil and allow to drain on a paper towel. After drained, place in a large bowl and add all the remaining ingredients. Before serving, pour the dressing over the salad and toss. Serve immediately. *Makes 4 serving.*

Prep. Time: 30 to 40 minutes.

PATIO CORN SALAD

Dressing:

¼	cup sour cream
2	tablespoons mayonnaise
1	tablespoon vinegar
½	teaspoon salt
¼	teaspoon dry mustard

Salad:

2	12 ounce cans white corn, drained
¼	cup onion, chopped or ¼ cup green onions, chopped
¾	cup cucumber, diced
2	small tomatoes, chopped
1	green bell pepper, chopped (optional)

In a small bowl, combine the dressing ingredients, mixing well. In a medium bowl, combine the salad ingredients. Stir in the dressing. *Makes 6 to 8 servings.*

Prep. Time: 15 to 20 minutes.

BLUE CHEESE VEGETABLE SALAD

Croutons:
½-1 cup margarine, melted
3-5 slices bread, cubed

Dressing:
½ cup mayonnaise
1 tablespoon lemon juice
crumbled blue cheese, to taste
2 tablespoons Parmesan cheese, grated
salt, to taste
fresh green pepper, to taste

Salad:
1 cup cauliflower florets
1 cup fresh broccoli florets
1 cup asparagus, cut into 1 inch pieces
1 bunch curly or romaine lettuce
4-5 cherry tomatoes, halved
4-5 slices bacon, cooked & crumbled
¼ cup green onions & tops, sliced

Place the melted margarine in a large frying pan. Place the bread cubes in the frying pan. Toss to thoroughly coat. Place in a 200° preheated oven, stirring occasionally, for several hours until golden brown. Spread out on a paper towel and allow to cool.

In a small bowl, combine the dressing ingredients. Set aside.

Bring a large pot of water to a rolling boil. Stir in cauliflower, broccoli and asparagus. Blanche for 45 seconds. Douse in cold water. Tear the lettuce into bite-sized pieces, discarding the stems. Add the cauliflower, broccoli, asparagus and tomatoes and toss. Gently stir in the salad dressing. Top with bacon pieces, chopped green onions and croutons.

Prep. Time: 30 minutes for salad.

Hint: *Peppercream dressing (page 96) is very good also with this salad.*

FROZEN CUCUMBERS

Salad:
7 cups fresh cucumbers, sliced (preferably without wax coating)
3 large onions, thinly sliced
2 green peppers, thinly sliced
2 tablespoons salt

Dressing:
1 cup vinegar
2 cups sugar
2 teaspoons mustard seed
2 teaspoons celery seed

In a large bowl, combine the salad ingredients. Let sit at room temperature for 1 hour. In a saucepan, combine the dressing ingredients and bring to a boil. Cool and pour over vegetables. Place in the freezer until frozen.

Prep. Time: 1 hour and 15 minutes.

VEGETABLE BOUQUET

1-2	bunches broccoli, broken into florets	1	14 ounce can hearts of palm
1	head cauliflower, broken into florets	1	8 ounce can water chestnuts, drained & sliced
2	zucchini, thinly sliced		cherry tomatoes, to taste, halved
	fresh mushrooms, to taste, thinly sliced	1	cup cooked shell macaroni
1	red onion, sliced & separated into rings	1	8 ounce bottle Italian salad dressing
1	14 ounce can artichoke hearts, drained		

I n a large bowl, combine all the vegetables. Marinate with the entire bottle of Italian dressing. Cover and refrigerate 4 to 6 hours. This will last for several days if it is kept refrigerated. *Makes 10 to 12 servings.*

Prep. Time: 30 minutes.
Refrigerating Time: 4 to 6 hours.

Hint: Add any of your favorite vegetables, taking away any you do not like.

WINTER SALAD

Dressing:
½	cup mayonnaise
⅓	cup vinegar
⅓	cup salad oil
¼	cup sugar
	salt, to taste
	pepper, to taste

Salad:
1	head cauliflower, cut into bite-sized pieces
1	bunch broccoli, cut into bite-sized pieces
½	cup onions, coarsely chopped
¼	cup green onions, chopped
½	cup carrots, sliced
¼	cup celery, chopped
1	cup Cheddar cheese, cut into ¼ inch cubes
¼	cup bacon, cooked & crumbled

C ombine all of the dressing ingredients in a jar and shake until thoroughly mixed. In a large bowl, combine all the salad ingredients. Pour the dressing over salad and stir well. Cover and refrigerate for 12 to 24 hours stirring several times.

Prep. Time: 1 hour,
              plus 12 to 24 hours to marinate.

CAULIFLOWER SALAD

¼	cup oil	1	cup stuffed green olives, chopped
⅓	cup ketchup		
2	tablespoons sugar	4	cups cauliflower florets
2	teaspoons lemon juice	½	cup green pepper, chopped
1	teaspoon salt		
1	teaspoon paprika	½	cup yellow onion, chopped

I n a large bowl, combine the oil, ketchup, sugar, lemon juice, salt and paprika. Mix well. Stir in the remaining ingredients and allow to marinate.

Prep. Time: 30 minutes,
plus several hours to marinate.

COTTAGE CHEESE SALAD

1	package lemon gelatin	1	green bell pepper, chopped
1	cup boiling water	1	tablespoon onion, grated
1	teaspoon sugar		
1	teaspoon salt	¼	cup celery, chopped
1	cup mayonnaise	1	cup cottage cheese
1	tablespoon pimentos, chopped		

M ix together gelatin, boiling water, sugar and salt. Set aside to cool. After the gelatin mixture is cooled, add the remaining ingredients. Whip in a blender or food processor until the mixture is smooth. Refrigerate overnight. *Makes 8 servings.*

Prep. Time: 20 minutes.
Refrigerating Time: Overnight.

BROCCOLI SALAD

Salad:		Dressing:	
1	large bunch broccoli, cut into florets	1	cup mayonnaise
½	pound crisp bacon, crumbled	¼	cup sugar
		2	tablespoons red wine
½	red onion, sliced in thin rings		
½	cup sunflower seeds, shelled		
½	cup raisins		
½	cup fresh mushrooms, sliced		

I n a large bowl, mix all of the salad ingredients. In a small bowl or jar, mix all of the dressing ingredients. Toss the salad with the dressing just before serving. *Makes 8 servings.*

Prep. Time: 30 minutes.

DELI POTATO SALAD

3	pounds new potatoes or plain potatoes	½	teaspoon pepper
¾	pound bacon	½	teaspoon celery salt
12	ounces sour cream	½	teaspoon onion salt
½	cup mayonnaise		grated cheese (optional)
1	teaspoon salt		green onion (optional)

Cut potatoes into chunks and boil in covered pot 20 to 30 minutes until tender, not mushy. Meanwhile, fry bacon and crumble. Add bacon and remaining ingredients to drained potatoes. Serve warm.

Prep. Time: 30 minutes.

Hint: Do not mash potatoes when mixing.

TATER SALAD

Grandma would be proud.

5	pounds potatoes, cubed (cooked in boiling water)	2-3	medium onions, chopped
6-10	boiled eggs	1	4 ounce jar pimentos, diced
1	medium bottle sweet pickles, chopped	1	pint or more salad dressing
1	small stalk celery, chopped		salt, to taste paprika

Mix all together carefully. Season. Sprinkle paprika over top. Chill before serving. Chill any leftovers.

Prep. Time: 45 minutes.
Refrigerating Time: 1 to 2 hours.

HOT GERMAN POTATO SALAD

4	medium potatoes	⅛	teaspoon pepper
¾	cup boiling water	6	tablespoons vinegar
6	slices bacon , cut up		water drained from potatoes
⅔	cup onion, chopped		
4	teaspoons sugar		
1 ½	teaspoons salt		
½	teaspoon celery seed		

Pare and cube potatoes. Add boiling water and cook, covered, until tender. Fry bacon until crisp. Remove from pan. Sauté chopped onion in the bacon fat until slightly brown. Blend in sugar, salt, celery seed, pepper, vinegar and water drained from the potatoes. Bring to a boil and cook for 2 to 3 minutes. Pour over the potatoes and add bacon. Stir lightly. If needed, add a little more water.

Prep. Time: 45 minutes.

DILL POTATO SALAD

Simply dill-icious!

2	medium potatoes, boiled with peeling left on		celery salt, to taste
		2	tablespoons dill pickle, finely chopped
2	medium hard-boiled eggs	¾	cup mayonnaise
		1	teaspoon mustard

salt, to taste
pepper, to taste

Peel and dice potatoes. Dice eggs. Mix remaining ingredients together and stir into potatoes and eggs. Chill.

Prep. Time: 1 hour.

Hint: Sprinkle paprika on top for color.

FROZEN FRUIT SALAD

6	ounces cream cheese, softened	½	cup maraschino cherries, drained & quartered
1	8 ounce carton non-dairy whipped topping	2 ½	cups tiny marshmallows
1	17 ounce can fruit cocktail, drained		few drops cherry juice for color

In a large bowl, fold all the above ingredients into the cream cheese. Place in the freezer until frozen. Serve partially frozen. *Makes 10 servings.*

Prep. Time: 5 minutes,
             plus time for mixture to freeze.

MORNING FRUIT SALAD

½	medium-sized cantaloupe	2-3	tablespoons fresh mint leaves
2	kiwi fruit	¼	cup freshly squeezed orange juice
1	pint strawberries		
½	pint fresh raspberries or blackberries	4	whole mint sprigs for garnishing

Scoop out cantaloupe with a melon baller and place melon balls in a medium bowl. Peel kiwi fruit and cut crosswise into thin slices. Add to the cantaloupe. Set aside 4 of the prettiest strawberries for garnishing. Hull and slice enough strawberries to make 1 cup. Add to the fruit in the bowl. Add the raspberries or blackberries. Sprinkle fruit with chopped mint leaves. Drizzle with orange juice. Toss gently. Refrigerate covered for a half hour. Divide among four bowls. Garnish each with a mint leaf and a strawberry. *Makes 4 servings.*

Prep. Time: 30 minutes.
             Chill for 30 minutes.

TROPICAL FRUIT SALAD

1	17 ounce can fruit cocktail, drained	1	cup pecans, chopped
1	8 ounce can pineapple tidbits, drained	2	cups buttermilk
		1	3 ounce package instant vanilla pudding
1	11 ounce can mandarin oranges, drained	1	8 ounce carton non-dairy whipped topping

I n a large bowl, combine the fruits and pecans and set aside. In another bowl, combine the buttermilk and vanilla pudding mixing until the pudding is dissolved. Fold in the non-dairy whipped topping. Pour over the fruit mixture and mix well. Refrigerate 24 hours.

Prep. Time: 14 minutes.

Hint: *Best if chilled for at least 24 hours.*
        Make certain the fruits are well-drained.

HAWAIIAN FRUIT SALAD

Salad:
1   15.25 ounce can pineapple chunks
1   can mandarin oranges
1   cup fresh green seedless grapes
2   bananas, sliced
1   avocado, chopped

Dressing:
1   cup sugar
1   tablespoon cornstarch
3   tablespoons lemon juice
1   egg, slightly beaten
¾   cup pineapple juice

D rain fruits, reserving liquids. Combine pineapple, oranges, grapes, bananas and avocado. Set aside. Mix ingredients for dressing. Cook slowly over medium heat, stirring constantly until thickened. Cool before pouring over fruit mixture. Chill before serving. *Makes 4 to 6 servings.*

Prep. Time: 20 minutes.

PEACH PIE FRUIT SALAD

1   11 ounce can mandarin oranges, drained
1   15.25 ounce can pineapple chunks, drained
1   29 ounce can large pears, drained
2   large bananas (or to taste), sliced

1   21 ounce can peach pie filling
add cherries for color
cantaloupe balls (optional)
miniature marshmallows (optional)
pecans, chopped (optional)
coconut (optional)

C ombine all the above ingredients in a large bowl and refrigerate until ready to serve.

Prep. Time: 20 minutes.

MARSHMALLOW FRUIT SALAD

3	eggs, beaten	2	5.25 ounce cans
4	tablespoons sugar		pineapple chunks,
3	tablespoons butter		drained
6	tablespoons vinegar	2	cups marshmallows
2	16 ounce cans	4	bananas, sliced
	cherries, drained	½	pint whipping cream
2	11 ounce cans		
	mandarin oranges,		
	drained		

In a small saucepan, combine the first four ingredients. Cook over a low heat until thick. Do not boil. Remove from heat and cool. Add canned fruit and let stand 18 to 24 hours. Add marshmallows and bananas mixing well. Stir in whipping cream until desired consistency. Serve immediately. *Makes 10 to 12 servings.*

Prep. Time: 20 minutes.
Refrigerating Time: 18 to 24 hours.

PUDDIN' SALAD

1	15.25 ounce can	1	11 ounce can
	pineapple chunks,		mandarin oranges,
	drained reserving		drained
	1 cup juice	2	bananas, sliced
1	17 ounce can apricot	1	3 ounce package
	halves, drained		vanilla pudding
1	16 ounce can peach		(not instant)
	slices, drained		

In a large bowl, combine all the fruit and mix well. In a small saucepan, dissolve the pudding in the cup of pineapple juice. Heat over a medium heat until the pudding and juice mixture starts to boil. Remove from heat and pour over fruit mixture.

Prep. Time: 15 minutes.

QUICK AND EASY FRUIT SALAD

1	15 ounce can	3	tablespoons instant
	pineapple chunks		orange drink mix
1	16 ounce can chunky	2	large sliced bananas
	mixed fruit		
1	3.75 ounce package		
	instant vanilla		
	pudding mix		

Drain pineapple and mixed fruits, reserving pineapple juice. Combine juice, pudding mix and orange drink mix. Stir well. Combine fruit with dressing, toss gently and chill.

Prep. Time: 20 minutes.

LO–CAL WALDORF SALAD

¾	cup non-fat yogurt	½	cup walnuts,
1	tablespoon sugar		chopped
1	teaspoon lemon juice	½	cup celery, chopped
3	medium apples, chopped into bite-sized pieces		

I n a small bowl, combine the yogurt, sugar and lemon juice mixing well. In a medium bowl, combine the apples, walnuts and celery. Pour the yogurt mixture over the apple mixture and toss. *Makes 4 servings.*

Prep. Time: 20 minutes.

PISTACHIO PERKY SALAD

1	9 ounce carton non-dairy whipped topping	2	cups mini marshmallows
1	3 ounce package pistachio instant pudding mix	1	20 ounce can crushed pineapple with juice, unsweetened
		½-1	cup pecans, chopped

I n a medium bowl, fold the dry ingredients into the non-dairy topping. Stir in the pineapple with juice and the pecans. Refrigerate until thoroughly chilled. *Makes 8 servings.*

Prep. Time: 10 minutes.
Refrigerating Time: 1 hour.

WALDORF SALAD WITH WHIPPED CREAM DRESSING

Dressing:

¼	cup mayonnaise	
1	tablespoon sugar	
½	teaspoon lemon juice	
dash of salt		
½	cup cream, whipped	

Frosted grapes:
red grapes
egg white, slightly beaten
granulated sugar

Salad:

2	cups apples, diced
1	cup celery, chopped
½	cup pecans, chopped
½	cup grapes, halved & seeded

F or dressing, in a small bowl, combine the mayonnaise, sugar, lemon juice and salt. Fold in the whipped cream and set aside until needed.

For salad: In a large bowl, combine all the salad ingredients. Fold in the dressing.

For frosted grapes: Brush the grapes with the beaten egg whites. Sprinkle with the sugar. Decorate the salad with frosted grapes.

Prep. Time: 30 minutes.

CHRISTMAS CRANBERRY SALAD

Will be a holiday tradition.

1	*pound fresh cranberries*	2	*cups sugar*
1	*pound grapes, chopped*	2	*cups pecans*
		½	*pint whipping cream, whipped*

Grind cranberries in food processor. Add sugar and let stand overnight in refrigerator. Drain in colander for 1 hour. Add grapes, pecans and whipping cream. *Makes 6 servings.*

Prep. Time: 20 minutes.
Refrigerating Time: Overnight.

CHERRY SALAD

1	*14 ounce can condensed milk*	1	*cup pecans, chopped*
1	*21 ounce can cherry pie filling*	1	*8 ounce carton non-dairy whipped topping*
1	*5.25 ounce can crushed pineapple, drained*		

In a large bowl, combine the condensed milk with the pie filling, mixing well. Stir in the pineapple and pecans mixing well. Fold in the non-dairy whipped topping. Refrigerate until thoroughly chilled. *Makes 10 to 12 servings.*

Prep. Time: 20 minutes.
Refrigerating Time: 1 to 2 hours.

LITE THANKSGIVING CRANBERRY SALAD

Low calories, but delicious.

1	*large package sugar-free gelatin*	2	*apples, chopped*
2	*cups boiling water*	2	*oranges, chopped*
2	*cups fresh cranberries, chopped or ground*	1	*capful lemon extract*
1	*cup crushed pineapple*	8	*packages artificial sweetener*

Dissolve gelatin in boiling water. Refrigerate until slightly thickened. Add the other ingredients. Chill until firm. *Makes 12 servings.*

Prep. Time: 30 minutes.
Refrigerating Time: 1 to 2 hours.

SIMPLE BANANA SALAD

Tastes like a popsicle.

4	medium ripe bananas, mashed	1	5.25 ounce can crushed pineapple, drained
½	cup buttermilk		
1	teaspoon vanilla	1	9 ounce carton non-dairy whipped topping
1	cup sugar		
1	cup pecans, chopped		

Thoroughly mix all of the ingredients. Place in a glass 9 x 13 inch baking dish. Freeze 1 hour. Cut into squares and serve. *Makes 8 to 10 servings.*

Prep. Time: 15 minutes.
Freezing Time: 1 hour.

GREEN GRAPES SUPREME

¼	cup firmly packed light brown sugar	5	cups seedless, washed green grapes
½	cup sour cream		mint sprigs

Combine brown sugar and sour cream in a large mixing bowl. Stir in grapes. Chill several hours. Spoon fruit into individual serving dishes. Garnish with sprigs of mint. *Makes 8 servings.*

Prep. Time: 15 minutes.
Refrigerating Time: Several hours.

STRAWBERRY JELLO SALAD

1	6 ounce package strawberry gelatin	1	15.25 ounce can crushed pineapple, drained
1	cup boiling water		
3	medium bananas, mashed	1	pint sour cream
1	cup pecans, chopped		
2	10 ounce packages frozen strawberries, thawed & drained		

In large bowl, combine the gelatin and boiling water. Stir until the gelatin is completely dissolved. Allow to cool. Add bananas, pecans, strawberries and pineapple. Pour half of this mixture into a 9 x 13 inch pan and refrigerate until set (45 minutes). Spread sour cream on top of the set strawberry gelatin. Spoon the remaining room temperature strawberry gelatin mixture on top of the sour cream. Place back into the refrigerator and chill until totally set. *Makes 12 servings.*

Prep. Time: 20 minutes.
Refrigerating Time: 1 to 2 hours.

ITALIAN PASTA SALAD

8	ounces shell or wheel pasta	½	cup parsley, chopped
1	tablespoon olive oil	½	cup celery, finely chopped
3	eggs, hard-boiled & sliced		
2	large tomatoes, diced		*Dressing:*
⅓	cup capers	¼	cup white wine vinegar
⅔	cup black olives, chopped	½	cup olive oil
2	onions, chopped	1	clove garlic, minced
1	large jar sliced pimentos		salt & pepper, to taste

Cook pasta until al dente. Drain and rinse under cold water. Toss with olive oil and then set aside. In another bowl, mix all dressing ingredients. In serving bow, mix all other ingredients. Toss with dressing mix. Chill until ready to serve. *Makes 6 servings.*

Prep. Time: 20 minutes.
Refrigerating Time: At least 1 hour.

Hint: *The longer the flavors marinate, the more flavorful.*

ITALIAN RODEO SALAD

1	pound curly vegetable pasta	8	ounces Monterey-Jack cheese, cubed
1	small bunch broccoli, cut into bite-sized pieces	1	6 ounce jar artichoke hearts in oil, cut each into 3 pieces
2	small zucchini, sliced	12	ounces Italian dressing with cheese
4	ounces pepperoni, sliced & pieces cut into 3 strips	¼	cup Italian cheese, grated

Cook pasta according to directions. Rinse in cold water. Toss in broccoli, zucchini, pepperoni, and Monterey-Jack cheese. Try to mix thoroughly. Mix in the artichoke hearts, including the oil that they are in. Toss with Italian dressing. After it is mixed well, toss again with the grated cheese. Cover and chill at least 2 hours before serving. Stir well before serving.

Prep. Time: 30 minutes.
Refrigerating Time: 2 hours.

VERMICELLI SALAD

1	14 ounce package vermicelli coils	½	teaspoon chives, chopped
1	medium red onion, chopped	¼	cup Italian dressing
1	medium green pepper, chopped	1	cup mayonnaise
1	tablespoon parsley, chopped		salt & pepper, to taste
1 ½	tablespoons celery seed	1	pound shrimp or crabmeat, cooked, rinsed & marinated in
½	teaspoon oregano		½ to 1 cup lemon juice (optional)

Cook vermicelli in boiling water, stirring constantly. Drain and blanch with cold water. Add onion, green pepper, parsley, celery seed, chives, oregano and Italian dressing. Moisten well with the mayonnaise. Add salt and pepper to taste. Toss in shrimp.

Prep. Time: 30 minutes.

MACARONI SALAD
Can't be beat.

1	8 ounce package shell macaroni	2-3	ounces blue cheese, crumbled
2-3	cups seedless green grapes, halved		salt & pepper, to taste
1	8 ounce can black olives, drained & halved	¼	teaspoon garlic powder
¾	cup green onions, chopped	3	tablespoons fresh lemon juice
		1	cup mayonnaise

Cook macaroni according to package directions. Drain. In large bowl, combine hot macaroni with grapes, olives, onion, cheese, salt, pepper and garlic powder. In small bowl, mix together lemon juice and mayonnaise until smooth. Combine macaroni and mayonnaise until evenly mixed. Refrigerate covered several hours or overnight. Add more mayonnaise if desired, before serving.

Prep. Time: 30 minutes.
Refrigerating Time: Several hours or overnight.

PARTY PASTA SALAD

1	3 pound fryer
1	small onion, quartered
water	
½	pound package rotelli or shell macaroni
salad oil	
2	large carrots, thinly sliced, diagonally
salt	
½	pound mushrooms, cut in quarters
½	small bunch broccoli, cut into bite-sized pieces

½	small head cauliflower, separated into florets
1	bunch green onions, cut in 1 inch pieces
2	tablespoons soy sauce

Rinse chicken and giblets with cold water. Place chicken breast side down in a saucepan, just large enough to hold chicken. Add giblets, onion and 2 inches water. Over high heat, heat to boiling. Reduce heat to low, cover pan and simmer 35 minutes or until chicken is fork tender. Remove chicken to large bowl. Refrigerate 30 minutes or until easy to handle. Discard skin and bones from chicken; cut meat and giblets into bite-sized pieces. Meanwhile prepare pasta and drain. In 8 quart Dutch oven or saucepan over medium-high heat, in 1 tablespoon hot salad oil, cook carrots and ½ teaspoon salt until carrots are tender crisp, for 3 to 5 minutes, stirring frequently. With slotted spoon, remove carrots to a large bowl. In same Dutch oven, in 2 more tablespoons hot salad oil, cook mushrooms and ¼ teaspoon salt until mushrooms are tender, for 5 minutes, stirring occasionally. With slotted spoon, remove mushrooms to bowl with carrots. In 2 more tablespoons salad oil, stir broccoli, cauliflower and onions until coated and add ¼ cup water and ½ teaspoon salt. Cover and cook 5 to 10 minutes until tender crisp. With slotted spoon remove to bowl with mushrooms and carrots. Discard liquid. Return all vegetables to Dutch oven. Add chicken, macaroni, soy sauce, and 3 tablespoons salad oil and ½ teaspoon salt. With rubber spatula, toss gently to mix. Spoon mixture onto a large platter. Serve salad at room temperature or cover and refrigerate to serve chilled later. *Makes 6 main dish servings.*

Prep. Time: 45 minutes.
Refrigerating Time: 30 minutes.

PASTA SALAD

Dressing:

1	cup olive oil	1	carrot
½	cup fresh parsley, minced	1	onion
		1	celery stalk
4	tablespoons Dijon mustard	½	teaspoon salt
		⅓	cup pine nuts
1	teaspoon curry (1 ½ teaspoons if needed)	1	cup butter
		⅓	pound fresh snowpeas
1 ½	teaspoons salt	1	15 ounce can garbanzo beans, drained
1	teaspoon pepper	1 ½	pounds mushrooms, washed & sliced
½	teaspoon garlic powder	1	2 ounce jar green olives, drained & sliced
5	tablespoons red wine vinegar	1	2 ounce jar black olives, drained & sliced
		1	red or green bell pepper, cut in strips

Pasta:

1	pound spiral macaroni	1	jar marinated artichoke hearts
1 ½	pound chicken		

Prepare the macaroni according to directions. Prepare the dressing mixture by mixing well. Set aside. Poach the chicken, carrot, onion, celery and salt. Allow to cool. Remove the skin from the chicken. Chop the chicken, carrot, onion and celery. Sauté the pine nuts; drain and cool. Blanche the snowpeas, then cool. In a large bowl, mix the dressing and pasta ingredients, except for the pine nuts. Refrigerate overnight. Add the pine nuts just before serving. *Makes 12 large servings.*

Prep. Time: 30 minutes.
Refrigerating Time: Overnight.

CHICKEN, RICE AND ARTICHOKE HEART SALAD

1	16 ounce box of rice	1	2 ounce jar pimentos, drained
2	chicken breasts, cooked & diced	½	cup green peppers, chopped
1	package Italian dressing mix	1	cup celery, chopped
		½	cup mayonnaise
1	16 ounce can artichoke hearts, drained & quartered	½	pound fresh mushrooms

Cook the rice according to the directions on the box using ¼ cup less water than called for. Set aside. Mix the Italian dressing according to the instructions on the package and set aside. In a large bowl, combine the rice, salad dressing and all the other ingredients, except the mushrooms. Cover and refrigerate overnight. Slice the mushrooms a ½ hour before serving and add to the salad. *Makes 8 servings.*

Prep. Time: 30 minutes.
Refrigerating Time: Overnight.

COLD RICE SALAD WITH SHRIMP AND ARTICHOKES

1	6 ounce package chicken-flavored rice with vermicelli	2	green (spring) onions, chopped
2	6 ounce jars marinated artichoke hearts	12	stuffed green olives, sliced
⅓	cup mayonnaise	1 ½	pounds shrimp, cooked & shelled
¾	teaspoon curry powder		

Cook rice as directed. Cool. Drain artichokes, reserving the liquid from 1 jar, and slice in halves. Combine reserved artichoke liquid with mayonnaise and curry powder. Combine rice, artichokes, mayonnaise mixture and shrimp. Chill overnight. You can make the cold salad up to 2 days ahead. *Serves 6 as an entrée.*

Prep. Time: 15 minutes.
Refrigerating Time: Overnight.

Hint: *To add color, cut the amount of shrimp and substitute chopped, fresh vegetables.*

BROWN RICE SALAD

1	cup brown rice, uncooked	¼	cup salad or olive oil
1	10 ounce package frozen corn	¼	cup red wine vinegar
1	10 ounce package frozen peas	1	teaspoon salt or ½ teaspoon dill weed
		¾	teaspoon sugar
			lettuce leaves

Prepare rice. Meanwhile, prepare the frozen vegetables and drain. In a large bowl, mix oil, vinegar, sugar and seasonings. Add rice, corn and peas. Toss to coat well with dressing. Cover and refrigerate mixture at least 1 hour to blend the flavors. To serve, arrange the lettuce leaves on a platter. Spoon the rice mixture on top. *Makes 8 servings.*

Prep. Time: 30 minutes.
Refrigerating Time: 1 hour.

CHICKEN SALAD

2	cups chicken (2 ½ cups if desired), cooked & cut into bite-sized pieces	½	cup sliced red grapes (optional)
1	cup celery, chopped	1	large apple, peeled & diced (optional)
1	cup mayonnaise	½	cup coconut (optional)
½	cup non-dairy whipped topping	1	cup pineapple, crushed & drained (optional)
½	cup almonds or pecans, slivered		

salt & pepper, to taste

In a large bowl, combine the first six ingredients. Add any or all of the options, depending on your tastes. Chill before serving. *Makes 6 to 8 servings.*

Prep. Time: 15 minutes.
Refrigerating Time: 1 to 2 hours.

Hint: *Serve on wheat bread, avocado halves, tomato shells or on a bed of fresh lettuce.*

GENERAL STUFF'S ORIENTAL CHICKEN SALAD

"General Stuff" was a popular specialty store and tearoom in Odessa.

	one head napa or boktay cabbage	¼	cup soy sauce
8	ounces fresh mushrooms, cleaned & sliced	16	ounces boneless chicken breasts, cooked & cut into bite-sized pieces
1	cup toasted slivered almonds	1	5 ounce can chow mein noodles
1	cup mayonnaise		

Tear the cabbage into bite-sized pieces and place in a large bowl. Toss in the mushrooms and almonds. In another bowl, combine the mayonnaise and soy sauce. Stir in the chicken. Pour this over the cabbage mixture and toss to coat. Before serving, add the can of chow mein noodles and toss to mix. *Makes 6 to 8 servings.*

Prep. Time: 30 minutes.

CURRIED CHICKEN SALAD

This recipe came from a grand Texas lady, Miss Ima Hogg, the daughter of Governor James Hogg. (Governor 1891-1895)

4	chicken breasts, cooked & diced	½	cup mayonnaise
2	cups cooked wild rice	1	teaspoon mango chutney
1	cup green seedless grapes (or raisins)	2	tablespoons soy sauce
1	cup celery, diced	2-3	teaspoons curry powder (dissolved in 2 tablespoons hot water)
1	cup unpeeled apples, diced		
1	cup almonds (or cashews or pecans), slivered		

In a large bowl, mix chicken, rice, grapes, celery, apples and nuts. Add mayonnaise and stir thoroughly. Add chutney, soy sauce and curry powder. Blend well. Adjust seasonings to taste. Chill for 2 hours. *Makes 10 servings.*

Prep. Time: 30 minutes.
Refrigerating Time: 2 hours.

HONEY MUSTARD DRESSING

¼	cup Dijon mustard
½	cup mayonnaise
¼	cup honey

In a small bowl, combine all ingredients until well blended. Cover and refrigerate. You may add more mustard or honey to taste. For salad dressing, use more honey to make it thinner. *Makes 1 cup.*

Prep. Time: 10 minutes.
Refrigerating Time: 30 to 60 minutes.

Hint: *Use as a spread for sandwiches or dip; add as salad dressing.*

HOMEMADE MAYONNAISE

1	egg		juice of 1 lemon
1	teaspoon salt	1 ½	cups oil

Except for oil, place all ingredients in bowl of food processor. Process 15 to 20 seconds. Leave processor on and gradually add oil in steady stream. *Makes 2 cups.*

Prep. Time: 2 minutes.

HERBED MUSTARD VINEGARETTE

1 ½ cups virgin olive oil
1 jar Dijon mustard
¾ cup sugar
1 tablespoon sweet basil leaves
1 tablespoon tarragon leaves
1 tablespoon garlic salt
1 tablespoon lemon pepper
1 tablespoon lemon juice
¾ cup red wine vinegar

U sing a wire whisk and large round mixing bowl, stir all ingredients briskly until smooth consistency is achieved. The mustard acts as a suspension agent to keep the oil from separating. This may also be extended with mayonnaise. This will keep up to 3 months if refrigerated. Never store vinegarette in metal; plastic or glass only. *Makes 5 cups.*

Note: Excellent on spinach salad, asparagus, avocados, tomatoes and cauliflower.

BLUE CHEESE SALAD DRESSING
One of the finest.

¾ cup sour cream
½ teaspoon dry mustard
½ teaspoon black pepper
½ teaspoon salt
⅓ teaspoon garlic powder
1 teaspoon Worcestershire sauce
1 ⅓ cups mayonnaise
4 ounces Danish blue cheese, crumbled by hand into small pieces

I n a small bowl, combine the first six ingredients. Blend 2 minutes at low speed. Add mayonnaise and continue to blend another ½ minute on low. Blend another 2 minutes on medium speed. Add crumbled blue cheese. Blend at low speed no longer than 4 minutes. Chill 24 hours before serving. *Makes 2 ½ cups.*

Prep. Time: 15 minutes
Refrigerating Time: 24 hours.

PEPPERCREAM DRESSING

1 ounce Parmesan cheese, grated
1 tablespoon black pepper, coarsely ground
¾ teaspoon MSG
1 tablespoon lemon juice
dash of Tabasco sauce
1 teaspoon Worcestershire sauce
6 tablespoons vinegar
1 tablespoon onion, grated
1 clove garlic, mashed
⅓ cup cold water
1 quart mayonnaise

M ix all ingredients in large jar. Keep refrigerated.

Prep. Time: 10 minutes.

Main Dishes

BEARNAISE SAUCE
A "bare necessity" for Châteaubriand.

2	tablespoons red wine vinegar	4	egg yolks
1 ½	teaspoons green onion, chopped	¾	cup butter or margarine, softened
1 ½	teaspoons tarragon	1	tablespoon parsley, chopped
⅛	teaspoon cracked black pepper		

In a double boiler top, combine the first four ingredients. Place the top directly on range. Over a high heat, bring to a boil. Boil until vinegar is reduced to about 1 tablespoon. Place the top into the bottom of the double boiler containing hot water, not boiling water. Add egg yolks and cook, beating constantly with a wire whisk until slightly thickened. Add butter, 2 tablespoons at a time, beating constantly with a wire whisk. Warm until mixture thickens. Stir in parsley.

Prep. Time: 15 to 20 minutes.

CHÂTEAUBRIAND
From the land where Beef is King.

8	large artichokes	1	tablespoon salt
2	2 pound beef loin tenderloin roasts		bearnaise sauce

Cut the stems from artichokes 1 inch straight across. With scissors, trim thorny tips of leaves. Brush edges with lemon juice to prevent discoloration. Pull loose leaves off around bottom. Place artichokes stem side down, in a pot with 1 inch of boiling salted water. Add a few lemon slices for flavor. Bring to a boil. Cover and boil over a low heat for 30 minutes or until the leaves can easily be pulled off. After cooking the artichokes, leave them in the water until needed. In the meantime, prepare the meat. Rub the roasts with the salt. Place on a broiler pan. Broil in the oven for 30 minutes turning once, for rare meat. Broil longer if desired. With a slotted spoon, remove the artichokes from the boiling water to a paper towel to drain. Slice the meat and arrange on a warm platter. With a spoon, scoop out the choke. Fill the hole with bearnaise sauce. Place the artichokes filled with bearnaise sauce around the meat. Serve immediately.

Prep. Time: 1 hour.

BLACK–EYED TEXAS CASSEROLE

1 ½	pounds ground round	1	can cream of mushroom soup
1	large onion, chopped		
2	cloves garlic	1	can cream of chicken soup
1	15 ounce can black-eyed peas with jalapeños, drained	14	corn tortillas, cut in eighths
		2	cups Cheddar cheese, grated
1	14 ounce can enchilada sauce		
1	10 ounce can tomatoes with green chilies, diced		

In a skillet, cook ground round, onion and garlic until browned. Drain. Add black-eyed peas, enchilada sauce, tomatoes, mushroom soup and chicken soup. Layer in greased casserole, meat mixture and tortillas. Top with grated Cheddar cheese. Bake in a preheated 350° oven for 30 minutes or until bubbly.

Prep. Time: 25 minutes.

THE ODESSA FIREMEN'S CHICKEN FRIED STEAK

Better than Mom's.

2	pounds round steak, tenderized by the store		pepper, to taste
			oil for frying
1	egg, beaten		**Gravy:**
1	tablespoon milk	4	tablespoons of drippings
1	12 ounce can evaporated milk	3	tablespoons flour
2-4	ounces water	½	teaspoon salt
	flour for dredging	½	teaspoon pepper
	garlic salt, to taste	2	cups milk

In a 9 x 13 inch cake pan, combine egg, milk and water. Remove excess fat from the round steak. Cut it into individual steaks, 4 x 4 inches each. Pound round steak with edge of a strong coffee cup. This step is very important for tenderizing, so do not leave it out. Place steak in egg and milk mixture and allow to soak for 10 minutes. Meanwhile, in a small flat bowl, combine flour, salt and pepper. Fill a large skillet with ¼ inch of oil. Heat oil until it is very hot. Remove steaks from egg mixture and roll them in the flour mixture until thoroughly coated. Place in skillet and fry until golden brown and meat is completely cooked, approximately 15 minutes per side. Remove from oil and place on a paper towel to drain.

For gravy: Drain off excess fat leaving 4 tablespoons. Stir in dry ingredients. Cook over a high heat, stirring constantly until mixture is lightly browned. Pour in milk. Continue to cook, stirring constantly, until thick. Pour over chicken fried steaks.

Prep. Time: 45 minutes.

COW POKE STEAK
So good it almost melts in your mouth.

2	pounds round steak, 1 to 1 ½ inches thick	1	28 ounce can tomatoes
1	teaspoon garlic salt	1	green bell pepper, sliced in rings
½	teaspoon black pepper		
½	cup flour	1	small yellow onion, sliced in rings
¼	cup oil		

Remove excess fat from round steak. Cut it into 6 to 8 individual steaks. In a small bowl, combine garlic salt, pepper and flour. Coat round steaks with flour mixture. In a skillet, heat oil until it is very hot. Brown round steaks on both sides. Remove from pan and place in a baking dish. Place tomatoes and juice in a blender. Purée until no lumps remain. Pour this over browned round steaks. Place peppers and onions on top. Cover and bake in a preheated 325˚ oven for 2 ½ hours or until meat is tender. *Makes 6 to 8 servings.*

Prep. Time: 30 minutes.

Hint: *For a variation, thoroughly drain tomatoes before placing in blender and add ½ cup red wine and ½ cup beef bouillon. Purée until smooth.*

BEEF AND BROCCOLI STIR-FRY
Sure beats woking your dog.

6	ounces boneless sirloin steak	1	tablespoon plus 1 ½ teaspoons rosé light wine
1	tablespoon vegetable oil		
2	cups blanched broccoli florets	1	tablespoon soy sauce
1	cup blanched carrots, sliced	½	teaspoon cornstarch
		¼	teaspoon sugar
½	cup onion, cut into ¼ inch strips	⅛	teaspoon salt
		1	cup cooked rice

In an oven, broil sirloin until cooked. Cut into thin strips. In a skillet or wok, heat oil until very hot. Add broccoli, carrots and onion. Cook, stirring constantly, until vegetables are cooked. Stir in beef strips and cook until warmed through. In a small bowl, combine remaining ingredients. Stir them until the lumps are gone. Add this to beef mixture. Cook, stirring constantly, until thick for 2 to 3 minutes. Serve over rice. *Makes 2 servings.*

Prep. Time: 30 minutes.

WESTERN BARBECUE SAUCE

The fixin's for a great bar-b-que!

1	12.5 ounce bottle Major Grey's chutney	2	5 ounce bottles steak sauce
½	bottle pickled walnuts (optional)	1	10 ounce bottle Worcestershire sauce
1	14 ounce bottle ketchup	1-1 ¼	cups chili sauce Tabasco, to taste

Chop chutney and walnuts in blender. Mix well with remaining ingredients. Will keep indefinitely refrigerated. *Makes 7 ½ cups.*

Prep. Time: 20 minutes.

PEPPERED RIB-EYE ROAST

Guaranteed to please the "cowboy" in every man.

5-6	pound rib-eye roast, fat removed	1	teaspoon paprika
½	cup pepper, coarsely cracked	1	cup soy sauce
1	tablespoon tomato paste	¾	cup red wine vinegar
½	teaspoon garlic powder	1	tablespoon cornstarch

Rub pepper over beef and press in with heel of hand. Place in a shallow baking dish. Shake remaining ingredients in a jar. Carefully pour over roast and marinate overnight. Remove from marinade and bake roast at 325° for 17 to 20 minutes per pound for rare. For best results use a meat thermometer. Add 1 cup water to meat juices after baking for "au jus", or thicken with 1 tablespoon cornstarch mixed with ¼ cup water. *Makes 10 to 12 servings.*

Prep. Time: 10 minutes,
plus marinating overnight.

MANHANDLER STEAK WITH GRAVY

Great after a long day of punching cows.

salt & pepper, to taste	1 can cream of
¾ pound round steak,	mushroom soup,
tenderized	slightly diluted with
small amount of oil	water
½ envelope of onion	¾ cup water
soup mix	

Salt and pepper steak. Lightly brown in small amount of oil. Remove steak and place it in a casserole dish. Sprinkle onion soup mix over steak. Pour mushroom soup and water over all. Cover and bake at 325° until steak is tender, for 2 hours. Check often and add water when needed. *Makes 2 to 4 servings.*

Prep. Time: 15 minutes.

ANNIE OAKLEY FILLETS

4 6 ounce beef	1 teaspoon olive oil
tenderloin fillets	¼ cup butter
2 teaspoons green	¼ cup shallots
peppercorns	1 tablespoon parsley,
few drops of olive oil	minced
soy sauce	dash of Worcestershire
1 cup beef broth	sauce
1 teaspoon cornstarch	dash of cognac
1 tablespoon Dijon	3 tablespoons heavy
mustard	whipping cream

Crush peppercorns and spread ¼ teaspoon on each side of steak with a few drops of olive oil and soy sauce. Refrigerate until ready to cook; can be done ahead of time. Combine broth, cornstarch and mustard. Set aside. In a heavy skillet, heat 1 teaspoon olive oil and 2 tablespoons butter. When hot, sauté steaks until done to your taste. Remove steaks to warm (low) oven. Add remaining 2 tablespoons butter to skillet and gently sauté shallots and parsley for 2 minutes. Stir in broth mixture, Worcestershire and cognac. Cook until thickened. Stir in cream. Serve sauce with steaks or over steaks. *Makes 4 servings.*

Prep. Time: 45 minutes.

SON-OF-A-GUN STEW

Great stew for cowhands.

1 ½	pounds stew meat		dash of pepper
1	cup carrots, sliced	1	can cream of
1	onion, chopped		mushroom soup
3	large potatoes,	½	can water
	peeled & cubed	1	bay leaf
1	cup celery, chopped	½	cup burgundy
	(optional)		(optional)
1 ½	teaspoons salt		

Combine all ingredients, except burgundy, in a covered casserole dish. Bake in a preheated 275° oven for 5 hours. During last half hour of cooking, add burgundy. Can be cooked in Crockpot for 10 hours on low. May need to thicken gravy. *Makes 4 to 6 servings.*

Prep. Time: 20 minutes.

BUENO BEEF STROGANOFF

3	onions, diced	4	small bay leaves
4	cloves garlic	½	teaspoon coriander
2	tablespoons cooking oil	1	teaspoon cayenne pepper
1 ½	pounds lean stew meat	½	red pepper
½	cup water	½	teaspoon cardamon
2	teaspoons cumin, ground	12	whole cloves
2	one-inch sticks cinnamon	1	pound, 12 ounces tomatoes, chopped
		1 ½	cups plain yogurt
			cooked rice

Sauté onions and garlic in oil. Add beef and simmer until brown. Add all remaining ingredients except yogurt. Cover tightly and simmer for 2 hours. Stir some sauce into the yogurt, then add yogurt to the meat. Cook uncovered without boiling until warm. Serve over rice. *Makes 6 servings.*

Prep. Time: 30 minutes.

LASAGNE

Even Texans love Italian classics.

1	pound ground beef	1	teaspoon garlic
1	cup onion, chopped		powder
2	tablespoons oil	1	teaspoon pepper
1	pound can tomatoes, drained	1/2	teaspoon oregano leaves
3	6 ounce cans tomato paste	1	box lasagne noodles
1 1/2	cups water	1	pound cottage cheese
1	tablespoon parsley	8	ounces Mozzarella cheese, shredded
1	teaspoon sugar	1	cup Parmesan cheese
2	teaspoons salt		

Place oil in a large skillet. Brown beef and onion. Add tomatoes, tomato paste, water, parsley, sugar and spices. Simmer, stirring occasionally, for 30 minutes. Cook noodles as directed. In a 9 x 13 inch pan, cover the bottom with noodles. Spread one-third of the sauce on top of noodles. Place one-third of the cheese on top of sauce. Repeat 2 more times ending with cheese. In a preheated 350° oven, bake for 45 minutes or until brown. *Makes 8 to 10 servings.*

Prep. Time: 45 minutes.

SPINACH LASAGNE

2	pounds fresh spinach	2	cloves garlic, crushed
4	tablespoons Parmesan cheese, freshly grated	1/2	cup onion, chopped
		2	cups tomato sauce
1	cup part-skim Ricotta cheese	1/2	teaspoon basil
		1/2	teaspoon oregano
dash of salt		1/2	teaspoon thyme
fresh ground pepper, to taste		1/2	pound lasagne noodles
1	tablespoon olive oil		

Wash the spinach. Steam until just limp. Can be microwaved for 1 minute. Squeeze out excess moisture. Chop the spinach. Mix with 2 tablespoons of the Parmesan, Ricotta, salt and pepper. Heat the oil in a large saucepan. Sauté the garlic and onions until the onions are translucent. Stir in the tomato sauce, basil, oregano and thyme. Cover and let simmer until ready to use. Cook the noodles according to the packaged directions. Layer the noodles alternately with the cheese/spinach mixture and the tomato sauce in a 9 x 13 inch baking dish. Sprinkle the top with the remaining Parmesan. Bake in a preheated 350° oven for 30 minutes, until bubbly. *Makes 8 servings.*

Prep. Time: 30 minutes.

SPAGHETTI AND MEATBALLS

Sauce:
¾	cup onion, chopped
1	clove garlic, minced
3	tablespoons oil
2	16 ounce cans stewed tomatoes, puréed in the blender
1	cup water
1 ⅓	cups tomato paste
1	tablespoon sugar
1 ½	teaspoons salt
½	teaspoon pepper
1 ½	teaspoons oregano, crushed
1	bay leaf

Meatballs:
4	slices dry bread
1	pound ground beef
2	eggs
½	cup Parmesan cheese
2	tablespoons dry parsley
1	clove garlic, minced
1	teaspoon oregano, crushed
1	teaspoon salt
	cooked spaghetti

Sauté onions and garlic in oil until tender. Add the next 8 ingredients and stir. Simmer uncovered over a low heat for 30 minutes. Remove the bay leaf. If you like a lot of sauce with spaghetti, then double this recipe.

For meatballs: Soak the slices of bread in the sauce. Tightly squeeze out extra sauce and place in a large bowl. Combine remaining ingredients. Form into 1 ½-2 inch balls. Brown in a skillet or broil in oven. Watch closely; they can burn quickly. When browned, add meatballs to sauce and cook an additional 30 minutes. Serve over cooked spaghetti. *Makes 6 to 8 servings.*

Prep. Time: 2 hours.

SPAGHETTI CASSEROLE

1 ½	pounds ground beef
2	medium green peppers, chopped
2	large yellow onions, chopped
½	cup salad oil
2	6 ounce cans tomato paste
2	28 ounce cans whole tomatoes, puréed in blender
1	8 ounce can mushrooms, chopped & drained

Seasonings to taste:
  salt, pepper, bay leaves, garlic powder, Worcestershire sauce parsley

1	pound spaghetti, cooked & drained
1-1 ½	pounds Cheddar cheese, grated

Sauté the first three ingredients in oil, drain well. Add the next 3 ingredients and seasonings. Simmer over low heat until thick, about 2 hours. Spray a deep 3 quart baking dish with a non-stick cooking spray. Fill baking dish with layers of spaghetti, sauce and cheese. Repeat until all ingredients are used, ending with cheese. Bake at 350° for 30 to 45 minutes or until bubbly. *Makes 10 to 12 servings.*

Prep. Time: 2 ½ hours.

BEEF AND MACARONI SCRAMBLE

1 ½ pounds ground beef
1   medium onion,
      chopped
¼   medium bell pepper,
      chopped
3   8 ounce cans
      tomato sauce
3   cups water

1   16 ounce can
      tomatoes with juice,
      chopped
2   cups elbow macaroni
2   bay leaves
1   tablespoons oregano
garlic, to taste
salt & pepper, to taste

In a 4 to 5 quart saucepan, cook the first three ingredients until brown. Drain. Add remaining ingredients and bring to a boil. Turn to low heat. Cook until macaroni is tender. *Makes 6 servings.*

Prep. Time: 10 minutes.

J-B RANCH CASSEROLE

2   pounds ground meat
2   cloves garlic, minced
salt & pepper, to taste
½   medium onion,
      chopped
½   medium bell pepper,
      chopped
2   tablespoons barbecue
      sauce

1   tablespoon
      Worcestershire sauce
1   16 ounce can
      ranch-style beans
⅓   cup cooked white rice
½   cup processed cheese,
      grated

Add garlic, salt and pepper to meat and mix well.   In large skillet, cook meat with onions and bell pepper until done. Add barbecue sauce, Worcestershire sauce and beans. Simmer about 5 minutes. Stir in cooked rice. Pour into a casserole dish and top with grated cheese. Bake in a preheated 350˚ oven until bubbly and cheese is melted. *Makes 8 servings.*

Prep. Time: 20 minutes.

SAUCY BRISKET

1	beef brisket	½-1	cup mushrooms, sliced
1-2	packages dry onion soup mix	1-2	cups red wine
½-1	cup onions, chopped		

Trim any unnecessary fat. Place brisket in baking dish or pan. Pour onion soup mix over and around brisket. Add onions, mushrooms and wine. Bake in a preheated 250° oven for at least 4 hours. Baste occasionally or leave alone.

Prep. Time: 10 minutes.

BEEF MUSHROOM LOAF

1	3 ounce can mushrooms, chopped & broiled	1 ½	cups soft bread crumbs
1	egg, slightly beaten	1 ½	pounds lean ground beef
1 ½	teaspoons Worcestershire sauce	2	tablespoons ketchup
1	teaspoon salt	1	tablespoon light corn syrup
½	teaspoon dry mustard		

Drain mushrooms, reserving liquid. Add enough milk to mushroom liquid to make ½ cup. In mixing bowl, combine liquids, egg, Worcestershire sauce, seasonings and bread crumbs. Let stand for 5 minutes. Stir in beef and chopped mushrooms. Shape into loaf in 9 x 13 x 2 inch baking dish. Bake in a preheated 350° oven for 1 hour. *Makes 6 servings.*

Prep. Time: 20 minutes.

BARBECUE BEEF MEATBALLS

Now that's a spicy meatball.

Meatballs:		Sauce:	
1	cup soft bread crumbs	¼	cup vinegar
½	cup milk	3	tablespoons sugar
1	pound ground meat	½	cup ketchup
1	teaspoon salt	½	cup water
½-1	teaspoon pepper	½	cup onion, chopped
1	tablespoon Worcestershire sauce	¼-½	cup green pepper, chopped

Soak bread crumbs in milk. Mix in meat, salt, pepper and Worcestershire sauce. Make into meat balls and place in baking dish.

For sauce: In a large bowl, combine all the sauce ingredients. Mix well. Pour over meatballs. Bake in a preheated 375° oven for 45 minutes. *Makes 5 servings.*

Prep. Time: 30 minutes.

SHERRIED BEEF

3	pounds round steak, cut into eleven 1 ½ inch cubes	2	cans cream of mushroom soup
½	cup teriyaki sauce	¼	cup cream sherry
¼	cup soy sauce	½	cup milk
¼	cup Worcestershire sauce	2	large jars mushrooms, drained
1	cup flour	1	8 ounce carton sour cream
½	teaspoon black pepper		cooked egg noodles
1	teaspoon garlic salt		
½-1	cup oil		
1	package dry onion soup mix		

Marinate round steak in teriyaki, soy and Worcestershire sauces overnight. Drain off excess liquid. Combine flour, pepper and garlic salt. Place marinated steak cubes in a large bag and pour flour mixture on top. Shake bag to thoroughly coat steak cubes. Heat oil over medium-high heat. Place coated steak cubes in oil to brown. Discard remaining flour mixture. Quickly brown steak cubes and transfer them to a large bowl. Add onion soup mix, cream of mushroom soup, sherry, milk and mushrooms. Mix thoroughly then pour into a baking dish, sprayed with a non-stick cooking spray. Bake in a preheated 325° oven for 2 hours. Remove from oven and stir in sour cream. Serve over cooked egg noodles.

Prep. Time: 30 minutes,
       plus marinating overnight.

DINNER BELL POT ROAST

½	cup all-purpose flour	8	small potatoes, peeled & halved
1	teaspoon salt	8	medium carrots, peeled & sliced
1 ¼	teaspoons pepper	8	small onions
4	pounds beef chuck pot roast	1	cup water
2	tablespoons shortening		
1	15 ounce jar horseradish		

S tir together flour, salt and pepper. Rub mixture on meat. Melt shortening in large skillet or Dutch oven. Brown meat over medium heat. Reduce heat. Spread horseradish on top of roast. Add potatoes, carrots, onions and water. Cover tightly and bake in a preheated 325° oven for 4 hours.

Prep. Time: 30 minutes.

HOP ALONG CASSEROLE

1	pound ground round	1	cup water
1	medium green pepper, chopped		salt & pepper, to taste
2	medium onions, chopped	½	cup salad olives
			Tabasco to taste
3	stalks celery, chopped	1	teaspoon basil
1	16 ounce bag noodles	1	teaspoon tarragon
1	16 ounce can tomatoes	1	teaspoon red pepper
1	16 ounce can tomato sauce	½	pound American cheese
		1	8 ounce can mushrooms, drained

B rown meat, green pepper, onions and celery in a large saucepan. Cook noodles according to the directions on the package. Drain. Add to beef mixture. Add tomatoes, tomato sauce, water, olives, Tabasco and spices. Add grated cheese and mushrooms. Pour into two 9 x 13 inch baking dishes. Bake in a preheated 350° oven for 30 to 40 minutes. *Makes 15 servings.*

Prep. Time: 30 minutes.

A COWBOY'S PIE

Wonderful after a cold snowy day's work.

Stew:		1	tablespoon
salad oil			all-purpose flour
2	pounds beef for stew,	2	tablespoons water
	cut into 1 inch	1	10 ounce package
	chunks		frozen peas
1	large onion, diced	1	10 ounce package
1	14.5 ounce can		frozen corn
	beef broth	1	egg, beaten
2	teaspoons		
	Worcestershire sauce	Pie Crust:	
½	cup water	1	cup flour, sifted
1	teaspoon salt	½	cup whole-wheat
¼	teaspoon ground		flour
	black pepper	dash of salt	
3	medium-sized	⅓	cup vegetable oil
	sweet potatoes	3	tablespoons milk
1	medium-sized		
	baking potato		

In a large pot, over medium-high heat, in 2 tablespoons of hot salad oil, cook beef chunks until well browned on all sides. Set aside in a bowl. Reduce heat to medium. In one more tablespoon hot salad oil, cook onion until almost tender, stirring occasionally. Stir in beef broth, Worcestershire sauce, ½ cup water, salt and pepper. Return meat to pot. Over high heat, heat to boiling. Reduce heat to low. Cover and simmer 45 minutes. While meat is simmering, peel and cut sweet potatoes into 1 inch chunks. Cut, but do not peel, the baking potato into 1 inch chunks. When the meat is ready, add sweet potatoes and baking potatoes. Cook 20 minutes longer or until meat and vegetables are tender.

Skim fat from beef mixture. In a cup, stir 1 tablespoon flour and 2 tablespoons water until blended. Gradually stir flour mixture into beef mixture. Cook until mixtures boil and slightly thickened, stirring constantly. Stir in frozen vegetables, heat through. Spoon beef mixture into a 2 quart casserole. Place the pie crust loosely over beef mixture. Flute the edge gently around the casserole rim. Cut several slits in pie crust for steam to escape during baking. Brush crust with beaten egg. Bake in a preheated 425° oven for 15 minutes or until crust is golden brown.

To prepare pie crust: Mix flours and salt. Pour oil and milk into measuring cup, but do not stir. Add to flour. Stir until mixed. Press into a smooth ball. Flatten and place between 2 sheets of wax paper. Roll out to a shape that matches the casserole pan the stew mixture will be placed in. Dough should be about 1 inch larger than pan. *Makes 8 servings.*

Prep. Time: 2 hours.

BEDROLL BEEF

1	tablespoon onion, minced	1	tablespoon Worcestershire sauce
¼	cup parsley, snipped	½	cup chili sauce
2 ¼	cups Bisquick	¼	cup water
⅔	cup milk		
1-1 ½	pounds ground beef		
½	teaspoon MSG		
1 ¼	teaspoons salt		
⅛	teaspoon pepper		

In a small bowl, add onion and parsley to Bisquick. Add milk and mix well. Roll dough into 12 inch square. With fork, mix meat lightly, but thoroughly, with rest of ingredients in bowl. Shape beef into a loaf about 9 x 5 inches and place on dough. Pull sides of dough up over loaf, overlapping edges. Pull ends up. Place in shallow baking dish with seam side down. Make a few slits in top of crust to make a design. Bake in a preheated 400° oven for 45 minutes or until crust is golden.

Prep. Time: 30 minutes.

BEEF ON A POKER

1 ½	pounds sirloin steak, cut into 1 inch cubes	½	pound fresh mushroom caps, washed & trimmed
2	cups tomato juice	1	large green pepper, cut into 1 inch pieces
½	cup vinegar		
¼	cup prepared mustard		
1	teaspoon sugar		
1	teaspoon salt	1	pint cherry tomatoes
½	teaspoon pepper		

Place steak cubes in shallow glass dish. Combine tomato juice, vinegar and seasonings. Pour over meat. Cover dish and refrigerate 2 hours. Remove meat from marinade, but reserve marinade. Alternate meat and vegetables on skewers. Place on grill 4 inches from hot coals. Cook 12 to 15 minutes, turning and basting frequently with reserved marinade. Meat should be browned and vegetables should be tender. *Makes 4 servings.*

Prep. Time: 15 minutes.
Marinating Time: 2 hours.

VEAL SCALLOPINI MARSALA

A good recipe for venison or game meat.

¾	*pound veal cutlets*	¼	*cup margarine*
¼	*teaspoon salt*	⅓	*cup Marsala wine*
⅛	*teaspoon pepper*	½	*cup beef broth*
flour			

Place cutlets on wax paper and flatten to ⅛ inch thickness with a meat mallet. Sprinkle with salt and pepper. Dredge in flour. Melt margarine in skillet. Sauté cutlets 2 or 3 minutes on each side or until brown. Reduce heat. Add wine and cook 1 minute over medium heat. Remove veal to a warmed serving platter. Add broth to skillet. Bring to a boil, stirring occasionally. Pour over veal. *Makes 2 servings.*

Prep. Time: 10 minutes.

VEAL OR CHICKEN PICCATA

1	*pound veal scalloppine or chicken breasts, skinned*	2	*tablespoons unsalted butter*
			juice of 1 lemon
¼	*cup flour*	¼	*cup dry white wine*
¼	*cup olive oil*		*(optional)*

Pound the veal or chicken until it is very thin, less than ¼ inch thick. Lightly flour the meat on both sides. In a large skillet, heat the oil and butter. When the butter begins to bubble, sauté the meat 2 minutes on each side. Do not overcook. Sprinkle with lemon juice just before removing from skillet. Add wine to the pan and deglaze by turning the heat on high. Stir constantly until the liquid is reduced to ¼ cup. Pour sauce over meat.

Prep. Time: 10 minutes.

PEPPERY VEAL

1-1½ *pounds veal chops,*   ¼   *cup vegetable oil*
     the equivalent of a   *salt*
     beef T-bone   *lots of fresh ground*
¼   *cup flour*   *black pepper*

V ery lightly flour veal. Shake off any excess flour. Dip veal into fresh ground black pepper. Gently rub in pepper. Heat the oil in a large, heavy skillet. Sauté the veal for 2 minutes on each side. Salt to taste. Serve hot. *Makes 2 to 4 servings.*

Prep. Time: 10 minutes.

COME AND GET IT STEW
Good ol' rib stickin' food.

1	pound beef stew meat, cut into 1 inch chunks	1	potato, peeled & coarsely chopped
salt & pepper		1	16 ounce bag frozen okra & tomatoes, chopped
3	tablespoons butter or margarine	4	tablespoons barley or rice
1	pound smoked continuous link sausage, sliced	3	beef bouillon cubes
1	30 ounce can tomato juice	1	10 ounce package frozen corn
1	30 ounce can tomatoes, coarsely chopped	3	tablespoons Worcestershire sauce
5	stalks celery, leaves included, chopped	2	tablespoons salt
2	carrots, peeled & sliced		
2	onions, thinly sliced		
2	cloves garlic, finely minced		

Sachet d'epice:
cheese cloth
12   *black peppercorns*
2   *bay leaves*
½   *teaspoon thyme*

L ightly salt and pepper beef. In a large skillet, sauté beef in butter over a medium-high heat until browned on all sides for 5 minutes. Wrap peppercorns, bay leaves and thyme in cheese cloth to form the Sachet d'epice. Place cooked beef in a Crockpot. Add all remaining ingredients including the Sachet d'epice and stir until mixed. Simmer on low all day. Remove the Sachet d'epice before serving. Serve with hard toasted French bread and butter.

Prep. Time: 20 minutes.

TERIYAKI STEAK

1 ⅓	cups cider vinegar	¼	teaspoon ginger,
1 ¼	cups tomato purée		ground
1	cup pineapple juice	¼	teaspoon garlic
1	cup soy sauce		powder
1	cup brown sugar,	6-8	sirloin steaks,
	firmly packed		1 inch thick
⅓	cup molasses		

In a medium saucepan, combine all the above ingredients, except the steaks, to make a teriyaki sauce. Bring sauce to a boil, stirring constantly to avoid sticking. Remove from heat and allow to cool. Place the steaks in a shallow baking dish making sure they do not overlap. Pour teriyaki sauce over steaks and marinate for 24 hours. Remove them from the sauce and cook over a hot grill. Baste every 5 minutes with the teriyaki sauce.

Prep. Time: 15 minutes,
plus 24 hours marinating time.

CHARCOALED ROAST

Wild stallions couldn't drive you away!

1	4 pound chuck or	½	teaspoon cayenne
	shoulder roast		pepper
meat tenderizer		¼	teaspoon garlic
1	large onion, chopped		powder
½	cup strong coffee,	¼	cup
	fresh brewed		Worcestershire sauce
½	cup soy sauce	1	tablespoon vinegar

Sprinkle the roast liberally with meat tenderizer. Combine all the other ingredients and pour over the roast. Marinate for 12 hours. Remove the roast from the marinade and place it on a hot grill. Pour the remaining marinade into a pan that can also go on the grill. Charcoal the meat and the marinade in the pan for 45 minutes. The meat will be cooked medium. Slice it into steaks and continue grilling until cooked in the desired way. Serve the marinade like a steak sauce.

Prep. Time: 10 minutes.
Marinating Time: 12 hours.

PEPPER STEAK

1	2 ½ to 3 pound eye of round roast	½	cup green onion, chopped
meat tenderizer		½	cup beef bouillon
2 ½	tablespoons peppercorns, crushed	⅓	cup red wine or brandy
2	tablespoons butter		
2	tablespoons vegetable oil		

Trim excess fat off the roast. Cut it crosswise into 6 steaks. Sprinkle each steak with meat tenderizer. Press peppercorns into both sides of steaks and lightly beat with a meat tenderizing mallet. Cover steaks and let stand for 1 hour.   In a large saucepan, combine butter and oil.   Heat over a high heat until almost smoking. Add steaks a few at a time so not to overlap them. Brown on each side for 3 to 4 minutes.   The meat will be cooked medium rare. Remove the meat and place it on a warm serving platter.   Add green onions to the juices and sauté 1 minute.   Add bouillon and wine and bring to a boil. Simmer for 2 minutes and then pour over steaks.   If steaks have cooled too much, then warm them just a little in the microwave. *Makes 6 servings.*

Prep. Time: 20 minutes.

SPICY HOT HOUSTON SAUCE FOR GRILLED CHICKEN

If you can't stand the heat, stay out of this chicken.

1	cup margarine	½	teaspoon garlic powder
2	teaspoons flour		
1	teaspoon black pepper	2	teaspoons prepared mustard
1	teaspoon cayenne pepper		juice of 1 lemon vinegar
½	teaspoon salt		

In a medium saucepan, melt the margarine. In a one cup measuring cup, add the next 7 ingredients and mix well. Fill measuring cup, to a level 1 cup, with vinegar and mix. Pour into melted margarine. Over a low heat, simmer for 10 minutes, stirring occasionally. Baste, every 5 to 10 minutes, on chicken while grilling.

Prep. Time: 15 minutes.

GARLIC GRILLED CHICKEN

4	chicken breast halves, skinned & deboned	2	cloves garlic, minced
		½	teaspoon cumin, ground
1	cup picante sauce	½	teaspoon dried oregano, crushed
2	tablespoons vegetable oil	¼	teaspoon salt
1	tablespoon lime juice		additional picante sauce

P lace each chicken breast between 2 pieces of plastic wrap. Flatten chicken to ¼ inch thickness, using a meat mallet or rolling pin; cut into 1 inch wide strips. Place chicken in shallow container. Combine next 7 ingredients, mixing well. Pour over chicken. Cover and chill 1 to 2 hours. Thread chicken onto skewers. Cook over hot coals 6 to 8 minutes or until done, turning occasionally and basting with remaining marinade. Serve with picante sauce. *Makes 4 servings.*

Prep. Time: 20 minutes,
            plus 1 to 2 hour marinating time.

PASTA FRITTATA

Ever wonder what to do with leftover spaghetti? Here you go.

3	eggs	½-1	cup fresh or frozen corn, peas or fresh asparagus, cut into 1 inch slices
2	cups cooked pasta, leftover spaghetti is perfect		
½	cup Parmesan cheese, freshly grated	½-1	cup chicken, turkey or ham, cooked & diced (optional)
¼	cup fresh parsley, chopped		
2	tablespoons olive oil		

B eat the eggs in a large bowl. Stir in the cheese, parsley, vegetables and pasta. Mix well. Place in a baking dish. Garnish with additional Parmesan cheese, if desired. Bake in a preheated 400° oven for 30 minutes. Can be served hot or cold. *Makes 6 servings.*

Prep. Time: 10 minutes.

CHICKEN FRICASSEE WITH DUMPLINGS

3	pounds cooked small chicken pieces		*Dumplings:*
⅓	cup flour	1 ½	cups packaged biscuit mix
1 ½	teaspoons salt	2	teaspoons parsley & chives, chopped
1	teaspoon marjoram leaves, diced	1	egg
¼	cup butter	¼	cup milk
2	onions, sliced	½	cup light cream
1	cup celery, chopped		
6	large carrots, pared & halved		
1	bay leaf		
4	whole cloves		
9	whole black peppers		
1	13.75 ounce can chicken broth		
1	cup water		

Combine flour, salt and marjoram. Dredge chicken in flour mix. Coat evenly, shake off excess and remove leftover flour. Reserve the flour for sauce. In a Dutch oven, sauté chicken in 2 tablespoons butter for 15 minutes, until lightly browned. Add butter as needed. Remove from Dutch oven and add onions, celery, carrots, bay leaf, cloves and black pepper to mixture. Sauté, stirring 5 minutes. Stir in broth and water. Bring to boil. Return chicken to Dutch oven. Reduce heat and simmer covered for 40 minutes to make fricassee.

To prepare dumplings: Combine biscuit mix and parsley. Blend in egg and milk. Drop batter by rounded tablespoonfuls on chicken (not liquid), 2 to 3 inches apart. Cook uncovered on low heat for 10 minutes. Cover tightly and cook 10 minutes until light and fluffy. With slotted spoon, remove dumplings to heated baking dish, keep warm in low oven. In small bowl combine reserved flour mix with light cream, stirring until smooth. Gradually stir in fricassee. Simmer 5 minutes until thickened. Replace dumplings on top of fricassee. Reheat gently, covered until hot. Before serving, sprinkle with chives.

Prep. Time: 35 minutes.

CHICKEN CORDON BLEU

4	boneless chicken breasts, skinned	1	egg
		¼	cup skim milk
4	thin slices baby Swiss cheese (deli cheese)	1	cup Italian bread crumbs
			salt & pepper, to taste
4	thin slices ham (deli ham)		paprika, to taste

Beat chicken breasts flat. Place a slice of cheese then a slice of ham on the chicken. Roll up and secure with two toothpicks. Combine the egg and milk and beat. Add salt, pepper and paprika to bread crumbs. Dip chicken in egg and milk mixture then roll in bread crumbs. Spray a 1 ½ quart casserole dish with a non-stick cooking spray. Add chicken breasts. Bake covered in a preheated 350° oven for 45 minutes or until chicken is tender. *Makes 4 servings.*

Prep. Time: 20 minutes.

TEXAS' BEST CHICK-N-DUMPLINGS
Good ol' home cookin'.

Broth:		Dumplings:	
1	whole chicken	3	cups flour
1	stick margarine	3	eggs
¾	cup milk	3	teaspoons salt
	salt & pepper		milk, enough to moisten dough

Cook chicken in a large soup pan until done. Remove chicken from pan and set aside to cool. Remove bone from chicken. Add 1 stick margarine, milk, salt and pepper to chicken broth. Bring to a boil.

To prepare dumplings: Mix ingredients and roll out as you would a pie crust. Cut into 1 x 4 inch strips and add to boiling broth. Add chicken to broth. Simmer for 35 minutes.

Prep. Time: 1 ½ hours.

HOME-FRIED CHICKEN
Good to the bone.

3   pounds chicken
solid vegetable shortening

First Coating:
½   cup flour
½   teaspoon salt
½   teaspoon pepper
½   teaspoon dried
      parsley
½   teaspoon basil
½   teaspoon oregano
½   teaspoon onion
      powder
½   teaspoon garlic
      powder

Second Coating:
1   cup flour
½   cup instant dry milk
1   tablespoon baking
      powder
1   tablespoon sugar
1   tablespoon salt
¼   teaspoon sage
¼   teaspoon celery salt
¼   teaspoon thyme
1   teaspoon paprika
1   teaspoon pepper

Dip for Coating:
1   egg
1   tablespoon club soda

Wash chicken and pat dry. Combine ingredients for first coating. Dredge chicken and let sit 45 minutes. Combine ingredients for second coating. Combine egg and club soda. Dip chicken in egg mixture, then in second mixture. Repeat second coating. Deep fry or skillet fry in very hot shortening. Turn after 15 or 20 minutes. Reduce heat slightly. Fry 15 to 20 minutes more or until cooked through. Drain well on paper towels. *Makes 6 to 8 servings.*

Prep. Time: 1 hour.

FAKE FRIED CHICKEN
Easy and your kids will love it.

1   5 ounce box
      Melba toast
1   cup Cheddar cheese,
      grated
6   tablespoons
      Parmesan cheese

1   cup butter, melted
      garlic salt, to taste
1   package boneless
      chicken breasts

Crush Melba toast to fine powder. Mix cheeses into Melba toast. Melt butter. Dip chicken in butter. Roll in Melba toast/cheese mixture. Sprinkle with garlic salt and place on greased cookie sheet. Bake in a preheated 350° oven for 30 minutes. *Makes 4 servings.*

Prep. Time: 20 minutes.

HOW TO STEW A CHICKEN

chicken
water
bay leaf
garlic powder
black pepper

stalk of celery
sliced carrot
sliced onion
sprig of parsley

Place chicken in a Crockpot. Add water, bay leaf, garlic powder, black pepper, celery, carrots, onion and parsley. Cook overnight on low. Debone chicken when done for use in chicken salads, etc. Strain the stock and refrigerate or freeze for use in soups. Beware of chicken stock, it spoils easily.

Prep. Time: 12 to 14 hours.

CHICKEN VEGETABLE STIR-FRY

A great low calorie dish.

3	teaspoons vegetable oil	1	teaspoon Chinese sesame oil
4	teaspoons chives, chopped	1	pound chicken, cut into strips
4	cloves garlic, minced	4	teaspoons soy sauce
1	cup mushrooms, chopped	4	teaspoons teriyaki sauce
1	cup snow peas, chopped	2	cups cooked rice
½	cup red bell pepper, in strips		

In a non-stick skillet or wok, heat 1 teaspoon of the vegetable oil. Sauté chives and garlic until tender. Add mushrooms, snow peas and bell pepper. Continue to sauté for 3 to 5 minutes until vegetables are tender yet crisp. Remove vegetables and set aside. In same skillet, heat remaining vegetable oil and sesame oil until hot. Add chicken strips and sauté until cooked and brown. Return vegetables to skillet and add soy sauce and teriyaki sauce. Cook for 5 minutes, stirring constantly until vegetables are heated through. Serve over cooked rice. *Makes 4 servings.*

Prep. Time: 1 hour.

HOME COOKIN' CHICKEN SPAGHETTI CASSEROLE

1	can cream of mushroom soup	2	green bell peppers, chopped
6	tablespoons flour	2	large chickens, cooked, deboned & cut into bite-sized pieces
1	quart milk		
1	pound American cheese, grated		
2	tablespoons butter or margarine	1	pound spaghetti, cooked & drained
2	onions, chopped		

In a large saucepan, combine the soup and flour. Stir in milk and ½ pound cheese. Over a low to medium heat, cook until sauce thickens. In a small skillet, sauté onions and green peppers in the butter. Add this to the milk mixture after it thickens. In a 9 x 13 x 2 inch pan (or larger), layer spaghetti, chicken and sauce. Repeat until everything is gone. This will not fit completely in a 9 x 13 x 2 inch pan. Leave out a little of spaghetti. Top with remaining cheese. Bake in a preheated 350° oven for 40 minutes or until hot and bubbly. *Makes 10 servings.*

Prep. Time: 45 minutes.

STERLING CHICKEN

3	cups cooked chicken	1	medium onion, chopped
1	5 ounce package combination wild and long grain rice, cooked	2	cups French-style green beans, drained
1	can cream of celery soup	1	cup mayonnaise
1	4 ounce jar pimentos, drained & sliced	1	6.5 ounce can water chestnuts, drained & diced
			salt & pepper, to taste

Mix all ingredients in a large bowl. Pour mixture into a 2 ½ or 3 quart casserole dish. Bake in a preheated 350° oven for 25 to 30 minutes. *Makes 16 servings.*

Prep. Time: 25 minutes.

LITTLE CHICKEN WELLINGTON

4	chicken breasts, deboned & skinned	1	tablespoon flour
4	tablespoons butter or margarine	4	tablespoons whipping cream
salt & pepper, to taste			squeeze of lemon juice
½	pound fresh mushrooms, finely chopped	1	frozen pre-rolled sheet frozen puff pastry, thawed
		1	egg, beaten

Heat butter in a heavy frying pan and cook chicken breasts over moderate heat for 3 minutes each side or until cooked through. Remove and season with salt and pepper. Add mushrooms to pan, sauté until they are browned. Sprinkle flour over, and stir in. Add cream, lemon juice, salt and pepper to taste. Continue stirring until mixture is smooth and thick. Allow to cool. Roll out pastry sheet to measure 12 inch square and ⅛ inch thick. Cut in four 6-inch squares. Chop the chicken into bite-sized pieces. Place a mound of chicken pieces on each square, and cover with mushroom mixture. Dampen edges of pastry and roll neatly around filling, tucking in the ends. Place seam-side down on a baking sheet. Brush tops with beaten egg. Cut a small slit in the top for steam to escape. Bake in a preheated 400° oven for 25 minutes or until golden brown. *Makes 4 servings.*

Prep. Time: 1 hour.

QUICK AND EASY CHICKEN

Cooks up in the microwave.

2 ½	pounds chicken, skinned	2	tablespoons fresh parsley
1	can cream of chicken or mushroom soup		

Arrange chicken in a 8 x 12 inch microwave safe baking dish, placing thicker portions toward edges. In small bowl, stir soup until smooth. Stir in parsley. Spread soup evenly over chicken. Cover with waxed paper. Microwave on high for 20 minutes or until chicken is nearly done, rearranging and basting chicken with pan juices once during cooking. Let stand covered 5 minutes or until chicken is no longer pink in center. *Makes 6 servings.*

Prep. Time: 5 minutes.

CHICKEN TARRAGON

4	chicken breasts, skinless & boneless	¼	cup white wine (optional)
2	tablespoons margarine	1	tablespoon tarragon
		½-¾	cup half-and-half

Melt margarine in skillet. Pound chicken breasts until ¼ inch thick. Brown each side in margarine for 2 minutes or until done. Remove to a warm plate. Add wine to drippings and bring to boil. Turn off heat and allow to cool somewhat. Add tarragon and slowly pour in half-and-half. Warm and pour over chicken. *Makes 2 to 4 servings.*

Prep. Time: 10 minutes.

ALMOND CHICKEN

4	whole chicken breasts, deboned	¼	teaspoon pepper
2	tablespoons celery, chopped	1	tablespoon fresh lemon juice
2	tablespoons onion, chopped	⅓	cup slivered almonds, toasted
¼	cup mushrooms, sliced	1	teaspoon flour
3	tablespoons butter	3	tablespoons butter, melted
¼	teaspoon salt	1 ¼	cups potato chips, crushed

Pound breasts to ⅜ inch thick and set aside. Sauté celery, onion and mushrooms in butter. Blend in salt and pepper, lemon juice and almonds. Stir in flour and cook until thick. Divide sautéed mixture evenly on each breast. Roll up breasts, coat with melted butter, roll in potato chips. Place seam-side down in baking dish. Cover and bake in a preheated 350° oven for 45 minutes. Uncover. Bake 15 minutes longer. Garnish with mushrooms and parsley. *Makes 4 servings.*

Prep. Time: 30 minutes.

CHICKEN WITH GRAPES

3	whole chicken breasts, halved, skinned & deboned	¼	teaspoon tarragon, crumbled
salt, to taste		1	green onion top, thinly sliced
ground nutmeg, to taste		⅓	cup dry white wine
2	tablespoons butter or margarine	½	cup seedless green grapes
1	tablespoon orange marmalade	¼	cup whipping cream

Sprinkle chicken breasts with salt and nutmeg. In large frying pan, brown lightly in heated butter. Add marmalade, tarragon, green onion and wine. Cover and reduce heat. Simmer 7 minutes. Add grapes, cover again and cook until done (7 minutes). Using slotted spoon, remove chicken and grapes to a warm serving dish. Keep warm. Add cream to liquid in pan. Bring to boil and stir. Cook until reduced and slightly thickened. Pour sauce over chicken and grapes. *Makes 6 servings.*

Prep. Time: 30 minutes.

SHERRIED CHICKEN

10	chicken breasts, skinned & deboned (12 if desired)	2	8 ounce jars mushrooms, drained
2	cans cream of mushroom soup	½	cup cream sherry
1	pint sour cream	1	tablespoon Worcestershire sauce
2	tablespoons margarine, melted	cooked rice	

Place chicken in a 9 x 13 inch baking dish. Do not stack chicken breasts. Mix remaining ingredients and pour over chicken breasts. Cover tightly. Bake in a preheated 350° oven for 2 hours. Serve over cooked rice. *Makes 10 to 12 servings.*

Prep. Time: 10 minutes.

CHICKEN WITH ARTICHOKES

3	whole chicken breasts, halved, skinned & deboned	1	6 ounce jar marinated artichokes
¼	cup oil	1	cup white wine
4	tablespoons margarine	½	cup pitted black olives, halved
¾	pound fresh mushrooms, sliced		
¼	cup flour seasoned with salt, pepper & garlic		

Pat chicken dry with a paper towel. Brown in oil and margarine until golden. Remove from pan and place in casserole dish. In same pan, sauté mushrooms. Remove from pan. Add flour and seasonings. Stir well. Add artichokes with liquid, and wine. Stir and smooth out flour in liquid. Add the olives. Cook for a few minutes on low stirring occasionally. Place mushrooms, olives and artichokes around chicken. Cover with foil. Heat in a preheated 300° oven for 30 minutes. *Makes 4 servings.*

Prep. Time: 10 minutes.

CHICKEN WITH LIME BUTTER

6	chicken breasts, skinned & deboned	1	lime, juiced
½	teaspoon salt	8	tablespoons butter
½	teaspoon pepper	½	teaspoon chives, minced
¼	cup oil	½	teaspoon dill weed

Sprinkle chicken on both sides with salt and pepper. In a large frying pan, place oil and heat to medium temperature. Add chicken and sauté 10 minutes or until lightly browned. Turn chicken, cover, reduce heat to low. Cook 10 minutes or until fork can be inserted into chicken with ease. Remove chicken and keep warm. Drain all oil. In same pan, add juice and heat on low heat until juice begins to bubble. Add butter, stirring until butter becomes opaque and forms a thickened sauce. Stir in chives and dill weed. Spoon over chicken and serve. *Makes 6 servings.*

Prep. Time: 30 minutes.

CHICKEN ROCHAMBEAU

8	boneless breasts of chicken	1	tablespoon Worcestershire sauce
flour		½	teaspoon salt
¾	cup butter	dash of cayenne pepper	
1	cup shallots, minced	½	cup burgundy wine
1	teaspoon garlic	cooked rice	
2	tablespoons flour	½	cup bearnaise sauce
2	cups chicken stock		
½	cup mushrooms, chopped		

Dredge chicken in flour. Melt butter in large skillet and sauté chicken until brown and tender. Remove to covered dish to keep warm. Sauté shallots and garlic in drippings. Add 2 tablespoons flour and brown well. Stir in stock until smooth. Add mushrooms and simmer 15 minutes. Add Worcestershire sauce, salt, cayenne pepper and wine. Heat through to make a wine sauce. Spoon wine sauce on top of rice. Place 2 deboned chicken breasts on top of rice and sauce. Cover with bearnaise sauce. (See Beef Section, page 97.) *Makes 4 to 6 servings.*

Prep. Time: 15 minutes.

SESAME CHICKEN

½	cup cooking oil	¼	teaspoon Accent
¼	cup soy sauce	chicken pieces	
3-4	pieces fresh garlic, diced	sesame seeds	

Combine cooking oil, soy sauce, garlic and Accent. Marinate chicken pieces 2 hours in oil mixture, turning occasionally. Broil or bake chicken until done. Sprinkle sesame seeds on chicken the last 10 minutes. *Makes 5 servings.*

Prep. Time: 20 minutes, plus 2 hours to marinate.

CHICKEN IN A POCKET

Do chickens have pockets? These do.

3	tablespoons olive oil		juice of 1 large lemon
2	large cloves garlic, minced	2	whole chicken breasts
1	teaspoon rosemary, dried & crumbled	1	medium onion, cut into eighths
½	teaspoon freshly ground pepper	4	whole pita bread

For marinade, combine first five ingredients in large shallow dish. Debone chicken and cut into 1 inch pieces. Add chicken and onion to marinade and stir to coat. Cover and refrigerate overnight, stirring once or twice. To cook, preheat broiler. Thread alternating pieces of chicken and onion on four 10-inch skewers. Reserve marinade. Broil until browned, basting frequently with marinade and turning skewers occasionally. About 10 minutes. Remove from skewers. Spoon into halved and warmed pita bread and serve immediately. *Makes 4 servings.*

Prep. Time: 20 minutes,
             plus marinating overnight.

CHICKEN DIVAN

4-6	chicken breasts, cooked, deboned & cut into bite-sized pieces	½	teaspoon fresh lemon juice
1	10 ounce package frozen broccoli, thawed & chopped	½	teaspoon curry powder
1	can cream of chicken soup	1	cup Cheddar cheese, grated
½	cup mayonnaise salad dressing	¼	cup margarine
		4	slices bread

Spray a 1 ½ quart casserole dish with a non-stick cooking spray. Place chicken on bottom of dish. Next place broccoli on top of chicken. In a small bowl, combine soup, mayonnaise, lemon juice and curry powder mixing well. Spread this mixture on top of broccoli. Sprinkle cheese on next. In a small skillet, melt margarine. Remove crusts from the bread and then cut it into ¼ inch cubes. Place this in skillet and cook until lightly browned. Place these on top of cheese. Bake in a preheated 350° oven for 30 minutes or until hot and bubbly. *Makes 4 to 6 servings.*

Prep. Time: 30 minutes.

LITTLE CHICKEN PIES

¼	cup green pepper, chopped	1	cup cooked chicken, diced
1	2 ounce jar mushrooms, drained & sliced	1	10 ounce package frozen mixed vegetables, thawed
¼	cup butter or margarine, melted	¼	cup pimento, chopped
¼	cup all-purpose flour	1	10 ounce package frozen pastry shells, baked (optional)
1	teaspoon salt		
⅛	teaspoon pepper		
1	cup chicken broth		
1	cup half-and-half (or milk)		

Sauté green pepper and mushrooms in butter in a 10 inch skillet until green pepper is tender. Combine flour, salt and pepper. Add to vegetables stirring until smooth. Cook 1 minute, stirring constantly. Gradually add chicken broth and half-and-half. Cook over medium heat, stirring constantly until thickened and bubbly. Stir in chicken, mixed vegetables and pimento. Cook until thoroughly heated. Divide filling among warm pastry shells. *Makes 6 servings.*

Prep. Time: 30 minutes.

TETRAZZINI

3-4	pound hen	½	cup celery, minced
1	onion	1	clove garlic, pressed
1	bay leaf	1	cup cream
2	ribs celery & tops	1	cup stock
salt & pepper		2	tablespoons white wine or sherry
¼	pound butter		
1	bunch green onions, minced	1	tablespoon lemon juice
½	cup bell pepper, minced	2	tablespoons flour
		2	tablespoons butter
¼	pound mushrooms, minced or 1 large can mushrooms, chopped	1	7 ounce package vermicelli
		¾	cup Parmesan cheese, grated
¼	cup parsley, minced		

Boil hen until tender with onion, bay leaf, celery, salt and pepper. Remove and cool. Strain stock and reserve the liquid. Cut chicken into bite-sized pieces and set aside. Sauté all vegetables and garlic in butter until soft. Add chicken, cream, stock, lemon juice and wine. Season to taste with salt and pepper and cook slowly over low heat, until heated through. Make a paste of additional butter and flour. Blend in and stir until smooth and thickened. Cook vermicelli in boiling stock until tender. Drain and spread on bottom of a shallow buttered casserole. Pour chicken mixture over vermicelli and sprinkle with Parmesan. Bake in a preheated 350° oven for 20 minutes. *Makes 6 to 8 servings.*

Prep. Time: 2 ½ hours.

SOUR CREAM CHICKEN

10	chicken breasts, skinned & deboned (12 if desired)	2	teaspoons paprika
		4	cloves garlic, crushed
2	cups sour cream	½	teaspoon pepper
¼	cup lemon juice	1	8 ounce package seasoned bread crumbs
4	teaspoons Worcestershire sauce		
1	teaspoon celery salt	2	sticks butter, melted

Mix all ingredients except, chicken, bread crumbs and butter in a large container with a lid. Dip chicken in mixture until completely covered. Cover dish and refrigerate overnight. After marinating, remove each piece of chicken retaining some of the mixture on each piece, dip in bread crumbs and coat completely. Place in a large casserole dish. Pour 1 stick of melted butter over chicken. Bake covered with foil in a preheated 350° oven for 45 minutes. Remove cover and pour remaining butter over chicken. Cook 15 minutes longer. *Makes 8 to 10 servings.*

Prep. Time: 30 minutes.
　　　　　　plus 10 hours marinating.

OVEN BARBECUED CHICKEN
Tastes like the great outdoors.

1	clove garlic, minced	1	tablespoon Worcestershire sauce
2	tablespoons margarine or butter	2½- 3	pound frying chicken, cut up & skinned
1	cup ketchup		
¼	cup water		
2	tablespoons brown sugar	3	small onions, sliced & separated into rings
½	teaspoon salt		
⅛	teaspoon pepper		

In small saucepan over medium heat, cook garlic in margarine for 1 minute or until tender. Stir in ketchup, water, brown sugar, salt, pepper and Worcestershire sauce. Bring to a boil. Reduce heat. Cover and simmer 5 minutes, stirring occasionally. Arrange chicken pieces in ungreased 8 x 12 inch baking dish. Place onion rings over chicken. Pour sauce over top. Bake in a preheated 375° oven for 1 hour or until chicken is fork tender and juice is clear, basting occasionally. *Makes 4 servings.*

Prep. Time: 15 minutes.

CHICKEN AND AVOCADO CASSEROLE

6	*chicken breasts*	*²/₃*	*cup chicken broth*
¼	*cup flour*	*½*	*chicken bouillon*
salt & pepper, to taste			*cube*
¼	*teaspoon thyme*	*1 ¼*	*tablespoons flour*
1	*lemon*	*²/₃*	*cup heavy cream*
6	*tablespoons butter*	*2-3*	*ripe avocados*
1 ¼	*cups dry white wine*		

Coat chicken in flour, seasoned with salt, pepper and thyme. Brown in 4 tablespoons of butter. Place in casserole dish. Add remaining butter to skillet and toss onions in this for several minutes. Add wine, chicken broth and bouillon cube, blended with flour. Bring to a boil and cook until thickened. Pour over chicken. Cover and cook for 1 hour in the oven, preheated to 375°. Remove from oven. Cool slightly so the liquid is no longer boiling. Stir in cream. Peel and slice the avocados, sprinkle with lemon juice. Place on chicken and brush with a small amount of oil. Return to oven for 10 minutes. *Makes 3 to 6 servings.*

Prep. Time: 20 minutes.

GRILLED DOVE
A dove with a bite (jalapeño).

12	*dove (15 if desired)*	*4-5*	*tablespoons*
milk			*Worcestershire sauce*
12	*jalapeño peppers*		*(1 bottle commercial*
	(15 if desired)		*BBQ sauce instead*
1	*pound bacon*		*of margarine &*
¼	*cup margarine*		*Worcestershire*
			sauce baste)

Place frozen or fresh dove in a pan. Fill the pan with milk until they are submersed. Place in the refrigerator and refrigerate overnight. When ready to cook, drain the milk off the dove and rinse. Place a jalapeño pepper inside of each dove in the breast cavity. Wrap a slice of bacon around each bird and secure with a toothpick. Combine the margarine and the Worcestershire sauce, or use a bottle of barbecue sauce of your choice. Baste the birds with the margarine mixture. In a grill, heat the charcoal to a low heat. Place the doves on the grill and slowly cook for 30 minutes to 1 hour or until the birds are tender. Turn and baste the dove throughout cooking. Eat immediately.

Prep. Time: 1 hour,
            plus marinating overnight.

CHARCOAL DOVE

Makes those hours of hunting worthwhile!

8	cleaned dove (12 if desired)	½	cup brown sugar pepper, to taste
1-2	tablespoons Coca-Cola®		

Clean dove well. Pat dry. Make a paste of brown sugar and Coca-Cola. Mixture will be very thick and pasty. Spread mixture on birds that have been peppered to taste. Grill over medium-hot fire until done. Cooking the birds rare, for 20 minutes, makes them more tender. The brown sugar marinade may be applied several hours before cooking or just prior to the grill time. Serve with cheese grits, green salad, green vegetables and hot homemade bread. *Makes 4 to 6 servings.*

Prep. Time: 15 minutes.

PROUD BIRD WITH A GOLDEN TASTE

4-6	quail	½	cup fresh mushrooms
3	tablespoons salt & pepper	1	tablespoon fresh parsley
1	cup flour	½	cup white wine
¼	cup butter or margarine	½	cup whipping cream
¼	cup onion		cooked rice

Dredge cleaned birds in flour mixed with seasoning. Sauté in butter until slightly browned. Remove birds. Sauté onion and mushrooms in butter. Add birds. Add wine. Cook 30 minutes. Add cream and blend well. Serve over white rice. *Makes 4 servings.*

Prep. Time: 20 minutes.

BAKED QUAIL

½	cup flour	8	ounces heavy whipping cream
½	teaspoon black pepper		
½	teaspoon salt		
8	quail, breasts & legs		
¼	cup oil		

Combine flour, pepper and salt. Coat the quail in the flour mixture. In a medium skillet, heat oil until very hot. Place quail in the oil and brown on all sides. Remove quail from the skillet and place in a baking dish. Pour the whipping cream over the quail. Bake in a preheated 325° oven for 1 hour.

Prep. Time: 10 minutes.

BREASTS OF WILD DUCK
Guaranteed to tame the wild in the duck.

4	wild duck breasts, skinned & deboned	1 ½	teaspoons red wine vinegar
1	cup milk	1	teaspoon soy sauce
½	cup red wine	¾	teaspoons Worcestershire sauce
¼	cup vegetable oil		
¼	cup soy sauce	¼	teaspoon cumin
		⅛	teaspoon pepper

Wild game sauce:
¾   cup currant jelly
2   teaspoons Dijon mustard

M arinate the duck breasts overnight in milk. Drain milk and pat dry. Combine red wine, oil and soy sauce. Place duck in this mixture and marinate for 3 hours. Drain marinade and pat dry. Broil in a preheated oven on a preheated broiler pan 5 inches from heat, 7 minutes on each side. Remove from heat and set aside for 5 minutes. Slice diagonally against the grain. Serve with wild game sauce.

For wild game sauce: In a small saucepan, combine all the sauce ingredients. Heat over low heat stirring constantly until jelly is melted. Serve over wild duck.

Prep. Time: 15 minutes,
             plus overnight marinating time.

WILD DUCK

¼	cup butter	½	pound butter
1	cup fresh mushrooms, chopped	1	jar currant jelly
		1 ½	cups bourbon
1	onion, chopped	1	ounce dry sherry
1	6.5 ounce can water chestnuts, drained & chopped		dash of Worcestershire sauce
			dash of salt & pepper
3	stalks celery, chopped	2	split duck breasts

I n a skillet, melt ¼ cup butter. Add mushrooms, onion, water chestnuts and celery. Sauté these until tender. In a large pan, melt ½ pound butter. Stir in currant jelly and cook until it is melted also. Add bourbon, sherry, Worcestershire sauce, salt and pepper. Bring to a boil. Add duck breasts. Lower heat, but continue to boil. Cook for 10 to 15 minutes. Turn duck over in pot. Continue to cook another 10 to 15 minutes. Stir in sautéed vegetables. Serve over rice.

Prep. Time: 30 minutes.

BAKED PHEASANT

1	cup sour cream	½	teaspoon ginger
¾	cup dry sherry	1	4 ounce can
5	ounces cream of		mushrooms,
	mushroom soup		drained & sliced
½	package dry onion	1	pheasant, cleaned &
	soup mix		cut into pieces
½	teaspoon curry		
	powder		

Combine all the above ingredients. Pour into a casserole dish and cover. Bake in a preheated 350° oven for 2 hours. Just before ready to serve, broil until lightly browned. Serve as is or over rice.

Prep. Time: 20 minutes.

SMOTHERED COUNTRY PHEASANT
None other quite as pleasant.

1 ½	cups flour	½	cup margarine
1	teaspoon salt	3	tablespoons oil
½	teaspoon pepper	½	onion, chopped
1	teaspoon thyme	1	cup chicken broth
3	pheasant breasts, deboned	½	cup white wine
3	pheasant legs with thighs	½	teaspoon sweet basil
			cornstarch

In a small bowl, combine flour, salt, pepper and thyme. Dip pheasant pieces in flour mixture. In a skillet heat margarine and oil. Cook pheasant in oil until brown. Add onions and cook until they are tender. Turn heat down to a low setting. Stir in chicken broth, wine and basil. Cover and cook slowly for 2 hours or until very tender. Add more chicken broth or wine if the other cooks off. When cooked, remove pheasant to another plate. Thicken remaining sauce with cornstarch. Pour this over the pheasant before serving.

Prep. Time: 20 minutes.

BURRITOS
A Southwest staple.

½	cup green bell pepper, chopped	1	8 ounce can tomato sauce
1	cup onion, chopped	1	15.5 ounce can refried beans
3	tablespoons oil		
1	pound ground round	1	4 ounce can green chilies, chopped
½	teaspoon cumin		
½	teaspoon salt	8	ounces Cheddar cheese, grated
¼	teaspoon garlic powder	6-8	burrito-sized flour tortillas
¼	teaspoon oregano		
½	teaspoon dry mustard	½-1	cup oil (plus)
2	tablespoons chili powder		guacamole (see Appetizers, page 9)
2	tablespoons picante sauce		sour cream

In a large pan, sauté peppers and onion in 3 tablespoons of oil until onions are clear. Add ground round and continue cooking until brown. Drain off excess fat. Add next 10 ingredients and continue to cook until hot and bubbly stirring constantly. Remove from heat and stir in Cheddar cheese. Divide evenly among flour tortillas. Pull ends of tortilla over the meat and roll sides up. Roll as tightly as possible to seal them. Serve as is or deep fry. To fry, heat ½ - 1 cup oil in a large skillet. Additional oil may be needed during frying the burritos. Place burritos seam-side down in hot oil and fry until lightly brown. Turn and fry other side until lightly brown. Remove from oil and place on a paper towel to drain. Serve hot. Top with guacamole and sour cream. *Makes 6 to 8 servings.*

Prep. Time: 30 minutes.

CHICKEN AND CHEESE CHIMICHANGAS

2	onions, chopped	½	teaspoon cumin
2	cloves garlic, finely minced	½	teaspoon oregano
		1	teaspoon salt
¼	cup oil	8	ounces Cheddar cheese, grated
3	cups cooked chicken, cut into bite-sized pieces		
		6-8	burrito-sized flour tortillas
4	tomatoes, skinned & chopped	½-1	cup oil (plus)
2	tablespoons chili powder		guacamole (see Appetizers, page 9)
			sour cream

In a large pan, sauté onions and garlic in ¼ cup oil until tender. Add next 6 ingredients and simmer over a medium heat until all liquid has evaporated, for 30 minutes. Remove from heat and stir in Cheddar cheese. Divide evenly among flour tortillas. Pull the ends of tortilla over the meat and roll the sides up. Roll as tightly as possible to seal them. In a skillet, heat ½-1 cup of oil. Additional oil may be needed while frying chimichangas. Place chimichangas seam-side down in hot oil and fry until lightly brown. Turn and fry other side until lightly brown. Remove from oil and place on a paper towel to drain. Serve hot. Top with guacamole and sour cream. *Makes 6 to 8 servings.*

Prep. Time: 1 ½ hours.

GREEN ENCHILADAS
Enchiladas verdes.

¼	cup flour		oil
¼	cup butter, melted	1	dozen corn tortillas
1	can chicken broth	2	cups Monterey-Jack
1	cup sour cream		cheese, grated
1	4 ounce can green chilies, chopped	¾	cup onion, chopped

In a medium saucepan, mix flour and melted butter. Add broth and stir. Heat until it begins to bubble. Do not boil. Add sour cream and peppers. Meanwhile, in a small skillet, heat oil until it is almost smoking. Dip tortillas in oil for just a few seconds to soften. Sprinkle cheese and onion in each tortilla and roll. Secure with toothpicks. Pour green chili sauce over enchiladas. Bake in a preheated 425° oven for 20 minutes. *Makes 4 to 6 servings.*

Prep. Time: 45 minutes.

Hint: *For a variation, add 3 cups cooked, deboned chicken. Divide among the tortillas then top with cheese and onion.*

RED ENCHILADAS
Enchiladas rojas de San Antonio.

Red chili sauce:		*Enchiladas:*	
1	package red chili pods	corn tortillas	
water		oil	
1	small onion, chopped	*Filling,*	
½	clove garlic, finely minced	*use one of the following:*	
1	teaspoon salt	cheese & onion	
1	teaspoon oregano	cooked ground beef with cheese, garlic, onion & red sauce	
water		cooked deboned chicken with cheese, onion & red sauce	
1	15 ounce can tomato sauce	red sauce	

Place chili pods in a small bowl. Fill with water until chili pods are covered. Soak overnight. Remove stems and seeds and place in a blender. Purée until smooth. Add onion, garlic, salt and oregano. Fill with water to top of blender. Purée on low until smooth. Pour through a strainer into a saucepan. Stir in tomato sauce. Bring to a boil. Reduce heat and simmer for 2 hours.

In a small skillet, heat oil until it is almost smoking. Dip tortillas in oil for just a few seconds to soften. Place filling of your choice in middle of tortilla and roll it into a log. Place this in a large baking dish. Spoon red sauce over filled tortilla. Bake in a preheated 350° oven for 30 minutes or until heated through. Garnish with cilantro.

Prep. Time: 15 minutes,
plus overnight soaking time.

SOUR CREAM ENCHILADAS
Enchiladas Suisa.

1/4	cup butter or margarine	1/2	teaspoon salt
1	large bunch green onions & tops, chopped	1/2	teaspoon oregano
		1/2	teaspoon basil
1	clove garlic, finely minced	3	cups chicken, cooked & cut into bite-sized pieces
1	15 ounce can tomato sauce	2	cups Cheddar cheese, grated
1	4 ounce can green chilies, chopped	2	cups Monterey-Jack cheese, grated
1	teaspoon sugar	1	16 ounce carton sour cream
1	teaspoon cumin	12	corn tortillas

In a large skillet, melt butter or margarine. Add onions and garlic and sauté until onions are tender. Stir in tomato sauce, green chilies, sugar, cumin, salt, oregano and basil. Bring to a boil. Reduce heat and simmer for 15 minutes. Meanwhile, combine chicken, with enough sour cream to moisten. In another bowl, mix the two cheeses. Dip each tortilla in the hot tomato sauce. Divide the chicken mixture between the 12 tortillas spreading it down the middle. Sprinkle cheeses on top of the chicken mixture reserving some to top the dish with. Roll tortilla into a log and place in baking dish seam-side down. Repeat until all 12 tortillas are filled. Combine the remaining tomato sauce and sour cream. Spread this over the tortillas. Sprinkle remaining cheeses on top. Bake in a preheated 350° oven for 45 minutes or until the dish is thoroughly heated. *Makes 6 servings of 2 enchiladas.*

Prep. Time: 1 hour.

CHILIES RELLENOS

1/2	pound Monterey-Jack cheese	2	eggs, separated
		2	tablespoons flour
6	whole green peppers, either fresh* or canned	1	tablespoon lard or olive oil

Cut 6 pieces of cheese 1 inch wide, half an inch thick and the length of the chili. Make a small slit in chili just big enough to insert cheese. Beat the egg whites until stiff. Beat the yolks and flour together. Fold into the egg whites. Drop the cheese stuffed peppers into the egg mixture one at a time. Take out with a spoon. Drop into the hot lard or olive oil. Fry until golden brown on both sides.

Prep. Time: 15 to 20 minutes.

Note: If fresh, chilies must be pierced with a fork, then placed on a cookie sheet. Broil 4 to 6 inches below heating unit. Turn often until the chilies are blistered on all sides. Remove from broiler and cover with a damp cloth for 10 minutes. Start at the stem and peel the skin downward. You may want to remove the stem and seeds.

TACOS

Shells:
12   corn tortillas
½   inch lard or
       vegetable oil, heated
       in large skillet

Filling:
1 ½   pounds ground beef
1   small onion,
       chopped
1   clove garlic, mashed
       or ⅓ teaspoon garlic
       powder
½   teaspoon garlic salt
½   teaspoon oregano
1   teaspoon salt

Garnish:
1   fresh tomato,
       chopped
1 ½   cups cheese, grated
       (2 cups if needed)
2   cups lettuce,
       shredded

Fry tortillas using medium-high heat. Fry on one side until slightly crisp, but still pliable. Turn and fold in half holding edges of tortillas open so inside can be filled. Fry until the remaining side becomes crisp. Drain on paper towels. Sauté the beef and onion (and garlic, if using a clove), crumbling the meat while cooking with a fork or potato masher. Drain off excess fat. Stir in remaining seasonings. Place meat in tortilla shells. Add garnishments. Warm in the oven until cheese melts.

Prep. Time: 15 to 20 minutes.

CHALUPAS

2   pounds pork roast
1   pound pinto beans
       (unsoaked)
2   cloves garlic, minced
2   tablespoons chili
       powder
1   tablespoon cumin
1   tablespoon oregano
1   tablespoon picante
       sauce
1   teaspoon salt
corn chips

1 ½   pounds Cheddar
       cheese, grated
1   head lettuce,
       shredded
12   bunches green onion
       & chives, chopped
5   tomatoes, chopped
guacamole (see Appetizers,
       page 9)
extra picante sauce

In a large pan or Crockpot, place the pork roast and cover with water. Add the next 7 ingredients and cook over a low heat for 8 hours; stirring occasionally to blend all ingredients well. Serve over corn chips. Top with Cheddar cheese, lettuce, onions, tomatoes, guacamole and extra picante sauce as desired. Let your guests build their own. *Makes 8 to 10 servings.*

Prep. Time: 15 minutes.

TOSTADOS

10	corn tortillas (12 if needed)	8	ounces Cheddar cheese, grated
	vegetable oil	1	cup green onion tops, chopped
1	pound ground round		
2	cloves garlic, finely minced	2-3	cups lettuce, shredded
1	15.5 ounce can refried beans	2-3	cups tomatoes, drained & chopped
2	tablespoons chili powder	2	cups guacamole (see Appetizers, page 9)
1	teaspoon dry mustard		
½	teaspoon paprika	1	cup sour cream
	pico de gallo (see Appetizers, page 10)		black olive slices

In a deep skillet, heat oil. Fry corn tortillas in oil until it holds shape. Remove from oil and place on a paper towel to drain. In a pan, cook ground round and garlic until beef is brown. Drain off excess fat. Stir in refried beans, pico de gallo to taste, chili powder, dry mustard and paprika. Heat until warmed through. Spread this on corn tortillas. Place them on a cookie sheet. Divide the Cheddar cheese and green onions among the tostados. Bake in a preheated 375° oven for 15 minutes until cheese is melted. Remove from oven. Top with lettuce, tomatoes, guacamole and sour cream. Garnish with sliced black olives. *Makes 10 to 12 servings.*

Prep. Time: 30 minutes.

FLAUTAS

1 ½	cups leftover roast beef	10	corn tortillas (12 if needed)
		2	tablespoons lard

Shred the roast beef. Spread 1 heaping tablespoon beef along a tortilla. Tightly roll up the tortilla so that it looks like a cigar. Secure with a toothpick. Place in hot lard for 2 minutes, turning so all sides are brown. Drain on paper towels. Serve with guacamole.

Prep. Time: 15 minutes.

FAJITAS

Marinade:
3   cups light soy sauce
1   cup water
1   cup brown sugar,
      firmly packed
2   tablespoons Liquid
      Smoke
1   teaspoon garlic
      powder
1   teaspoon onion
      powder
1   teaspoon cayenne
      powder
1   teaspoon seasoned
      pepper

½   cup lemon juice
4   teaspoons ginger

Fixin's:
1   skirt steak
mesquite or hickory chips
flour tortillas
grilled onions &
      green peppers
guacamole (see Appetizers,
      page 9)
pico de gallo
      (see Appetizers,
      page 10)
Cheddar cheese, grated
      (optional)

Combine first ten ingredients in a inner-lock plastic bag to form a marinade. Shake to mix well. Let marinade stand overnight to blend flavors. Trim excess fat off skirt steak. Place it into marinade. Place this in refrigerator. Let marinate for 2 hours, but is best if marinated overnight. Meanwhile, soak mesquite or hickory chips in water, but is best if done night before needed. In an outdoor grill, heat charcoal until very hot. Before cooking, drain mesquite or hickory chips and place in coals. Remove meat from marinade and grill 5 minutes per side over hot coals. Place lid on grill while grilling to help keep mesquite or hickory chip smoke inside grill. Remove from heat. Slice in thin strips. Place on a flour tortilla. Place condiments of your choice on top. Roll up and enjoy!

Prep. Time: 10 minutes,
           plus marinating time of 2 days.

SANTA FE STYLE CHICKEN OR BEEF TENDERLOIN

⅓   cup fresh lime juice
3   tablespoons olive oil
dash of salt
dash of black pepper,
      freshly ground
4   chicken breasts,
      deboned but with
      skin or four 1-inch
      thick tenderloins
1 ½   cups canned whole
      peeled tomatillos
      (green tomatoes),
      drained & rinsed
½   cup cream

Salsa:
5   small tomatoes,
      diced
1   small onion, diced
1   fresh jalapeño,
      seeded, deribbed &
      minced
¼   cup fresh cilantro,
      minced
2   tablespoons red
      wine vinegar

In a small bowl, whisk together the lime juice, olive oil, salt and black pepper until blended. Brush marinade on both sides of chicken or beef. In food processor or blender, process tomatillos until finely chopped. Pour into a glass saucepan and stir in cream. Bring to a simmer over moderately high heat. Cook, stirring occasionally, until slightly reduced and thickened, for 5 minutes. Remove from heat. Meanwhile, in a medium bowl, combine the tomatoes, onion, jalapeño, cilantro and vinegar. Refrigerate until needed. To cook the chicken or beef, arrange the breasts skin-side down on a preheated grill or in a broiler pan, 4 inches from the broiler. Cook for 5 minutes on each side, turning once. Do not over cook. To serve, divide the tomatillo sauce among 4 plates. Place chicken or beef in the center. Garnish with salsa on top.

Prep. Time: 20 to 30 minutes.

TEXAS–STYLE CHILI

Chili is the State dish of Texas. It is a fiery beef dish that is fixed by Texans with lots of Texas pride. If you can stand the heat, then rustle up some for your bunch today!

1	green bell pepper, chopped	2	teaspoons garlic salt
1	red bell pepper, chopped	2	tablespoons cumin
2	onions, chopped	12	ounce bottle Texas beer
2	cloves garlic, chopped	8-10	whole tomatoes, skinned & chopped
3	stalks celery, chopped	1	6 ounce can tomato paste
4-6	fresh jalapeño peppers, seeded & chopped (if you can find them, use red jalapeños for a better flavor)	1	8 ounce can tomato sauce
		1	4 ounce can green chilies, chopped
		1 1/4	cups water
		1/4	teaspoon pequin peppers (or to taste)
1/4	cup oil	2	15 ounce cans ranch-style beans, drained & rinsed
3	pounds chili meat		corn chips
1/2	teaspoon Tabasco sauce (or to taste)		Cheddar cheese, grated
1/4	cup hot (Mexican) chili powder		Monterey-Jack cheese, grated
1/4	teaspoon black pepper		

Place bell peppers, onion, garlic, celery, jalapeños and oil in a large Dutch oven or stock pan. Cook over a high heat until all vegetables are tender. Crumble in chili meat and continue cooking until brown. Drain off excess fat (optional). Turn the heat off and stir in Tabasco, chili powder, black pepper, garlic salt, cumin and 8 ounces of beer. The other 4 ounces are for the cook. Let this mixture stand for 5 minutes. Add tomatoes, tomato paste, tomato sauce, green chilies and water. Turn heat back on and bring to a boil. Meanwhile, place the pequin peppers in a blender and grind them until they are a fine powder. These are very hot peppers so add them a little at a time. Reduce heat and simmer for 2 1/2 hours. Stir in beans* and continue cooking an additional 30 minutes. Serve with corn chips and top with cheeses. *Makes 6 large bowls.*

Prep. Time: 1 hour.

* *To bean or not bean is a Texas-sized controversy. Follow the independence of the West and make your own decision.*

SOUTHWEST MINI-INDEX

You will find the following Southwest recipes in other sections as follows:

TO PEPPER OR NOT TO PEPPER?

In Spanish, there are two words meaning "hot". "Caliente" means hot to touch; "picante" means hot to taste. But different chilies are more "picante" than others.

Here is a listing of chilies, according to their spiciness:

1. *Habañero: beyond mucho picante.*
2. *Pequin: mucho picante.*
3. *Tabasco, cayenne peppers: too hot to handle for most people.*
4. *Jalapeño: picante enough for everyday souls.*
5. *Serrano: used in table salsas.*
6. *Ancho: used to make paprika.*
7. *Anaheim: mild, fresh green chili usually bought in cans.*
8. *Bell peppers, pimento: sissy stuff.*

CHILI AND RICE

1	pound ground beef	1	16 ounce can
1	cup onion, chopped		ranch-style beans
1	clove garlic, minced	1	16 ounce can
1	tablespoon chili		stewed tomatoes
	powder	½	cup water
¼	teaspoon red pepper		cooked rice
½	teaspoon oregano		

In a large skillet, brown meat, onion and garlic. Drain and add remaining ingredients, stirring well. Reduce heat and simmer 1 hour.   Serve over rice. If desired, sprinkle grated cheese over chili and rice before serving. *Makes 6 to 8 servings.*

Prep. Time: 15 minutes.

CHICKEN TORTILLA CASSEROLE

3	cups cooked chicken, cut into bite-sized pieces	2	tablespoons margarine, melted
1	onion, chopped	12	small flour tortillas, quartered
1	4 ounce can green chilies, drained & chopped	1	pound American cheese, grated
1	cup milk		
1	can each cream of mushroom & cream of chicken soup		

Combine chicken, onion, green chilies, milk and soups. Set aside. Pour margarine in a 9 x 13 inch pan and coat bottom. Layer bottom of pan with flour tortilla quarters, chicken mixture and cheese. Repeat, ending with cheese on top. Refrigerate overnight. Bake in a preheated 350° oven for 1 hour or until hot and bubbly. *Makes 8 servings.*

Prep. Time: 15 minutes.
Marinating Time: Overnight.

KING RANCH CHICKEN

1	(3 ½-4 pound) chicken, cooked, deboned & cut into bite-sized pieces	1 ½	teaspoons chili powder
1	large onion, chopped		garlic salt, to taste
1	large green bell pepper, chopped	1	can cream of chicken soup
1	8 ounce package corn tortillas	1	can cream of mushroom soup
	broth from cooked chicken or canned broth	1	can Rotel tomatoes with green chilies, diced
8	ounces Cheddar cheese, grated		

Combine chicken, onion and pepper. Layer alternately with tortillas, which have been dipped into hot chicken broth just long enough to soften, in a shallow 3 quart casserole dish. Top with grated cheese. Sprinkle with chili powder and garlic salt. Mix soups and Rotel tomatoes. Spoon over chicken and tortillas. Bake in a preheated 350° oven for 30 to 45 minutes or until hot and bubbly. *Makes 8 to 10 servings.*

Prep. Time: 30 minutes.

CHILIES RELLENOS BURRITOS
A new twist on an old favorite.

5	tablespoons butter	4	eggs, beaten to blend
1	medium onion, finely chopped	12	whole green chilies
2	cups sour cream	3	cups Monterey-Jack cheese, grated
¼	teaspoon cayenne pepper	12	8 inch flour tortillas
	dash of salt	12	slices avocado
	dash of pepper, freshly ground		mild or hot salsa
1	15 ounce can refried beans		

Heat 2 tablespoons butter in medium skillet over medium heat. Add onion and sauté until soft, 5 to 7 minutes. Stir in 2 tablespoons sour cream, cayenne pepper, salt and pepper. Mix in refried beans. Remove from heat, cover and keep warm. Melt 1 tablespoon butter in another medium skillet over medium heat. Pour one-third of eggs into skillet. Arrange 4 chilies over eggs in half of pan. Sprinkle with 1 cup cheese. Cook until just set, about 2 minutes. Fold other half over (as for omelet) and cook until firmly set, about 1 minute. Slice into 12 pieces, cutting between chilies. Keep warm. Warm tortillas in dry skillet over medium heat, 1 minute per side. Fill each with egg strip, bean mixture, sour cream and avocado slice. Add salsa to taste. Roll up, then fold in edges. Serve burritos immediately.

Prep. Time: 20 minutes.

SOUTHWEST CHICKEN

2	whole chickens, boiled & deboned	2	cloves garlic, minced
1	teaspoon salt	1	tablespoon flour
¼	teaspoon pepper	¾	cup chicken broth
2	tablespoons butter	½	cup plain yogurt
½	pound fresh mushrooms, sliced	½	cup Monterey-Jack cheese, grated
½	cup chicken broth	¼	cup pine or sunflower nuts
1	tablespoon butter		
1	onion, chopped		
2	4 ounce cans diced green chilies, drained		

Season chicken with salt and pepper. Spread chicken in a casserole dish. In a skillet, sauté mushrooms in ½ tablespoon of butter for 3 minutes. Scatter mushrooms over chicken and pour ½ cup broth overall. Cover and bake in a preheated 350° oven for 10 minutes. Melt remaining butter in skillet and sauté onion for 3 minutes. Add chilies, garlic and flour. Cook for 1 minute, stirring constantly. Remove chicken from oven. Combine pan drippings and ¾ cup broth in a measuring cup to measure 1 cup. Stir into onion mixture. Mix in yogurt and heat thoroughly. Spoon mixture over chicken. Sprinkle with cheese and return to oven. Bake in a preheated 350° for 15 minutes more. To serve, sprinkle with nuts. *Makes 6 to 8 servings.*

Prep. Time: 20 minutes.

MEXICAN POTATO CASSEROLE
A great low-cal meal.

12	ounces potatoes, peeled & shredded	1	4 ounce can green chili peppers, drained & chopped
2	ounces Cheddar cheese, shredded	½	cup taco sauce
¼	teaspoon pepper	⅛	teaspoon onion salt
⅛	teaspoon onion powder	4	ounces Cheddar cheese, shredded
10	ounces ground turkey		picante sauce (optional)
1 ½	cups cabbage, shredded		

In large bowl, toss together potatoes, 2 ounces cheese, pepper and onion powder. Press into the bottom and up the sides of a 9 x 9 x 2 inch baking dish that has been sprayed with a non-stick cooking spray. Bake in a preheated 350° oven for 30 minutes. In large skillet, brown turkey and set aside. In same skillet stir fry cabbage over high heat for 2 to 3 minutes. Remove from heat and stir in turkey, green chilies, taco sauce, pepper and onion salt. Top with 4 ounces cheese. Pour into the baking dish lined with potatoes. Bake 2 to 3 minutes to melt cheese. Let stand 10 minutes before serving. Serve with picante sauce. *Makes 4 servings.*

Prep. Time: 20 minutes.

COMANCHE CHICKEN CASSEROLE

1	cup dairy sour cream
1/3	cup milk
1/4	cup onion, chopped
1/2	teaspoon garlic salt or 1/4 teaspoon garlic powder
1/4	teaspoon cumin
dash	Tabasco sauce
1	can cream of chicken soup
10	ounce package frozen spinach, thawed , chopped & well drained
4	ounce can green chilies, drained & chopped
2	ounce jar pimento, drained & chopped
2-3	cups chicken, cooked & cubed
4	ounces Monterey-Jack cheese, shredded
2	ounces Cheddar cheese, shredded

Topping:

2	eggs, separated
1	cup all-purpose or unbleached flour
1 1/2	teaspoons baking powder
3/4	cup milk
1/4	cup margarine or butter, softened
paprika	

Lightly grease 2 quart deep casserole. In large bowl, combine sour cream, 1/3 cup milk, onion, garlic salt, cumin, Tabasco sauce, soup, spinach, chilies and pimento. Blend well. Combine chicken with cheeses. Toss lightly. Spoon half of spinach mixture into greased casserole dish. Sprinkle with half of chicken mixture. Repeat layers.

For topping: In small bowl, beat egg whites until stiff peaks form. Remove whites from bowl. Set aside. Lightly spoon flour into measuring cup and level off. In small bowl, with same beaters, combine flour, baking powder, 3/4 cup milk, margarine and egg yolks. Beat at low speed until moistened. Beat 4 minutes at highest speed, scraping sides of bowl occasionally. Fold in beaten egg whites. Pour topping over chicken and spinach layers. Sprinkle with paprika. Bake in a preheated 375° oven for 40 to 45 minutes or until deep golden brown. *Makes 6 to 8 servings.*

Prep. Time: 30 minutes.

SHRIMP AND CHICKEN OLE'

1	*medium onion, diced*		*dash of cayenne pepper*
½	*cup green pepper, diced*	*2*	*5-6 ounce cans boned chicken*
3	*cloves garlic, minced*	*2*	*cans shrimp, drained*
1 ½	*cups quick-cooking rice*	*¾*	*cup sharp Cheddar cheese, grated*
¼	*cup butter*	*¼*	*pound sharp Cheddar cheese, sliced*
1	*1 pound can tomatoes, chopped*		
1	*teaspoon salt*		

In a skillet, cook onion, green pepper, garlic and rice in butter until vegetables are tender. Add tomatoes, salt and cayenne. Add chicken, cut into bite-sized pieces, liquid and drained shrimp. Put half of mixture into 3 quart casserole dish and sprinkle with grated cheese. Add remaining mixture. Cover and bake in a preheated 350° oven for 15 to 20 minutes. Arrange 1 inch wide strips of sliced cheese over top of casserole. Return to oven for 2 to 3 minutes or until cheese melts. *Makes 6 servings.*

Prep. Time: 30 minutes.

CHEESY CHICKEN MEXICANA

2	*medium onions, chopped*	*1*	*pound processed cheese, cut in chunks*
1	*clove garlic, minced*		
1	*tablespoon oil*	*1*	*pound Cheddar cheese, grated*
1	*bell pepper, seeded & chopped*		
2	*10 ounce cans tomatoes & green chilies, chopped*	*6*	*cups chicken, cooked & chopped*
		1	*pint sour cream*
			tostados or rice

In a skillet, cook the onion and garlic in oil until transparent. Add the tomatoes and green chilies and bring to a boil. Reduce heat and simmer until thick for 20 minutes. Add cheeses and heat slowly until melted. Then add chicken and sour cream. Heat until smooth, but do not boil. Serve over layer of rice or crisp tostado chips.

Prep. Time: 20 minutes.

MEXICAN TACO SALAD

1	15.5 ounce can refried beans	¼	pound Cheddar cheese, grated
1	pound ground beef	¼	pound Monterey-Jack cheese, grated
½	onion, chopped		
2	tablespoons chili powder	1	small head lettuce, shredded
1	teaspoon paprika	4	tomatoes, chopped
1	teaspoon cumin	1	small bunch green onions & tops, chopped
½	teaspoon salt		
¼	teaspoon garlic powder		avocado slices or guacamole (see Appetizers, page 9)
4	tostado salad shells or tostado chips, broken		
	salsa picante sauce (see Appetizers, page 9)		sour cream
			black olives, sliced

Over a low heat, warm refried beans until bubbly. In a medium skillet, cook ground beef and onion until beef is brown. Drain excess fat. Stir in chili powder, paprika, cumin, salt and garlic powder. Divide refried beans between the tostado salad shells or crumbled tostado chips. Top with meat mixture and spoon a little salsa on top. Next place cheeses on, then lettuce, tomato and green onions. Place avocados or guacamole on top and a spoonful of sour cream. Garnish with the black olives. *Makes 4 servings.*

Prep. Time: 20 minutes.

PANCHO PIE

1	green pepper, diced	½	cup cornmeal
3	clove garlic, crushed	1	cup milk
2	tablespoons oil	½	cup black olives, minced
1	pound ground beef		
1	teaspoon chili powder	1	cup mushrooms
2	teaspoons salt		corn chips
1½	cups stewed tomatoes		lettuce, shredded (optional)
1	can cream corn		

In a skillet, sauté peppers, garlic and oil. Add 1 pound ground meat, chili powder and salt. Cook 10 minutes and add tomatoes and corn. Boil briskly and add cornmeal, milk, olives and mushrooms. Bake in a greased, uncovered casserole dish in a preheated 350° oven for 1 hour or until set. Serve over corn chips. Garnish with shredded lettuce. *Makes 8 servings.*

Prep. Time: 30 minutes.

Variation: *This can also be made on campouts in a cast iron kettle with a lid. Sauté the peppers, garlic and oil over hot coals. Add the ground meat, chili powder and salt. Cook 10 minutes. Add tomatoes, corn, cornmeal, milk, olives and mushrooms. Place the lid on the cast iron kettle. Bury in very hot coals and bake for 1 hour. Serve over corn chips.*

MEXICAN MEAT SAUCE

This is great for a "serve-yourself" buffet for a crowd.

2	pounds ground round
1 ¾	pounds onions, diced
1	tablespoon garlic salt
2	tablespoons chili sauce
1	28 ounce can tomatoes
1	12 ounce can tomato purée
1	cup tomato sauce
1	15 ounce can ranch-style beans

Garnishes:
flour tortillas
fresh tomatoes, chopped
fresh lettuce, shredded
Cheddar cheese, grated
black (ripe) olives, sliced
sour cream

Sauté ground round in large pot. Add onions and stir. Add remaining 6 ingredients and stir. Simmer for 2 hours until flavors are well mixed. Serve with warm flour tortillas, chopped fresh tomatoes, chopped lettuce, grated cheese, sliced ripe olives, sour cream and more, for "make-your-own" burritos! *Makes 12 servings.*

Prep. Time: 20 minutes.

CRISPY ENCHILADA CASSEROLE

2	cups Longhorn cheese, shredded	½	cup water
1	can (1 ⅔ cups) enchilada sauce, mild, medium or hot	2	tablespoons onion, minced
1	15 ounce can chili with beans	1	6 ounce package corn chips (small ones)
1	6 ounce can tomato paste	1	cup sour cream

Combine 1 ½ cups shredded cheese, enchilada sauce, chili, tomato paste, water, onion and all but 1 cup of corn chips. Pour into lightly greased oblong baking dish. Bake uncovered in a preheated 375° oven for 30 minutes. Spread sour cream over top. Sprinkle with remaining cheese. Circle corn chips around edge. Bake an additional 5 minutes. *Makes 6 servings.*

Prep. Time: 10 minutes.

ONION-SMOTHERED PORK TENDERLOIN

2	*½ pound pork tenderloins*	*½*	*teaspoon dried whole thyme*
2	*teaspoons margarine, melted*	*¼*	*teaspoon salt*
2	*cups onion, diced*	*¼*	*teaspoon pepper*

Trim fat from tenderloins. Cut a lengthwise slit down center of each tenderloin about two-thirds of the way through the meat. Place tenderloins in opposite directions side-by-side on a rack that is coated with a non-stick cooking spray. Place the rack in a shallow roasting pan. Coat a large skillet with a non-stick cooking spray. Add margarine and place over medium heat until hot. Add onion, and sauté until tender, stirring frequently. Add seasonings, stirring well. Spread onion mixture evenly over tenderloins. Bake in a preheated 400° Dutch oven for 40 minutes or until done. *Makes 4 servings.*

Prep. Time: 30 minutes.

PORK CHOPS WITH MUSHROOMS

4	*pork chops, ¾" thick*	*½*	*teaspoon chervil*
1	*tablespoon oil*	*⅛*	*teaspoon black pepper, freshly ground*
½	*pound fresh mushrooms, sliced*		
1	*medium onion, sliced*	*¼*	*cup water*
2	*tablespoons butter*	1	*tablespoon cornstarch*
⅔	*cup dry vermouth*	*¼*	*cup parsley, chopped*
⅔	*cup water*		
¾	*teaspoon salt*		

In large skillet, brown the chops in 1 tablespoon oil. Remove and drain off fat. Sauté mushrooms and sliced onion in butter over medium heat for 2 minutes. Return chops to pan and add vermouth, ⅔ cup water, salt, chervil and pepper. Simmer covered, 45 minutes or until meat is tender. Remove chops and place on serving dish. Keep warm. Blend the ¼ cup water and cornstarch. Stir into mushroom mixture. Cook and stir until sauce boils about ½ minute. Stir in the parsley. Pour sauce over chops. Serve immediately. *Makes 4 servings.*

Prep. Time: 30 minutes.

PORK CHOPS WITH RICE

6	pork chops	1	cup milk
1	small box quick-cooking rice	1	package onion soup mix
1	can cream of celery soup	1	10 ounce package frozen broccoli spears, thawed
1	can cheese soup		

Sprinkle rice in buttered casserole dish. Place pork chops on rice. Mix soups and milk. Pour over pork chops. Sprinkle dry soup mix over casserole. Lay broccoli spears over this. Cover and seal with foil. Bake in a preheated 350° oven for 2 hours.

Prep. Time: 10 minutes.

SKEWERED SMOKED PORK TENDERS

	pork tenderloins		salt & pepper, to taste
	barbecue sauce	1	cup pineapple chunks, undrained
2/3	cup brown sugar		
2	tablespoons cornstarch	2	green peppers, chopped to size of pineapple chunks
2	teaspoons dry mustard		
2/3	cup vinegar	2	onions, chopped to size of pineapple chunks
1/2	cup ketchup		
1/2	cup water		
2	tablespoons soy sauce		

Place pork tenderloins on grill over hot coals. Baste with your favorite barbecue sauce. Close lid of grill. Turn about every 30 minutes, basting each time. Watch closely as tails of tenderloins will dry out. Cover tails with foil if they are cooking too fast. Grill 1 hour. Remove from grill and cut into 1 - 1 1/2 inch cubes. Cover bottom of stainless steel or foil lined pan with barbecue sauce. Place tenders in pan and place on grill for 30 minutes and let simmer.

Combine the brown sugar, cornstarch, mustard, vinegar, ketchup, water, soy sauce, salt and pepper. Add pineapple, onion and bell pepper and marinate 12 hours. Place on 8 inch wooden skewers, alternating with meat. Place back on the grill and cook until vegetables are warmed.

Prep. Time: 30 minutes,
plus marinating time of 12 hours.

LONE STAR SPICED AND SMOKED RIBS

Good grub for the whole bunch of ya'll!

4	cups hickory or mesquite chips		
water			
4	pounds farmer's-style pork ribs		
water			
1	tablespoon brown sugar		
1	teaspoon parsley		
1/4	teaspoon garlic powder		
1/4	teaspoon dry mustard		
1/4	teaspoon thyme		
1/4	teaspoon basil		
1/2	teaspoon salt		
1/2	teaspoon paprika		
1/4	teaspoon celery seed		
1/4	teaspoon black pepper		
1	recipe of molasses or teriyaki glaze		

Molasses glaze:
1/2	cup ketchup
2	tablespoons light molasses
1	tablespoon lemon juice
1	tablespoon soy sauce

Tabasco sauce, to taste

Teriyaki glaze:
2	tablespoons brown sugar
1	tablespoon cornstarch
1/2	teaspoon ground ginger
1	clove garlic, minced
1/4	cup unsweetened pineapple juice
1/4	cup soy sauce
1/4	cup dry sherry

Place the hickory or mesquite chips in a bucket of water. Soak at least 4 hours. Place the ribs in a large Dutch oven. Cover with water. Boil 1-1 1/2 hours or until thoroughly cooked or cook them in a pressure cooker for 30 to 45 minutes. Drain and cool the ribs slightly. While the ribs are cooling, combine the next 10 ingredients except the recipe of glaze. When the ribs are cool to the touch, rub the dry spice mixture on both sides of the ribs. In a covered grill, preheat your charcoal to a slow heat. To test for a slow heat, hold your hand palm side down, above the coals at the height your food will be cooked. If you can keep your hand in this position for 3 seconds then you have a slow heat. Arrange the preheated coals in the grill around a drip pan. Pour 1 inch of water or pineapple juice in the drip pan. Drain the hickory or mesquite chips and place them on top of coals. Place ribs on grill rack over drip pan but not over coals. Lower grill hood and cook for 30 minutes or until ribs are thoroughly heated, turning once. Meanwhile, prepare either molasses* or teriyaki** glaze. After 30 minutes of grilling, brush glaze on both sides of ribs. Lower grill cover and continue cooking for another 15 minutes. Turn once and brush with glaze occasionally until all glaze is used.

Molasses glaze: Stir all molasses glaze ingredients together. Brush on ribs during the last 15 minutes of grilling.

**Teriyaki glaze:* In small saucepan, combine first four ingredients mixing well. Slowly stir in remaining 3 ingredients until all lumps are gone. Bring to a boil over a medium heat. Boil, stirring constantly, for 2 minutes. Brush on ribs during last 15 minutes of grilling.

Prep. Time: 2 hours.

COUNTRY–STYLE PORK RIBS

4 ½	pounds country-style pork ribs (5 pounds can also be used)		*Barbecue Sauce:*	
		3 ½	ounces ketchup	
		3	ounces chili sauce	
Marinating Sauce:		2	tablespoons brown sugar	
½	cup soy sauce			
¼	cup water	1	teaspoon dry mustard	
2	tablespoons brown sugar			
1	teaspoon dark molasses			
¼	teaspoon salt			

Trim fat from ribs. Mix together marinating sauce and bring to a boil. Let cool. Place ribs in 9 x 13 inch glass dish. Pour sauce over pork, making sure ribs are well covered. Cover. Refrigerate overnight, turning once. Next day, drain sauce off of ribs and cover tightly with foil. Bake in 375˚ oven until tender for 2 hours. While ribs are baking, make barbecue sauce.

To prepare barbecue sauce: Combine and bring to boil all remaining sauce ingredients. When pork is tender, remove from oven. Dip each rib in sauce and return to baking dish. Bake an additional 30 minutes in 350˚ oven.

Prep. Time: 2 hours,
     plus overnight marinating.

EGGROLLS

A change of pace for Texans and want-to-be Texans.

1	pound pork sausage	6	green onions, including tops, chopped	
¼	teaspoon curry powder			
1	4 ounce can mushroom stems and pieces, drained	16	eggroll wraps (up to 20 wraps can be used)	
1	16 ounce can bean sprouts, drained	1	egg	
1	tablespoon oil	2	teaspoons water	
½	head cabbage, shredded		oil to deep fry in	
			soy sauce	

Brown sausage and drain well. Add next 3 ingredients, mix and set aside. In a large skillet, stir fry the cabbage and onions in the oil. Stir into the sausage mixture. Place ¼ cup filling in center of each eggroll wrap. Wrap each eggroll up. Mix egg with 2 teaspoons of water. Lightly brush each eggroll with this mixture. Deep fry until golden brown for 2 to 3 minutes. Serve warm with soy sauce. *Makes 4 servings.*

Prep. Time: 30 minutes.

FANCY FISH AND SAUCE

4-6	firm white fish fillets	1	onion, chopped
2	tablespoons oil	1	28 ounce can
1	green pepper,		tomatoes, drained &
	chopped		chopped
1	stalk celery, sliced		thyme, dried not ground
½	pound fresh		Tabasco
	mushrooms, sliced		salt & pepper

Sauté fish fillets in oil to brown only. Place in a casserole dish. Bake in a preheated 350° oven for 15 to 20 minutes until nearly done. Mix remaining ingredients and pour over and around fish. Continue baking for 5 minutes, or until fish are done. Fish are done when no longer translucent and when meat is flaky and tender. *Makes 4 to 6 servings.*

Prep. Time: 10 minutes.

STUFFED FISH FILLETS

½	cup onion, finely		salt & pepper
	chopped	2	tablespoons lemon
1	tablespoon butter		juice
	or margarine	1	can cream of
1	10 ounce package		mushroom soup
	broccoli, chopped,	½	cup water
	cooked & drained	½	cup Cheddar cheese,
½	cup soft bread		grated
	crumbs	2	tablespoons dry
¼	teaspoon ground		white wine
	thyme	3	cups cooked rice
6	fillets flounder or	2	tablespoons
	other white fish		pimento, diced
	(1 ½ pounds)		

In a skillet, cook onions in butter until tender but not brown. Stir in broccoli, bread crumbs and thyme. Set aside. Season fish with salt and pepper. Sprinkle with lemon juice. Place ¼ cup broccoli mixture on each fillet. Roll up and secure with toothpicks. Place in greased shallow baking dish. Bake in a preheated 350° oven for 15 minutes. Blend soup, water, cheese and wine. Pour over fish rolls. Bake 20 minutes longer. Combine rice and pimento. Serve stuffed fillets with sauce and mounds of pimento rice. *Makes 6 servings.*

Prep. Time: 15 minutes.

FLOUNDER WITH SHRIMP SAUCE

4	tablespoons butter	1	green onion, sliced
2	teaspoons all-purpose flour	2	tablespoons parsley, finely chopped
½	cup milk		pinch of dill weed
3	tablespoons dry sherry		pinch of paprika
			pinch of rosemary, crumbled & dried
salt		2	teaspoons butter
pepper, freshly ground		½	lemon, juice only
6	medium shrimp	2	flounder fillets
4	large mushrooms, sliced		freshly cooked rice

Melt 2 tablespoons butter in heavy small saucepan over low heat. Stir in flour and cook 3 minutes. Add milk and sherry. Increase heat to medium-high and continue cooking, stirring constantly, until sauce boils and is moderately thick. Season with salt and freshly ground pepper. Set aside and keep warm. Shell, devein and cut shrimp in half. Melt 2 tablespoons butter in heavy large skillet over medium-high heat. Add shrimp, mushrooms, green onion, parsley, dill weed, paprika, rosemary, salt and pepper and sauté 3 minutes until shrimp turn pink (add more sherry if liquid is needed). Remove shrimp mixture from skillet and set aside.

Melt remaining 2 teaspoons butter in same skillet over medium heat. Stir in lemon juice. Add flounder and cook for 1 to 2 minutes per side until fish turns opaque. Season with salt and pepper. Arrange fillets on heated platter. Spoon half of shrimp mixture over fillets. Whisk fish cooking liquid into white sauce and pour over fish. Spoon remaining shrimp over top. Serve immediately with hot rice. *Makes 2 servings.*

Prep. Time: 15 minutes.

SALMON CROQUETS

1	can salmon	½	cup cracker crumbs
1	egg (2 if needed to hold mixture together)		dash of salt & pepper
		¼	cup onions, chopped

In a large bowl mix all ingredients together. Make into patties. Fry in shallow skillet with oil until lightly browned. *Makes 2 to 4 servings.*

Prep. Time: 10 minutes.

RED SNAPPER CASSEROLE

1 ½	pounds (6 4-ounce fillets) red snapper, or other firm-fleshed fish	12	ounces Monterey-Jack cheese, grated
½-1	cup flour, seasoned with salt & freshly ground pepper	6	ounces Cheddar cheese, grated
3-4	tablespoons butter	2	tablespoons fresh parsley, minced
6	ounces green chili sauce		

Coat fillets with seasoned flour. Heat butter in medium skillet, and lightly sauté fillets on both sides, two at a time, adding more butter as needed. Transfer fillets to individual casserole dishes. Divide sauce and then cheeses among them. Bake in a preheated 350° oven for 12 minutes. Sprinkle with parsley. *Makes 6 servings.*

Prep. Time: 15 minutes.

GRILLED SHRIMP

2	pounds shrimp	½	cup margarine,
	soy sauce		melted
1	cup ketchup or	½	teaspoon garlic
	chili sauce		powder
	prepared horseradish sauce		

Peel and devein shrimp leaving tail section on. Place in a bowl and cover with soy sauce. Marinate for 3 hours. Meanwhile, combine ketchup (or chili sauce) and horseradish sauce to taste to make shrimp sauce. Place in refrigerator to chill until needed. Remove shrimp from marinade. Place shrimp on skewers by running them through the top of shrimp and then through the tail so they pass through the shrimp twice. In a bowl, combine margarine and garlic powder. Baste both sides of the shrimp. Heat coals in a charcoal grill to a medium heat. Place skewers on grill and grill for 5 to 8 minutes per side or until cooked through. Baste every couple minutes with garlic butter. Serve with shrimp sauce for dipping in.

Prep. Time: 30 minute.
plus marinating time of 2 hours.

TROUT ALMONDINE

½	cup flour	½	cup almonds,
¼	teaspoon salt		slivered
¼	teaspoon pepper	6	sprigs parsley
8	trout fillets	12	lemon wedges
1	cup milk	3	tablespoons dry
⅓	cup butter (not		white wine
	margarine)		

In a small bowl, combine flour, salt and pepper. Dip trout in milk and then roll it in flour mixture. Melt butter in a skillet. Place trout in skillet and brown on both sides and cook through. Remove trout, place on a serving tray and keep warm. Place almonds in remaining butter and sauté them. Stir in wine. Pour this over trout. Garnish with parsley and lemon wedges.

Prep. Time: 30 minutes.

SPICY SAUCE FOR SEAFOOD

¼	pound butter,	1	tablespoon whiskey
	softened		pinch of paprika
1	teaspoon dry		pinch of nutmeg
	mustard		dash or two of Tabasco
1	teaspoon lime juice		sauce
1 ¼	teaspoons sugar		dash of Worcestershire
⅔	cup ketchup		sauce

In a small bowl, combine all ingredients, mixing well. Serve with cooked seafood.

Prep. Time: 5 minutes.

BEER BATTER FRIED SHRIMP

2	pounds uncooked shrimp in shells or 1 ½ pounds raw shrimp, peeled & deveined	2	teaspoons paprika pinch of cayenne pepper
1	cup flour	1	teaspoon salt
		1 ½	cups flat beer extra flour vegetable oil

In mixing bowl, combine flour, paprika, cayenne pepper and salt. Gradually beat in beer until batter is quite thin. Dip shrimp first in extra flour, then into beer batter. Deep fry in oil at 400° for 2 minutes. Drain on paper towels and keep warm. Serve immediately. *Makes 4 to 6 servings.*

Prep. Time: 15 minutes.

MARINATED SHRIMP

½	cup butter	½	teaspoon celery salt
½	cup Worcestershire sauce	1	teaspoon olive oil
1	teaspoon salt	50	fresh shrimp in shells (up to 60 shrimp can be used)
1	teaspoon black pepper		
1	teaspoon red pepper		
2	teaspoons garlic purée		
1	teaspoon thyme		
2	teaspoons rosemary		

In a large saucepan, melt butter. Stir in remaining ingredients except shrimp. Cook slowly, 10 to 15 minutes. Do not bring to a boil. Allow to cool slightly. Pour in a 1½ quart casserole dish. Add shrimp, stirring well. In order for seasoning to take effect, do not cook for at least 2 to 3 hours or even better overnight. When ready to cook, preheat oven to 400°. When oven is hot, place shrimp in for 18 to 20 minutes, stirring several times. Cooking time depends on size of shrimp. Do not overcook. Shrimp are hard to peel if overcooked.

Prep. Time: 20 minutes,
          plus 2 to 12 hours to marinate.

SHRIMP CURRY

1/3	cup butter	1	tablespoon candied
2	tablespoons onion		ginger, finely
	flakes		chopped
3	tablespoons flour	1	tablespoon lemon
2	tablespoons curry		juice
	powder	1	teaspoon sherry
1/2	teaspoon salt		dash of Worcestershire
dash of nutmeg and			sauce
	paprika		cooked rice
2	cups half-and-half		
3	cups shrimp, cooked,		
	peeled & deveined		

P lace butter in a saucepan and melt. Blend in onion flakes, flour, curry powder, salt, paprika and nutmeg. Gradually stir in cream. Cook until mixture thickens, stirring constantly. Add remaining ingredients. Heat through. Serve over rice. *Makes 4 to 6 servings.*

Prep. Time: 30 minutes.

SHRIMP GREEK–STYLE

1	teaspoon garlic,	1/8	teaspoon hot
	minced		pepper flakes
5	tablespoons olive oil	1/2	pound Feta cheese,
2	cups tomatoes,		crumbled
	chopped	1/3	pound angel hair or
1/2	cup dry white wine		rigatoni pasta
1/4	cup fresh basil	2	tablespoons butter
1	teaspoon		
	dried oregano		
1 1/2	pounds shrimp,		
	uncooked & peeled		

I n a skillet, cook garlic in 2 tablespoons oil. Add tomatoes, wine and spices. Simmer 10 minutes. Cook shrimp in remaining oil for 5 minutes. Sprinkle with pepper flakes. Transfer shrimp to baking dish and cover with sauce. Sprinkle with Feta cheese and bake in a preheated 400° oven for 10 minutes. Cook pasta and toss with butter. Serve shrimp over pasta. *Makes 4 to 6 servings.*

Prep. Time: 30 minutes.

SPICY SHRIMP SPAGHETTI

¼	cup olive oil	1	teaspoon dried basil
½	pound shrimp, peeled, deveined & uncooked		salt & pepper, to taste
		8	ounces spaghetti, cooked
½	cup onion, chopped	1	small can black olives, sliced
2	cloves garlic, crushed		
2	teaspoons cajun seafood seasonings		fresh Parmesan cheese, grated
1	16 ounce can tomatoes, undrained & diced		

P lace olive oil in a skillet and heat until hot. Add shrimp, onion, garlic and 1 teaspoon cajun seasoning. Sauté until shrimp is pink. Remove shrimp with slotted spoon. Set aside. Add tomatoes, remaining cajun seasoning, salt, pepper and basil. Bring to a boil, then turn down heat and simmer uncovered for 5 minutes. Return shrimp to pan and cook 2 minutes. Pour mixture over spaghetti and toss well. Garnish with black olives and Parmesan cheese. *Makes 4 servings.*

Prep. Time: 30 minutes.

SHRIMP CREOLE

½	pound shrimp, peeled & deveined	6	ounces tomato paste
¼	pound butter	3	cups water
1	cup green onions & tops, chopped	½	cup bell pepper
1	cup celery, chopped	4	cloves garlic
1	cup onion, chopped	1	teaspoon sugar
8	ounces tomato sauce		salt & pepper

S eason shrimp with salt and pepper and set aside. Melt butter in a skillet. Sauté green onions and tops, celery and onions. Add tomato paste and cook 5 minutes, stirring constantly. Add tomato sauce and water. Cook 40 minutes, stirring constantly. Add remaining ingredients and simmer 30 minutes or until shrimp is done. Serve over rice. *Makes 4 servings.*

Prep. Time: 20 minutes.

SHRIMP ETOUFFÉE

6	tablespoons butter	3	pounds shrimp, peeled & deveined
3	tablespoons flour		
1	cup onion, chopped	¼	cup parsley, chopped
6	green onions & tops, chopped		salt & pepper, to taste
½	cup bell pepper, chopped	1	small bay leaf
½	cup celery, chopped		Tabasco, to taste
2	cups water		cooked rice

In a skillet, melt butter and stir in flour. Cook, stirring constantly, until this is a rich brown roux. Add vegetables and cook until tender. Stir in water, shrimp, parsley and seasonings. Simmer uncovered for 20 minutes or until the shrimp are cooked. Serve over hot rice. *Makes 4 to 6 servings.*

Prep. Time: 20 minutes.

CLASSIC CRAB NEWBURG

¼	cup butter	3	egg yolks, slightly beaten
2	tablespoons flour		
½	teaspoon salt	1	6 ounce package frozen crabmeat, thawed, save liquid
⅛	teaspoon nutmeg		
⅛	teaspoon cayenne pepper		
2	cups half-and-half or light cream	1 ½	tablespoons dry sherry
			hot, cooked rice

Melt butter in medium saucepan. Add flour, salt, nutmeg and cayenne pepper. Stir until smooth. Gradually add half-and-half. Cook over medium heat 8 to 10 minutes or until slightly thickened, stirring constantly. Gradually add a half cup hot mixture to egg yolks, beating to blend. Add egg yolk mixture back into sauce mixture, mix well. Add crab and crab liquid. Cook 1 to 2 minutes or until thickened, stirring constantly. Remove from heat. Stir in sherry. Serve over hot, cooked rice. Garnish with parsley if desired. *Makes 4 to 5 servings.*

Prep. Time: 30 minutes.

DEVILED CRAB

1	dozen fresh crabs	1	teaspoon cayenne	
water			pepper	
1/4	teaspoon soda	1/2	teaspoon salt	
1/4	cup margarine	1	8 ounce package	
1	onion, finely		herb stuffing mix	
	chopped	melted margarine for		
1/2	red bell pepper,		brushing crabs	
	finely chopped			
1/4	green bell pepper,			
	finely chopped			
1	teaspoon Kitchen			
	Bouquet spice			
3	cloves garlic,			
	finely minced			
4	stalks celery,			
	finely chopped			
2	tablespoons			
	margarine			
1	tablespoon fresh			
	parsley			

P lace the crabs in a large heavy saucepan. Fill with water until crabs are totally covered. Bring to a boil and boil until cooked for 30 minutes. Pry the crabs open with a knife and remove all white meat plus a little of fat. Set aside. Scrub crab shells and remove legs. Place them back in boiling water with soda and boil an additional 20 minutes. Remove from water and drain thoroughly. Melt the 1/4 cup margarine in a large skillet. Add onion, peppers, garlic and celery and sauté until tender. Add crabmeat and sauté an additional 5 minutes until crab is lightly browned. Add crab fat, 2 tablespoons margarine plus a little water to moisten. Stir in parsley, cayenne pepper, salt and Kitchen Bouquet. Cover and simmer for 30 minutes until all liquid is absorbed. Remove from heat and stir in stuffing, reserving 1/2 cup. Stuff crab shells with this mixture and place them in a large baking dish. Lightly brush each crab with melted margarine. Sprinkle 1/2 cup of stuffing on top of crabs. Bake in a preheated 350° oven for 20 to 25 minutes or until lightly brown. *Makes 6 servings, 2 crabs each.*

Prep. Time: 30 minutes.

COCONUT SEAFOOD SALAD

1	cup cooked crabmeat (or 6 ounces water packed tuna)	1	tablespoon lime juice
1	rib celery, minced	½	teaspoon coconut flavoring
2	tablespoons low-calorie mayonnaise		

Combine crabmeat, celery, mayonnaise, lime juice and coconut flavoring. Mix lightly. Serve on beds of lettuce, or in fruit cups. *Makes 3 servings.*

Prep. Time: 10 minutes.

RANCH GRILLED RACK OF LAMB

	rack of lamb (or leg of lamb, beef prime rib, whole beef tenderloin)	2	bottles tarragon vinegar (preferably with the tarragon stalk in it)
1	32 ounce bottle olive oil (not extra virgin)		fresh cracked pepper

One to two days before cooking, in a large bowl or pan, cover meat with olive oil, tarragon vinegar and pepper. Stir the mixture. Cover with a cloth or lid and set aside until ready to cook.

Cook 1: Preheat oven to 450°. Cook for 15 minutes. Turn oven down to 375°. Cook for another 20 to 30 minutes. Cooking time depends on how done you like your meat.

Cook 2: On outside grill, start a large fire of mesquite wood. When flaming fire is half-way burned down, put meat on. Close cover on grill and let fire burn out. Remove meat when ashes are warm. If meat is not done enough, finish cooking in oven at 350°. *One rack will serve 2 people. One leg of lamb will serve 6 people. Each rib in prime rib will serve 2 people. One whole tenderloin will serve 6 to 8 people.*

Prep. Time: 1 hour,
          plus 2 days marinating.

HOLLANDAISE SAUCE

Great on asparagus and broccoli.

3	egg yolks	¼	teaspoon Tabasco
2	tablespoons fresh		sauce
	lemon juice	½	cup margarine,
dash of salt			melted

Combine the first four ingredients in a blender. Blend until smooth. Add margarine a third at a time blending well. Mix thoroughly. Serve immediately.

Prep. Time: 5 minutes.

BAKED FRESH ASPARAGUS

1 pound asparagus
salt & pepper, to taste
3-4   tablespoons butter

Trim and peel the asparagus. Place asparagus in 1 or 2 layers in a shallow baking dish that has been buttered. Salt and pepper to taste, then dot with butter. Cover the dish. Bake in a preheated 300° oven for 30 minutes. Asparagus should still be crunchy. *Makes 4 servings.*

Prep. Time: 5 minutes.

BOILING FRESH ASPARAGUS

fresh asparagus, any amount
butter

Trim and peel the asparagus. To protect tender tips, wrap 6 to 8 peeled asparagus stalks with kitchen string into a bundle. For a neater appearance, cut off ends of stalks to make them all even. Place asparagus bundles into a large pot of boiling water. After water returns to a boil, cook uncovered for 8 minutes. Remove when bundles turn bright green and are tender, yet firm to the bite. Place bundles on a serving dish. Remove string. Place pats of butter on tips and stalks. Serve immediately.

Prep. Time: 5 minutes.

Hint: *Leave one stalk loose from the bundle for*
        testing purposes.

FRESH ASPARAGUS WITH CHEESE TIPS

1	pound asparagus	⅓	cup grated fresh
8	tablespoons butter, melted		Parmesan cheese
			salt & pepper

T rim and peel the asparagus. Bundle asparagus into groups of 6 to 8 stalks. Cook asparagus in salted, boiling water for 8 to 10 minutes, or until tender. Drain asparagus on a kitchen towel. Remove the string. Dip each asparagus tip in melted butter. Place asparagus in layers in a buttered gratin dish. Sprinkle grated cheese over the tips of each layer. Season with pepper. Brown the asparagus under a preheated broiler. *Makes 2 to 4 servings.*

Prep. Time: 5 minutes.

STEAMED GREEN BEANS

¾	pound green beans, snapped into bite-sized pieces	1	small onion, chopped
		½-1	tablespoon butter

B ring to a boil a few tablespoons of water mixed with butter. Add beans and onions. Season with salt. Mix well. Cover tightly. Let the beans steam for 5 to 7 minutes. The moisture should have dried off. Serve immediately. Do not overcook the beans.

Prep. Time: 5 minutes.

GREEN BEAN CASSEROLE

3	15.5 ounce cans french cut green beans, drained	8	ounces processed cheese, sliced
	garlic salt	24	butter flavored crackers, crushed
1	8 ounce carton sour cream	½	cup butter, melted
1	can cream of mushroom soup		

P lace beans in 9 x 13 inch dish. Sprinkle with garlic salt. Mix soup with sour cream and pour over beans. Top with sliced cheese. Sprinkle with crackers. Dribble butter on top. Bake uncovered in a preheated 375°oven for 30 minutes. *Makes 10 servings.*

Prep. Time: 20 minutes.

BROCCOLI AND CHEDDAR TIMBALES

¾	pound (3 cups) fresh broccoli florets	½	cup plain bread crumbs
2	tablespoons butter or margarine	½	cup Italian seasoned bread crumbs
½	cup green onion, chopped	1 ½	cups sharp Cheddar cheese, grated
1 ½	cups prepared non-fat dry milk	¾	teaspoon salt
4	eggs	¼	teaspoon pepper

Place the broccoli in a large saucepan and cover with water. Over a high heat, bring to a boil and cook for 5 minutes. Drain and place in a mixing bowl. In a skillet, melt the butter. Add green onions and sauté until tender. Add this to the broccoli and toss. In another bowl add milk and eggs. Beat and pour over broccoli mixture. Add all remaining ingredients and stir well. Spoon into 8 custard dishes that have been lightly buttered or 12 cup cakes. Place custard dishes in a cake pan. Fill the cake pan with water to reach two-thirds of the way up the sides of custard dishes. Bake in a preheated 325° oven for 35 to 40 minutes or until set. Unmold and serve hot or cold. *Makes 8 servings.*

Prep. Time: 20 minutes.

RICE AND CHEESE BROCCOLI CASSEROLE

½	cup rice	1	can cream of mushroom soup
1	10 ounce package frozen broccoli, chopped	1	8 ounce jar processed cheese
½	cup margarine	1	cup Cheddar cheese, grated
½	cup onion, chopped		
½	cup celery, chopped		

Cook the rice and broccoli according to the directions on the boxes. After cooking, drain the broccoli thoroughly on a paper towel. In a large saucepan melt the margarine. Add the onions and celery. Sauté until the vegetables are tender. Add rice, broccoli, soup, and processed cheese. Continue to cook until heated through and the cheese is melted. Pour into a 1½ quart casserole dish that has been sprayed with a non-stick cooking spray. Sprinkle the Cheddar cheese on top. Bake in a preheated 325° oven for 30 minutes or until bubbly.

Prep. Time: 30 to 45 minutes.

BROCCOLI CASSEROLE

1-2	bunches broccoli	1	teaspoon oregano
1	14.5 ounce can tomatoes, drained		salt & pepper, to taste
1	can Cheddar cheese soup	½	cup Parmesan cheese

Steam broccoli 5 to 8 minutes. Drain. Mix peeled tomatoes and soup. Add seasonings then broccoli. Top with cheese. Bake in a preheated 350° oven for 30 minutes. *Makes 6 servings.*

Prep. Time: 10 minutes.

GOLDEN NUGGET CORN

2	tablespoons butter	2	16 ounce packages frozen corn kernels
1	bunch green onions, stems only, finely chopped	1	8 ounce carton sour cream
3	4 ounce cans mushrooms, sliced		salt & pepper, to taste

In a skillet melt butter. Sauté green onions and mushrooms until onions are translucent. Stir in corn. Cook on medium-high heat until corn is tender. Stir in sour cream. Salt and pepper to taste. Lower heat to warm and cook until hot.

Prep. Time: 15 minutes.

CAMPFIRE CORN

This is great for camp-outs because it can be prepared ahead of time.

1	ear of corn per person, shucked & rinsed	1	tablespoon butter or margarine per ear, melted
	salt & pepper, to taste	2	tablespoons water per ear

Salt and pepper each ear of corn to taste. Place on a square sheet of foil. Drizzle the butter over the ear of corn. Fold the foil around the corn and seal one end. Pour the water in the other end and seal it. Place on the coals of a campfire (or grill). Cook for 30 to 45 minutes.

Prep. Time: 5 minutes.

SAVORY BRUSSELS SPROUTS

Brussels sprouts even your kids will like.

2	10 ounce packages brussels sprouts	1	can cream of chicken soup
2	chicken bouillon cubes	½	teaspoon thyme, crushed
2	tablespoons butter or margarine	1	2 ounce jar pimentos, drained & chopped
½	cup almonds, slivered		pepper, to taste

Place the brussels sprouts in a large pan with the bouillon cubes. Prepare them as directed on package. Drain and set aside. In a skillet, sauté the almonds in the butter until lightly toasted. Stir in the remaining ingredients. Pour this over the brussels sprouts and mix well. Pour this into a 1½ quart casserole dish that has been sprayed with a non-stick cooking spray. Bake in a preheated 350° oven for 30 minutes. *Makes 6 servings.*

Prep. Time: 20 minutes,
   plus 30 minutes cooking time.

CABBAGE BAKE

1	head cabbage, sliced		salt & pepper, to taste
4	tablespoons margarine	1	cup warm milk
3	tablespoons flour	1	cup Cheddar cheese, shredded
2	tablespoons sugar		

Steam cabbage until tender. Drain. Pour steamed cabbage into a 2 quart casserole dish. Dot with margarine. Mix flour, sugar, salt and pepper. Sprinkle on top. Pour milk over cabbage and top with cheese. Bake in a preheated 375° oven for 30 to 35 minutes.

Prep. Time: 30 minutes.

DILLY BRUSSELS SPROUTS

2	10 ounce packages frozen brussels sprouts	1	teaspoon dill weed
		2	tablespoons chives
		6	black olives
1	cup Italian salad dressing		salt & pepper, to taste

In boiling water, cook brussels sprouts until tender (5 minutes). Drain. Add other ingredients. Chill overnight in a covered container. Serve chilled.

Prep. Time: 10 minutes.
Refrigerating Time: Overnight.

COWBOY PENNIES

Scalloped carrots.

2	pounds carrots, thinly sliced	1	tablespoon margarine
1	can cream of celery soup	1	medium onion, chopped
½	soup can of milk	1	8 ounce package Cheddar cheese, sliced
½	teaspoon salt		
⅛	teaspoon dry mustard		buttered bread crumbs

Cook sliced carrots until tender. Drain. Dilute the soup with milk. Add salt and mustard. Sauté the onion in butter, add to the soup mixture. Arrange layers of carrots and cheese in a 2 quart casserole dish. Pour soup mixture over the carrots and cheese. Top with bread crumbs. Bake in a preheated 350° oven for 20 minutes until cheese melts and bubbles.

Prep. Time: 20 minutes.

CELERY ALMONDINE

1	large bunch of celery, cut into 1 inch slices	1	2 ounce jar pimentos, chopped & drained
¼	cup butter	1	cup chicken broth
¼	cup flour	1	cup half-and-half
½	teaspoon salt	1	cup Swiss cheese, grated
¼	teaspoon pepper		
3	whole green onions, chopped	1	tablespoon butter
		¾	cup almonds, slivered

Place celery in a medium saucepan and cover with water. Cook for 5 minutes. Drain and rinse in cold water. Drain. In the same pan, melt the ¼ cup of butter. Stir in flour, salt and pepper and mix to form a paste. Stir in the green onions, pimentos, chicken broth, half-and-half, and ½ cup Swiss cheese. Cook stirring constantly until sauce thickens. In a small skillet, melt butter. Add almonds and cook until they are toasted. Add half of the almonds to celery mixture. Pour celery mixture in a 9 x 13 inch cake pan that has been sprayed with a non-stick cooking spray. Sprinkle remaining cheese on top followed by remaining almonds. Bake in a preheated 350° oven for 35 minutes. *Makes 8 servings.*

Prep. Time: 25 minutes.

CHUCK WAGON CORN CASSEROLE

2	eggs, well beaten	½	cup corn oil
1	16 ounce can cream-style corn	1	tablespoon sugar green chilies, to taste
1	cup cornbread mix	¾	cup Cheddar cheese, grated
½	cup onion, chopped		
1	2 ounce jar pimentos		

Mix together all ingredients, except cheese. Pour into an 8 x 8 inch pan that has been sprayed with a non-stick cooking spray. Top with grated cheese. In a preheated oven, bake at 350° for 45 minutes. *Makes 6 to 8 servings.*

Prep. Time: 10 minutes.

CREAMED CORN

2	10 ounce packages frozen kernel corn	6	teaspoons sugar
8	ounces whipping cream	1	pinch of white or cayenne pepper
8	ounces milk	2	tablespoons butter, melted
1	teaspoon salt	2	tablespoons flour
¼	teaspoon Accent		

Combine all ingredients except last 2 in a pot and bring to a boil. Simmer 5 minutes. Blend butter with flour and add to the corn. Mix well and remove from heat. *Makes 8 servings.*

Prep. Time: 10 minutes.

Variation: Substitute frozen peas for the corn to make creamed peas.

FRIED OKRA

2	cups fresh okra, sliced	½	cup flour
1	egg, slightly beaten	½	teaspoon salt shortening for frying
1	tablespoon water		
¾	cup cornmeal, more if needed		

In a medium bowl, combine egg and water. Stir in okra making sure it is thoroughly coated with egg mixture. In a plastic bag, combine cornmeal, flour and salt. With a slotted spoon, remove okra from egg mixture and place it in the plastic bag with cornmeal mixture. Shake vigorously so that okra is totally coated. Add more cornmeal if needed. In a large skillet heat ¼ inch of oil until it is hot. Add okra, reduce heat to medium. Place a cover on skillet and cook for about 30 minutes or until okra is browned on all sides, turning okra every 10 minutes. You may need to add more oil if skillet dries out.

Prep. Time: 15 minutes.

ONION PIE

1	cup crackers, crushed	¾	teaspoon salt
6	tablespoons margarine, melted	½	teaspoon pepper
2	large yellow onions, sliced	½-1	teaspoon Worcestershire sauce
2	eggs, beaten	1	cup Cheddar cheese, grated
1	8 ounce carton sour cream or Ricotta cheese	6	slices bacon, cooked & crumbled
1-2	tablespoons fresh dill		

In a small bowl, combine crackers and 4 tablespoons margarine. Press into a 9 inch pie pan. In the remaining butter, sauté onions. Pour these into pie pan. In another bowl, combine eggs, sour cream, dill, salt, pepper and Worcestershire sauce. Pour this over onions. Sprinkle cheese on top of this and then the bacon. Bake in a preheated 350° oven for 30 minutes or until set. *Makes 8 servings.*

Prep. Time: 20 minutes.

ONION CASSEROLE

5-6	yellow onions, sliced		salt & pepper, to taste
½	cup butter or margarine	1	can cream of mushroom soup
¼	cup Parmesan cheese, grated	1	cup Cheddar cheese, grated
¾	cup butter flavored crackers, crushed	¼	cup Parmesan cheese, grated
¾	cup cheese crackers, crushed		paprika

In a large skillet, sauté onions in butter. Place half of the onions in a 1½ quart casserole dish that has been sprayed with a non-stick cooking spray. Place ⅛ cup Parmesan cheese on next then half butter flavored crackers, half the cheese crackers, then sprinkle with salt and pepper. Repeat layering. Spread cream of mushroom soup on top of this. Sprinkle Cheddar cheese on next and then top with Parmesan cheese. Garnish with paprika. Bake in a preheated 350° oven for 30 minutes or until cheese is lightly browned. *Makes 8 servings.*

Prep. Time: 15 minutes.

BAKED OKRA

1	pound fresh okra, washed	lemon pepper or cajun seasoning

Place okra on a cookie sheet sprayed with a non-stick cooking spray. Sprinkle with either lemon pepper or cajun seasoning and bake at 350° until tender (30 minutes). Serve on a platter and eat with fingers like french fries. *Makes 6 servings.*

Prep. Time: 10 minutes.

BANDIT PEAS

Western-style black-eyed peas.

½	pound bacon, chopped into bite-sized pieces	½	yellow onion, chopped
1 ½	quarts water	2	tablespoons sugar
5	cups black-eyed peas, fresh shelled	1	teaspoon salt
2	jalapeños, seeded & chopped	½	teaspoon black pepper

Combine all the above ingredients in a large saucepan. Bring to a boil over a medium-high heat. Reduce the heat to low. Cover. Simmer for 2 to 2 ½ hours or until peas almost fall apart.

Prep. Time: 5 minutes.

BAKED POTATO CASSEROLE

8	medium baking potatoes	1	large onion, chopped
8	ounce carton sour cream	2	cups Cheddar cheese, shredded
1	can cream of mushroom soup		

Scrub potatoes well. Do not peel. Boil for 20 minutes. Combine sour cream and soup. Slice potatoes and arrange half in a 3 quart casserole dish that has been sprayed with a non-stick cooking spray. Place half of the onions on top of potatoes and pour half of soup mixture over. Sprinkle with half of the cheese. Repeat layers with remaining ingredients. In a preheated 350° oven, bake for 45 minutes to 1 hour or until bubbly. *Makes 6 to 8 servings.*

Prep. Time: 30 minutes.

CHEESY POTATOES

4	tablespoons margarine	1	4 ounce jar of pimentos, drained & chopped
3	tablespoons flour	4-6	cups boiled potatoes
¾	cup green peppers or chili peppers, chopped		
2	cups milk		
1 ½	cups processed cheese, cubed		

Make white sauce using margarine and flour. Add peppers and simmer 5 minutes. Add milk and cook until sauce begins to thicken.

Add processed cheese. Add pimentos. Arrange potatoes in casserole dish and pour sauce over potatoes. In a preheated 350° oven bake uncovered for 30 minutes. *Makes 6 to 8 servings.*

Prep. Time: 30 minutes.

Hint: For a variation, omit pimentos and green chilies for basic au gratin dish.

JACK RABBIT POTATOES

Rustle some up for supper tonight.

2	pounds frozen hash browns	8	ounces sharp Cheddar cheese, grated
1	can cream of chicken soup	1	cup onion, chopped
2	cups sour cream	1	cup corn flakes, crushed
½	cup butter or margarine, melted		

T haw potatoes for 30 minutes. Grease a 9 x 13 inch pan or spray with a non-stick cooking spray. In a greased pan, combine cream of chicken soup, sour cream, butter, cheese, and onion. Fold in the potatoes. Sprinkle the corn flakes on top. Bake in a preheated 375˚ oven for 45 to 60 minutes.

Prep. Time: 20 minutes.

SCALLOPED POTATOES

3	large potatoes, peeled	½	onion, chopped
1	can cream of mushroom soup		salt & pepper, to taste
⅔	cup milk		

C ut potatoes in half. Cut each half into slices. In a small bowl, combine soup, milk and onion. Spray a 1 ½ quart casserole dish with a non-stick cooking spray. Place a third of potato slices in bottom of the dish. Top with a third of soup and onion mixture. Sprinkle salt and pepper on top. Repeat this process two more times. In a preheated 350˚ oven, bake for 1 ½ hours.

Prep. Time: 20 minutes.

GARLIC POTATOES

6	potatoes, unpeeled, cut each into 8 pieces	2	teaspoons garlic powder
1	stick butter	¼	cup Parmesan cheese (optional)
2	teaspoons black pepper		

M elt butter in bottom of 9 x 13 pan. Place potatoes in pan. Sprinkle pepper, garlic powder, and Parmesan cheese, and toss. In a preheated 300˚ oven bake for 1 ½ to 2 hours.

Prep. Time: 20 minutes.

COWHAND POTATOES

2	pounds frozen hash browns, thawed	¼	cup bacon, cooked & crumbled
1	bunch green onions plus tops, chopped	1	pound processed cheese, melted
1	8 ounce jar mayonnaise		

Combine all of the ingredients in a large bowl. Pour into a 9 x 13 x 2 inch pan that has been sprayed with a non-stick cooking spray. Bake in a preheat 350° oven for 30 minutes or until lightly browned and bubbly.

Prep. Time: 20 minutes.

DEEP-FRIED SWEET POTATOES

6	medium sweet potatoes	1	cup sugar
3	cups peanut oil	2	teaspoons cinnamon
		½	teaspoon nutmeg

Scrub potatoes, quarter lengthwise and pat dry. Heat oil in deep fryer to 375°. Add potatoes and fry until golden brown, 6 to 8 minutes. Drain briefly on paper towels. Combine remaining ingredients in shallow plate. Roll potato pieces in sugar mixture. Serve potatoes immediately. *Makes 8 servings.*

Prep. Time: 10 minutes.

CANDIED SWEET POTATOES

3	large sweet potatoes	4	tablespoons margarine, melted
water		½	cup water
1	cup brown sugar cinnamon, ground		

Place potatoes in a large pan. Add enough water to cover the potatoes plus about an inch. Over a high heat, bring to a boil. Reduce heat and boil until cooked, approximately 45 minutes. Remove from water. Peel and slice potatoes. Place a layer of potatoes in a buttered 1½ quart casserole dish. Sprinkle brown sugar, cinnamon and butter on top. Repeat until all potatoes are used, ending with cinnamon and butter. Pour ½ cup water on top. Bake in a preheated 350° for 30 minutes or until brown and well candied. *Makes 4 servings.*

Prep. Time: 10 minutes.

TWICE BAKED SWEET POTATOES

6-8	sweet potatoes, medium size	¼	cup margarine, melted
vegetable oil		½	cup whipping cream
¼	cup maple syrup	¼	teaspoon cinnamon
		⅛	teaspoon nutmeg

Rub potatoes with vegetable oil and cook in a preheated 400° oven. Bake for 45 minutes. Do not overcook. Let potatoes cool. Cut away skin from top of potato and spoon out insides, leaving the shells intact. Add all other ingredients to potato pulp and beat until fluffy. Fill potato skins with this mixture. In a preheated 375° oven bake for 15 to 20 minutes. *Makes 6 to 8 servings.*

Prep. Time: 20 minutes.

PAN–FRIED SWEET POTATOES

4	large sweet potatoes	confectioners' sugar
⅓	cup salad oil	

Peel potatoes, cut each lengthwise into 3 to 4 wedges. In 12 inch skillet over medium heat in hot oil, cook half the wedges in a single layer until golden brown on both sides, turning with a spatula. Reduce heat to low, cover and cook 15 minutes or until fork tender. Remove potatoes from skillet to warm platter. Keep warm while cooking remaining potatoes. Before serving, sprinkle lightly with sugar. *Makes 8 servings.*

Prep. Time: 10 minutes.

WRANGLER SPINACH

Even people who do not like spinach love it!

2	10 ounce packages frozen spinach	1	6 ounce package jalapeño cheese
4	tablespoons margarine	1	teaspoon Worcestershire sauce
2	tablespoons flour	½	teaspoon pepper
½	cup vegetable liquid from spinach	½	teaspoon celery salt
½	cup half-and-half	½	teaspoon garlic salt
2	tablespoons onion, chopped		

Cook spinach and drain, saving ½ cup juice. Make sauce of margarine, flour, vegetable liquid and half-and-half. Cook until thick. Add cheese and seasonings and heat until cheese melts. Combine with spinach. Pour into greased casserole dish. Chill 6 hours. Bake in a preheated 350° oven uncovered for 25 to 30 minutes. *Makes 4 servings.*

Prep. Time: 30 minutes.
Refrigerating Time: 6 hours.

SPINACH DUMPLINGS

2	pounds spinach	¾	cup flour
5	tablespoons butter	¼	cup Parmesan
1	cup Ricotta cheese		cheese, freshly grated
1	egg, beaten		

Sauté the spinach in 3 tablespoons of butter for 5 minutes. Remove the pan from heat. Add Ricotta cheese, egg, and 3 tablespoons of flour. Mix thoroughly. Shape mixture into small, round dumplings. Roll dumplings in remaining flour. Cook them, a small batch at a time, in a large pan of simmering salted water. The dumplings should float to the surface in 5 to 8 minutes. Lift them out with a perforated spoon. To serve, melt remaining butter. Pour it over dumplings. Sprinkle them with grated Parmesan. *Makes 4 to 6 servings.*

Prep. Time: 15 minutes.

CREAMED FRESH SPINACH

2	pounds spinach	3-4	tablespoons heavy
1	teaspoon salt		cream
	nutmeg, grated		salt & pepper

Remove stems from the spinach. Wash and pat dry. Heat a large, heavy pan. Place spinach, salt and nutmeg in pan. Cook spinach for 2 to 3 minutes. Drain spinach, pressing out any excess moisture. Place the spinach in a blender or food processor. Add the cream. Blend until smooth. Do not over blend. Reheat creamed spinach in a saucepan. Add more seasonings, if necessary. *Makes 4 to 6 servings.*

Prep. Time: 10 minutes.

GRINGO SPINACH

3	10 ounce packages frozen spinach	¼	cup Parmesan cheese
1	tablespoon butter or margarine	¼	cup green onion, chopped
3	3 ounce packages cream cheese, melted	1	egg, beaten
1	cup Cheddar cheese, grated	¼	cup seasoned croutons (optional)

Thaw spinach in hot water or in microwave, drain well. In a medium bowl, combine butter, cream cheese, Cheddar, Parmesan, green onions and egg. Stir in hot spinach. Mix well. Pour into casserole dish that has been sprayed with a non-stick cooking spray. Sprinkle croutons on top. Bake in a preheated 350° oven for 30 minutes. *Makes 8 servings.*

Prep. Time: 15 minutes.

Hint: *For a variation add sliced sautéed mushrooms. Substitute Swiss cheese for Parmesan cheese.*

WESTERN SQUASH CASSEROLE

10	(or 12) summer yellow squash, sliced	1	4 ounce can green chilies, chopped
1	medium onion, chopped in eighths		garlic salt, to taste
water			pepper, to taste
1	pound American cheese, sliced		

Boil squash and onion until tender, drain well. (Needs to be dry.) Grate American cheese and add to cooked squash. Allow to melt. Add green chilies, garlic salt and pepper. Pour into a buttered casserole dish. In a preheated 350° oven bake, until cheese is browned and bubbly, for 30 to 40 minutes. *Makes 6 to 8 servings.*

Prep. Time: 10 minutes.

SCRUMPTOUS SQUASH CASSEROLE

3	pounds squash	1	tablespoon sugar
½	cup onion, chopped	1	teaspoon salt
½	cup bread crumbs	½	teaspoon pepper
2	eggs		bread crumbs
½	cup butter		

Wash and remove ends from squash, cut squash into pieces. Boil until cooked. Drain and mash. Add everything else except ¼ cup of the butter and bread crumbs. Mix well. Pour into casserole dish. Melt remaining butter. Pour on top. Sprinkle with bread crumbs. In a preheated 375° oven, bake for 1 hour. *Makes 6 servings.*

Prep. Time: 30 minutes.

Hint: For a variation, add 1 cup grated Cheddar or processed cheese and one 4-ounce can green chilies, chopped.

SQUASH PATTIES

This is a down-home country-style dish.

3	cups yellow or zucchini squash, grated	1	egg
		1	cup flour
		¾	cup milk
3	tablespoons green pepper, chopped	3	tablespoons oil
		⅛-¼	cup sugar
1	onion, chopped	½	teaspoon salt
dash of black pepper			oil for cooking

Mix together first four ingredients. In separate bowl, combine the next 6 ingredients. Pour this into the vegetable mixture and mix well. Pour enough oil in a skillet to cover the bottom. Heat until hot. Drop by spoonfuls in hot oil and brown. *Makes 6 servings.*

Prep. Time: 20 minutes.

SQUASH AU GRATIN

4-5	medium zucchini, sliced thin	½	teaspoon cumin
4	tablespoons butter or margarine		salt & pepper, to taste
			dash of Tabasco sauce
1	medium onion, chopped	⅓	cup Cheddar cheese, grated
1	small green pepper, seeds removed & chopped	½	cup dry bread crumbs
2	tablespoons tomato paste	¼	cup butter or margarine

Steam zucchini until tender. While zucchini is steaming, sauté onion and green pepper in 4 tablespoons butter until tender. Add tomato paste, cumin, salt, pepper and Tabasco sauce. Cook on a low heat for 5 minutes and set aside. Drain and mash zucchini. Stir into onion mixture. Place in 8 x 8 inch square casserole dish that has been sprayed with a non-stick cooking spray. Top with cheese, then bread crumbs. Dot with butter. Bake in a 325° preheated oven for 20 minutes or until slightly brown. *Makes 4 to 6 servings.*

Prep. Time: 20 minutes.

TOMATOES A LA PROVENÇALE

6	firm ripe tomatoes	⅛	teaspoon thyme
	salt & pepper, to taste	¼	teaspoon salt
½	clove garlic, mashed	⅛	teaspoon cayenne pepper
3	tablespoons chives, finely minced	½	cup dry bread crumbs
2	tablespoons fresh basil, finely minced	¼	cup olive oil
2	tablespoons fresh parsley, finely minced	1	cup Mozzarella cheese, grated

Cut tomatoes in half. Gently squeeze juice and seeds out. Lightly salt and pepper each half. In a small bowl, combine the garlic, chives, basil, parsley, thyme, salt, cayenne pepper and bread crumbs. Mix well. Fill each tomato half with dry spice mixture. Arrange the filled tomatoes in a roasting pan that has been sprayed with a non-stick cooking spray. Sprinkle a few drops of olive oil on each. Bake in a preheated 400° oven for 10 minutes. Top with Mozzarella cheese. Turn the oven to broil and continue to cook them until the cheese is lightly browned.

Prep. Time: 15 minutes.

FRONTIER FRITTERS

4	medium zucchini, grated (or 2 large zucchini)	½-1	cup flour cayenne pepper, to taste (put in more than normally used) pepper, to taste
2	ears of corn (or 2 cups frozen corn kernels, thawed)	4-8	tablespoons olive oil salt, to taste
1	egg (or 2 egg whites if cholesterol is a problem)		

I f using corn on the cob, cut the corn from the cob. Mix all of the ingredients together. Use however much flour is necessary to hold the corn and zucchini together. You do not need a lot. The total amount depends on the size of the corn and zucchini. Put 2 tablespoons of olive oil in a skillet (enough to cover the bottom of the skillet). Heat over medium-high heat. When the olive oil is hot, drop tablespoonfuls of the mixture into the oil and flatten the mixture so it will look like a pancake. Make the pancake diameters whatever size you desire, keeping the thickness ¼ to ½ inch. Cook each side 3 minutes or until golden. Cooking time depends on the thickness. Add more oil if it is needed. If the oil is very hot, the corn will pop. *Makes 4 to 6 servings.*

Prep. Time: 20 minutes.

BREADED ZUCCHINI SLICES WITH CHEESE

1	pound zucchini black pepper, freshly ground	1	tablespoon fresh parsley, chopped
½	cup Parmesan cheese, freshly grated	3	egg whites, beat until frothy
½	cup fresh bread crumbs	2	tablespoons olive oil

G rind the pepper liberally over zucchini slices. In a shallow bowl, combine cheese, bread crumbs and parsley. Dip half of zucchini slices into beaten egg whites. Then coat them evenly with cheese/crumb mixture. Set aside. Use 1 tablespoon of olive oil to coat a cookie sheet with sides. Place half the breaded slices on the cookie sheet. Place in a preheated 325° oven. Bake for 5 minutes, then carefully turn over the slices. Bake for another 5 to 7 minutes, until golden brown. Remove the slices. Repeat the process. *Makes 12 servings.*

Prep. Time: 30 minutes.

ZUCCHINI CASSEROLE EGYPTIAN–STYLE

7   large zucchini, sliced
salt, to taste

Meat Sauce:
1   medium onion, chopped
1   clove garlic, finely minced
¼   pound lean ground beef
2-3 ounces tomato paste
dash of cinnamon
dash of allspice
salt & pepper, to taste
water

White Sauce:
3   tablespoons margarine
3   tablespoons flour
¼   teaspoon salt
¼   teaspoon pepper
1 ½ cups milk
1   egg

P lace the zucchini in a pot. Fill with water until the zucchini is completely covered. Add salt to taste. Bring to a boil and cook until tender.

Meat Sauce: In a large pan, combine onion and garlic. Add a small amount of cooking oil or spray with a non-stick cooking spray. Sauté vegetables over a medium-high heat until tender. Add the ground beef and continue to cook until browned. Stir in tomato paste, cinnamon, allspice, salt and pepper. Add enough water to make a thick sauce. Over a medium-high heat, bring to a boil. Reduce the heat and simmer for 15 to 20 minutes to allow flavors to blend.

White Sauce: In a saucepan, melt the margarine. Stir in flour, salt and pepper to make a paste. Stir in the milk. Cook over a high heat, stirring constantly, until mixture thickens. Place the egg in a cup. Add a little of the white sauce and stir well. This will keep the egg from cooking when added to the hot mixture. Pour this mixture into the white sauce and stir to blend.

Drain zucchini and place it in a large casserole dish. Stir ¼ cup of white sauce into meat sauce. Pour this over zucchini and gently mix. Pour remaining white sauce on top of this. Spread it evenly over meat and zucchini mixture. Bake in a preheated 350° oven for 30 minutes. Turn the broiler on and broil until lightly browned.

Prep. Time: 45 minutes.

EASY ZUCCHINI AND NUTMEG

3	medium zucchini, sliced		nutmeg, freshly grated
2	tablespoons butter		salt & pepper, to taste

Melt the butter in a large skillet. Sauté the zucchini in the butter 3 minutes, or until tender. Season with nutmeg, salt and pepper. Serve immediately. *Makes 4 servings.*

Prep. Time: 10 minutes.

COLD VEGETABLE MEDLEY

¾	cup sugar	1	pound frozen or canned vegetables, drained
⅓	cup oil		
⅔	cup vinegar		
salt & pepper, to taste			

In a medium bowl, combine the sugar and oil. Mix until the sugar is dissolved. Add vinegar, salt and pepper. Stir in the vegetables. Cover and refrigerate. Marinate vegetables at least 4 hours; but, preferably overnight.

Prep. Time: 10 minutes.
Marinating Time: 4 to 12 hours.

VEGETABLE WHIRLWIND

An excellent dish to serve at a dinner party.

1-2	bunches broccoli (broken into florets)	1	16 ounce can hearts of palm, drained
1	head cauliflower (broken into florets)	1	8 ounce can water chestnuts, drained & sliced
2	zucchini, sliced thin		
	fresh mushrooms, to taste (sliced thin)		cherry tomatoes, halved (to your taste)
1	red onion, sliced thin & separated	1	cup cooked shell macaroni
1	16 ounce can artichoke hearts, drained	1	8 ounce bottle Italian dressing

Combine all ingredients except Italian dressing in a large bowl. Add the Italian dressing and mix well. Cover and refrigerate 4 to 6 hours. It can be made several days ahead, just keep it refrigerated and covered. *Makes 10 to 12 servings.*

Prep. Time: 30 to 45 minutes.
Refrigerating Time: 4 to 6 hours.

RUSTLER RED BEANS WITH RICE

2-3	(1 pound) cans red kidney beans, undrained	4	stalks celery, chopped
1	pound ham, cut into bite-sized pieces	1	bay leaf
			dash of red pepper
1	ham bone (optional)		dash of Tabasco sauce
4	cloves garlic	2	whole jalapeño peppers
1	teaspoon oregano		seasoned salt
1	medium green pepper, chopped	2	cups cooked rice

P lace all ingredients, except the rice, in a large kettle and simmer for about 4 hours, or until the gravy thickens. Remove the ham bone, garlic cloves, bay leaf and pepper before serving. Serve over rice. *Makes 12 servings.*

Prep. Time: 20 minutes.

COWPOKE BEANS

2	pounds pinto beans	2	onions, chopped
1	teaspoon cayenne pepper	½	pound bacon, chopped into bite-sized pieces
¼	teaspoon Tabasco sauce	1	16 ounce can tomatoes
¼	cup chili powder		
2	teaspoons salt	1	teaspoon cumin
1	clove garlic, finely minced	1	teaspoon marjoram
		½	can beer (optional)
4-6	jalapeño peppers, seeds removed & chopped		

I n a large pot, combine all the ingredients. Bring to a boil over a high heat. Reduce the heat, cover, and simmer for 2 hours.

Prep. Time: 20 minutes.

CHUCK WAGON BEANS

1	16 ounce package dried pinto beans	2	tablespoons ground cumin
6	cups water	1	tablespoon chili powder (or less)
1	pound bacon, cut in half	1	tablespoon celery seed
2	medium onions, chopped	1-2	teaspoons Tabasco sauce
½	cup green pepper, chopped	1	bay leaf
3	cloves garlic, minced	1	16 ounce can tomatoes, undrained
¼	cup Worcestershire sauce		

S ort and wash beans, put in large pot. Cover with water, 2 inches above beans; let soak overnight. Drain beans, return to pot; add 6 cups water. In a skillet combine next 4 ingredients; cook until bacon is browned. Drain and add to beans. Add remaining ingredients, except tomatoes. Bring to boil, cover and reduce heat and simmer 2 hours or until beans are tender, stirring occasionally. Add tomatoes and cook 30 minutes more.

Prep. Time: 20 minutes, plus soak the beans the night before.

FRIJOLES MEXICANA (MEXICAN REFRIED BEANS)

2	cups Mexican or pinto beans	2	medium tomatoes, skinned
5	cups water		chili powder (optional)
4	tablespoons lard		
1	tablespoon onion, chopped		

P lace the beans in a large saucepan. Fill with water until beans are totally submerged. Soak overnight. Rinse beans then add 5 cups of water. Cover and cook for 2 hours or until tender. Drain reserving liquid. Heat 2 tablespoons of lard in a large skillet. Add beans and fry for 10 minutes, mashing with a fork. Add bean water a little at a time, stirring constantly. Cook until water has evaporated. Put in another bowl, cover and place in refrigerator overnight. The next day, melt remaining 2 tablespoons of lard in a large skillet and add onions. Place tomatoes in a blender and process until smooth. Measure out ½ cup. Cook for a few minutes and then add remaining half of the tomatoes and chili powder. Cook until onions are tender. Stir in refried beans and continue cooking until hot and bubbly. *Makes 6 servings.*

Prep. Time: 30 minutes,
        plus 2 days soaking and refrigerating.

AUTHENTIC SPANISH RICE

2	cups uncooked rice	1	can green chilies
2	tablespoons lard		salt, to taste
1	small onion, chopped	½	cup Monterey-Jack cheese
1	stalk celery, chopped		
1	small can tomatoes	3	cups cold water

B rown rice in hot lard. Add onions, celery, tomatoes, chilies, salt, cheese and enough water to cover rice. Cover tightly and simmer slowly until rice is almost dry. Add remaining water a little at a time, cooking over low heat until fluffy. *Makes 4 to 6 servings.*

Prep. Time: 10 minutes.

BARBECUED BEANS

2	16 ounce cans pork & beans	1	tablespoon Worcestershire sauce
1	cup canned tomatoes, drained	1	teaspoon seasoned salt
1	cup apple cider	1	teaspoon dry mustard
½	cup ketchup		
½	cup brown sugar	½	teaspoon pepper
½	onion, chopped	¼	teaspoon MSG
2	tablespoons horseradish (optional)		

Mix all ingredients in shallow 3 quart baking pan. Bake uncovered at 350° for 1½ to 2 hours. *Makes 10 to 12 servings.*

Prep. Time: 10 minutes.

CHEESE GARLIC GRITS

1	cup instant grits	½	cup milk
3	cups water	2	eggs, beaten
½	stick margarine	2	tablespoons parsley
1	6 ounce roll garlic cheese		paprika

Cook grits in water. Add margarine, garlic cheese, milk and eggs and mix until well blended. Stir in parsley and pour into greased casserole dish. Sprinkle with paprika and bake in a preheated 350° oven for 30 minutes.

Prep. Time: 15 minutes.

Note: For a variation substitute 8 ounces of processed cheese or jalapeño cheese for garlic roll, or add chopped green chilies to taste and crumbled fried bacon.

MUY BUENO REFRIED BEANS

16	ounces dried black beans	6	tablespoons margarine (not butter)
water			
1	large garlic clove, minced	12	ounces Monterey-Jack cheese
2	tablespoons red vinegar		
1	slice bacon		

Cook beans in a large amount of water with garlic, vinegar and bacon until beans are very tender. Drain beans and take out bacon. Mash beans until smooth. (This can be done in a food processor). Melt margarine in large skillet. Add mashed beans and fry beans until they thicken slightly. Be sure to stir the beans often, scraping the bottom and sides of the pan. Add two-thirds of the cheese and stir constantly until the cheese melts. Transfer beans to a casserole dish and top with the remaining cheese. Serve immediately or refrigerate and reheat for 30 to 45 minutes at 350°.

Prep. Time: 5 minutes.

WILD RICE WITH MUSHROOMS AND ALMONDS

1	cup wild rice	2	cups fresh mushrooms, sliced
¼	cup butter or margarine		(1 - 8 ounce can of mushrooms,
½	cup almonds, slivered		drained & sliced can
2	tablespoons chives, finely chopped		be substituted)
		3	cups chicken broth

Wash and drain the wild rice. In a large skillet, melt the butter. Add the rice, almonds, chives and mushrooms. Over a medium-high heat, sauté rice mixture until the almonds are golden brown, about 20 minutes. Pour this into an ungreased 1½ quart casserole dish. Heat the chicken broth until it boils. Pour this over the rice mixture. Cover tightly and bake in a preheated 325° oven for 1½ hours or until all the liquid is absorbed. *Makes 6 to 8 servings.*

Prep. Time: 2 hours.

Note: For a variation add ½ green pepper, chopped, to the rice mixture before frying. Stir in cooked cubed chicken before baking.

BAKED SPANISH RICE

4	slices of bacon	1	8 ounce can tomato sauce
1	cup onion, chopped		
½	cup green peppers, chopped	2	teaspoons sugar
		1	teaspoon salt
1	16 ounce can tomatoes	1⅓	cups rice
water		1	cup Cheddar cheese, grated

Cook the bacon until crisp. Place on a paper towel to drain and then crumble. In the bacon drippings, sauté the onion and pepper until tender. Into a measuring cup, drain tomatoes and add enough water to make 1¾ cups of liquid. Cut the tomatoes up into small chunks. Pour the tomato liquid into the skillet with the onions and peppers. Add the tomatoes, tomato sauce, sugar and salt. Bring to a boil. Remove from heat and stir in the rice. Pour into a 1½ quart casserole dish that has been sprayed with a non-stick cooking spray. Cover and bake in a preheated 350° oven for 35 minutes or until the rice absorbs all the liquid. Fluff rice with a fork and stir in the cheese. Bake an additional 5 minutes. Remove from the oven and garnish with bacon. *Makes 6 servings.*

Prep. Time: 15 minutes.

SHRIMP FRIED RICE

1	cup rice	1	8 ounce package
6	eggs		sliced bacon, cooked
1/4	teaspoon salt		& crumbled
1/4	cup raw shrimp,	1	tablespoon soy sauce
	peeled & chopped	2	tablespoons green
salad oil			onions, chopped

Prepare the rice according to the label directions. Refrigerate until cold. In a medium bowl, beat the eggs, salt and shrimp with a fork. Pour 3 tablespoons oil into a wok or 12 inch skillet. Heat until very hot. Pour in the egg mixture. Cook, stirring quickly with a spoon, until eggs are the size of peas. Reduce the heat to low. Push the eggs to the side of the wok. In the middle of the wok, place 2 tablespoons oil. Add the rice and stir until thoroughly coated. Add the bacon, soy sauce and eggs. Continue to cook until everything is heated through. Spoon into warm bowls and garnish with the green onions.

Prep. Time: 10 minutes.

PECAN RICE

2	cups chicken broth	1/2	teaspoon white
1	cup uncooked rice		pepper
2/3	cup pecans, chopped	6	orange shells,
2	tablespoons butter		if desired
2	tablespoons minced		
	fresh parsley		

Combine broth and rice in saucepan. Bring to boil and cover. Reduce heat and simmer 20 minutes or until liquid is absorbed and rice is tender. Remove from heat and stir in pecans, butter, parsley and pepper. If desired, spoon into orange shells when ready to serve.

Prep. Time: 10 minutes.

JALAPEÑO PEPPER RICE

4	cups rice, cooked	1	cup Cheddar cheese,
2	cups sour cream		grated
1	4 ounce can of		
	jalapeño peppers		
	(or 4 fresh, seeded &		
	chopped)		

Combine the rice, sour cream and jalapeño peppers. Pour this mixture into a casserole dish that has been greased with butter or margarine. Top with grated cheese. Bake in a preheated 350° oven for 20 minutes or until heated through.

Prep. Time: 25 minutes.

Note: If you do not like jalapeño peppers, substitute green chilies.

WILD RICE STUFFING

¾	cup wild rice	1	4 ounce can
1	14.5 ounce can chicken broth		mushrooms, drained & liquid reserved
1	onion, chopped	1 ½	8 ounce packages herb stuffing
1	tablespoon butter or margarine		salt & pepper

Wash and drain the wild rice. In a large pan, combine the rice, chicken broth, onion, butter and mushroom liquid. Heat to a boil then turn the heat down to low. Cover and simmer for 45 minutes to 1 hour. Watch carefully. If the rice gets too dry then add more chicken broth. While this is simmering, prepare the stuffing according to the directions on the package. After the rice is cooked, remove from heat and add mushrooms. Season with salt and pepper to taste. Replace the lid and allow to cool. When cool, add the stuffing.

Prep. Time: 15 minutes.

CHRISTMAS TURKEY STUFFING

1	8 ounce package plain stuffing	⅛	teaspoon garlic powder
1	8 ounce package cubed stuffing	2	cans cream of chicken soup
1	8 ounce package cornbread stuffing	3	14.5 ounce cans chicken broth (buy an extra can
1	8 ounce package herb seasoned stuffing		because sometimes it needs more)
1	large onion, chopped		
2	eggs	½	pound ground beef (optional)
1	tablespoon sage		
½	teaspoon celery salt	¼	cup pecans, chopped (optional)

Combine all the above ingredients and mix well. Add as much chicken broth as needed to make it as moist as desired. Stuff into the breast cavity of turkey. Pour the remaining stuffing into a large cake pan or roasting pan. Bake in a preheated 325° oven for 1½ hours.

Prep. Time: 30 minutes.

PRAIRIE RICE

2	cups rice	2	cloves garlic, chopped
2	cups milk	2	eggs, beaten
1	cup fresh parsley, chopped	½	cup oil
2	green peppers, chopped	2	cups sharp Cheddar cheese, grated
1	cup green onions & tops, chopped		salt & pepper, to taste

Cook rice according to directions. Combine remaining ingredients, mix with rice and pour into casserole dish. Bake in a preheated 350° oven for 45 minutes. *Makes 10 to 12 servings.*

Prep. Time: 15 minutes.

HOMEMADE TURKEY STUFFING
Enough stuffing for an 8 pound turkey.

16	slices white bread	6	tablespoons yellow
2	teaspoons salt		onion, chopped
½	teaspoon leaf sage	4	stalks celery, chopped
	(more if desired)		turkey giblets (optional)
½	teaspoon pepper	1 ½	cups water
¼	cup margarine	½	cup stock from giblets

Toast the bread and cut it into cubes with an electric knife. Place these in a large mixing bowl. Add the salt, sage and pepper and toss to mix. In a small skillet, sauté the onions and celery in the margarine until lightly browned. Add this to bread mixture. In a small pan place the turkey giblets and add the water. Bring to a boil and cook until the giblets are cooked through. Remove the giblets and discard the gizzard. If desired, dice up the liver and add it to the bread mixture. Measure out ½ cup of stock from giblets and pour this into the bread mixture. Toss until completely mixed. Add more giblet stock for moister dressing but not too much or the stuffing will end up soggy after cooking. Stuff it in the chest cavity of the turkey and bake with the turkey.

Prep. Time: 20 minutes.

FRESH HOLIDAY CRANBERRY SAUCE
Best in the West.

1 ½	pound fresh	1	12 ounce bottle
	cranberries		orange marmalade
2 ½	cups sugar	¾	cup brandy
3	tablespoons water		
6	tablespoons fresh		
	lemon juice		

Combine the cranberries, sugar and water mixing well. Place them in a 9 x 13 inch cake pan. Bake in a preheated 350° oven until the cranberries start to pop, about 40 minutes. Stir in the remaining ingredients and allow to cool. Pour in a bowl with an airtight lid and refrigerate. This stores for up to 3 weeks.

Prep. Time: 15 minutes.

CRANBERRY CHUTNEY

4	cups cranberries,	½	cup almonds,
	chopped		chopped
2	cups brown sugar	½	cup green pepper,
1	cup onion, chopped		chopped
1	cup golden raisins	¼	cup ginger, chopped
1	cup cider vinegar	1	medium clove garlic

In large saucepan, combine ingredients. Bring to boil, reduce heat and simmer 15 minutes. Stir occasionally. Chill. *Makes 4½ cups.*

Prep. Time: 20 minutes.

CANDIED BRANDY CRANBERRIES

A nice addition to a Christmas gift food basket.

1	pound fresh or frozen cranberries	4	tablespoons brandy extra sugar
2	cups sugar		

Pick over cranberries to eliminate any stray stems or imperfect berries. Place in a shallow baking dish, large enough so the fruit can lie flat. Sprinkle 2 generous cups of sugar over the berries. Cover tightly. Bake in a preheated 350° oven for 1 hour. Cool. Then mix in the brandy or cognac and sprinkle lightly with more sugar. *Makes 8 to 10 servings.*

Prep. Time: 10 minutes.

LINGUINE WITH ARTICHOKES

6	tablespoons olive oil, divided	1	4 ounce can mushrooms
¾	cup butter	3	tablespoons Parmesan cheese, grated
1	tablespoon flour		
1	cup chicken broth		
1	clove garlic, mashed	12	ounces linguine
salt & pepper, to taste		4	slices bacon, crumbled
2	teaspoons lemon juice		
1	teaspoon parsley		
1	16 ounce can artichoke hearts, sliced		

In heavy saucepan, heat 4 tablespoons olive oil over low heat. Add ½ cup butter and melt. Add flour. Cook stirring continuously for 3 minutes. Stir in chicken broth. Increase heat and cook 1 minute. Add garlic, salt, pepper, lemon juice and parsley and cook 5 minutes. Add artichoke hearts, mushrooms and 2 tablespoons Parmesan cheese. Simmer sauce. Cook linguine according to package directions. Drain linguine and top with remaining 2 tablespoons olive oil, ¼ cup butter and 1 tablespoon Parmesan cheese. Pour sauce over linguine and sprinkle with bacon. *Makes 6 servings.*

Prep. Time: 20 minutes.

PASTA PRIMAVERA

1 1/2	cups broccoli florets	1/4	teaspoon salt	
12	stalks asparagus, cut into 2 inch pieces (2 cups)	1/4	teaspoon ground pepper	
1	cup zucchini, sliced	4	cups mushrooms, sliced	
1	cup brussels sprouts, halved	pine nuts (or sunflower seeds)		
1 1/2	cups snow peas (green beans may be used)	1	cup fresh or frozen baby peas, thawed & drained	
3	tablespoons olive oil	1/2	cup butter	
1	carton cherry tomatoes, halved	1	cup heavy cream	
		1/2	teaspoon salt	
1/4	cup parsley, chopped	1/2	teaspoon pepper	
1/2	cup fresh basil, chopped	3/4	cup Parmesan cheese, grated	
2	teaspoons garlic, minced	1	pound spaghetti, cooked & drained	

S team broccoli, asparagus, zucchini, brussels sprouts and snow peas in large steamer for 3 to 4 minutes until tender-crisp. Immediately run cold water over vegetables and set aside to drain. In a 14 to 15 inch skillet heat 1 tablespoon of oil over medium heat. Add tomatoes, parsley, 2 tablespoons basil, 1 teaspoon garlic, and 1/8 teaspoon salt and pepper. Cook 1 to 2 minutes, stirring constantly, until tomatoes are hot. Transfer to a bowl and cover to keep warm. Add remaining 2 tablespoons oil to skillet. Add mushrooms, pine nuts and 1 teaspoon garlic and cook 1 to 2 minutes stirring constantly, until nuts are golden brown and mushrooms are just cooked. Add peas and steamed vegetables to mushrooms and cook stirring constantly for 4 to 5 minutes until very hot. Transfer to a large bowl and cover to keep warm. Add butter to skillet and heat over medium heat. When melted, stir in cream, 1/2 teaspoon each salt and pepper and 6 tablespoons basil. Cook 1 minute stirring constantly. Remove from heat, stir in Parmesan cheese, pasta and two-thirds of the vegetables. Toss and top with remaining vegetables.

Prep. Time: 20 minutes.

FETTUCINE ALFREDO

1	package fettucine noodles	3/4	cup whipping cream
		white pepper	
1	cup butter, softened (not margarine)	basil	
		additional fresh Parmesan cheese, grated	
2	cups fresh Parmesan cheese, grated		

C ook noodles according to directions on package. Drain and transfer to casserole dish. In saucepan, over low heat, add butter, cheese and whipped cream. Cook stirring constantly until sauce thickens. Add to noodles and toss gently. Season with pepper and basil. Serve immediately and top with additional grated Parmesan. *Makes 8 to 10 servings.*

Prep. Time: 25 minutes.

LEAN FETTUCCINI

8	ounces fettucini	1/4	teaspoon lemon peel, grated
1	teaspoon olive oil		
3/4	cup evaporated skim milk	1	clove garlic, chopped
			white pepper
1/3	cup fresh Parmesan cheese, grated		additional fresh Parmesan cheese, grated
1/4	cup green onion, chopped		lemon slices
2	tablespoons fresh basil or 1/2 teaspoon dried basil, chopped		

Cook pasta according to package directions. Drain; immediately return to pan. Add olive oil; toss to coat. Add the evaporated skim milk, Parmesan cheese, onion, basil, lemon peel, garlic and pepper to taste. Cook over medium-high heat until bubbly, stirring constantly. Top with extra Parmesan, fresh basil, and lemon slices, if desired. *Makes 6 side dishes.*

Prep. Time: 20 minutes.

RATATOUILLE

1	small onion, finely chopped	1	tomato, peeled & chopped
2	cloves garlic, chopped	1/2	cup black olives
3 1/2	tablespoons olive oil	2	tablespoons fresh parsley, chopped
1	cup egg plant, chopped		
1/2	pound mushrooms, sliced	1/2	teaspoon dried oregano
		1	bay leaf
2	small zucchini, chopped	1/2	cup Parmesan cheese, grated
1	small yellow squash, chopped		

Sauté onion and garlic in olive oil. Add eggplant, mushrooms, zucchini and yellow squash. Sauté until lightly brown. Add next 5 ingredients and simmer 25 to 30 minutes over medium heat. Remove bay leaf. Sprinkle with Parmesan cheese and serve. *Makes 6 to 8 servings.*

Prep. Time: 20 minutes.

SOUR CREAM MACARONI

3/4	pound Monterey-Jack cheese	3	cups large macaroni, cooked (1 1/2 cups uncooked)
2	cups sour cream		
2	4 ounce cans green chilies, chopped	1/2	cup Cheddar cheese, grated
	salt & pepper, to taste		

Cut Monterey-Jack cheese in strips. Mix sour cream, chilies, salt and pepper. Butter 2 1/2 quart casserole dish well. Put in layer of macaroni then a layer of sour cream mixture and strips of cheese. Continue to layer, finish with layer of macaroni on top. Cover and bake in a preheated 350° oven for 20 to 30 minutes until hot and bubbly. Add grated Cheddar cheese and melt. *Makes 8 servings.*

Prep. Time: 20 to 30 minutes.

STUFFED PASTA SHELLS

1	10 ounce package frozen spinach	1	teaspoon lemon juice
1/8	cup reduced calorie Italian dressing		dash of salt
			dash of pepper
2/3	cup cottage cheese	12	jumbo macaroni shells
1/2	cup part skim Ricotta cheese	1	16 ounce can tomatoes
2	tablespoons Parmesan cheese	4	ounces Mozzarella cheese, grated
2	tablespoons green onion tops, finely chopped		

Cook the spinach according to instructions. Allow to cool a little and drain. Place on several paper towels and squeeze to get as much water out as possible. Place in a large bowl. Add next 8 ingredients, mixing well. Meanwhile, cook the shells according to instructions. Drain. Stuff each shell with spinach mixture and place in a 9 x 13 inch baking dish that has been sprayed with a non-stick cooking spray. Place tomatoes and juice in a blender and process until smooth. Pour this over shells. Sprinkle Mozzarella on top. Bake in a preheated 350° oven for 30 minutes or until hot. *Makes 6 servings, 2 shells each.*

Prep. Time: 20 minutes.

GARDEN VEGETABLE SOUFFLÉ
(Corn Soufflé)

3	tablespoons butter	1	teaspoon salt
1/4	cup onion, minced	1/2	teaspoon nutmeg
3	tablespoons flour	6	egg whites
1	cup milk, or 1/2 cup milk plus 1/2 cup chicken broth to yield 1 cup	1/8	teaspoon salt
		1/4	teaspoon cream of tartar (if not using a copper bowl)
4	egg yolks		
1	cup fresh uncooked corn, cut from the cob		

Prepare a 1 1/2 quart soufflé dish. Heat the butter. Add the minced onion and cook until it is soft but not brown. Whisk in the flour. Gradually whisk in the liquid and cook until the mixture thickens. Remove from heat. Then whisk in the yolks one at a time. Stir in the corn and seasonings. Beat the egg whites with 1/8 teaspoon of salt and the optional cream of tartar until stiff, moist peaks form. Gently stir the corn mixture with 1 cup of the beaten egg whites. Fold the corn mixture into the egg whites. Scoop the mixture into the soufflé dish. Bake in a preheated 375° oven for 30 to 35 minutes.

Prep. Time: 30 minutes.

Note: Add less salt when using chicken broth.

JALAPEÑO HUSHPUPPIES

1	onion, finely chopped	1	8 ounce can cream-style corn
1	bell pepper, finely chopped	1 ½	tablespoons pickled jalapeño juice (optional)
2	jalapeño peppers, seeded & finely chopped		buttermilk
2	tablespoons margarine		vegetable oil for deep frying
½	cup self-rising flour		
1	cup cornmeal		

In a small skillet, sauté onions and peppers in margarine, over a medium-high heat for 5 minutes. Pour this into a mixing bowl. Add to this mixture, the flour, cornmeal and cream corn. Mix well. Stir in jalapeño juice (optional). Add enough buttermilk to make consistency pasty. Heat oil. Drop by spoonfuls into hot oil and fry until golden brown on all sides. Place on a paper towel to drain.

Prep. Time: 15 minutes.

CURRIED FRUIT

1	16 ounce can pear halves or slices, drained	1	16 ounce can peach halves or slices, drained
1	16 ounce can apricot halves, drained	⅓	cup butter
1	16 ounce can pineapple chunks, drained	½	cup brown sugar
		2	teaspoons curry powder

In a 2 quart casserole dish, add all fruits and stir. In a small saucepan, melt butter. Stir in brown sugar and curry powder and mix well. Pour this over fruit mixture. Allow to stand for 1 hour. Bake in a preheated 325° oven for 20 minutes or until hot and bubbly. *Makes 8 to 10 servings.*

Prep. Time: 10 minutes,
plus 1 hour standing time.

Vegetable Microwave Chart

Vegetable	Quantity	Preparation	Time: Microwave on High	Amount of Water	Time Standing in Water	Hints
Artichokes 3 1/2 inch diam.	1 2	Wash. Cut tops of each leaf.	7-8 mins. 11-12 mins.	1/4 cup 1/2 cup	2-3 mins. 2-3 mins.	When done, leaves peel off easily.
Asparagus spears and pieces	1 pound	Wash. Cut off the hard ends.	2-3 mins.	1/4 cup	None	Stir once during cooking.
Green beans	1 pound	Wash. Cut ends off. Snap or leave whole.	12-14 mins.	1/4 cup	2-3 mins.	Stir once during cooking.
Beets	4 medium	Wash. Leave 1 inch of beet top.	16-18 mins.	1/4 cup	None	Peel after cooking.
Broccoli: whole chopped	1 - 2 1/2 lbs. 1 - 1 1/2 lbs.	Remove outer leaves and split stalks.	9-10 mins.	1/4 cup	3 mins.	Stir during cooking.
Brussels Sprouts	1 pound	Wash. Remove outside leaves & stems.	8-9 mins.	1/4 cup	2-3 mins.	Stir once during cooking.
Cabbage	1/2 medium hd., grated 1 medium hd., wedged	Remove outside leaves.	5-6 mins. 13-15 mins.	1/4 cup 1/4 cup	2-3 mins. 2-3 mins.	Stir once during cooking. Stir after 7 minutes.
Carrots	4 sliced 6 sliced 8 sliced	Peel and cut tops off.	7-9 mins. 9-10 mins. 10-11 mins.	1 Tbl. 2 Tbls. 3 Tbls.	2-3 mins. 2-3 mins. 2-3 mins.	Stir once during cooking.
Cauliflower	1 medium florets 1 medium whole	Wash. Cut into florets. Remove core.	7-8 mins. 8-9 mins.	1/4 cup 1/2 cup	2-3 mins. 3 mins.	Stir after 5 minutes. Stir once during cooking.
Celery	2 1/2 cups 1 inch slices	Wash and slice.	8-9 mins.	1/4 cup	2 mins.	Stir once during cooking.
Corn on Cob	1 ear 2 ears 3 ears 4 ears	Husk and cook no more than four at a time.	3-4 mins. 6-7 mins. 9-10 mins. 11-12 mins.	1/4 cup 1/4 cup 1/4 cup 1/4 cup	2 mins. 2 mins. 2 mins. 2 mins.	Cook in a covered dish. Rotate once during cooking.
Egg Plant	1 medium sliced 1 medium whole	Wash, peel and cut into slices. Pierce skin several times.	5-6 mins. 6-7 mins.	2 Tbls. None	3 mins. None	Rotate once during cooking. Place on microproof rack.

Vegetable Microwave Chart

Vegetable	Quantity	Preparation	Time: Microwave on High	Amount of Water	Time Standing in Water	Hints
Mushrooms	1/2 pound sliced	Wash, slice. Add margarine.	2-4 mins.	None	2 mins.	Stir once during cooking.
Okra	1/2 pound	Wash, trim stems. Leave whole or cut.	3-5 mins.	1/4 cup	2 mins.	
Onions	1 pound tiny, whole 1 pound med. to lg.	Peel. Add margarine. Peel and quarter. Add margarine.	6-7 mins. 7-9 mins.	None None	3 mins. 3 mins.	Stir once during cooking.
Parsnips	4 medium quartered	Peel and quarter.	8-9 mins.	1/4 cup	2 mins.	Stir once during cooking.
Green Peas	1 pound 2 pounds	Shell and rinse.	7-8 mins. 8-9 mins.	1/4 cup 1/2 cup	2 mins. 2-3 mins.	Stir once during cooking.
Sweet Potatoes	1 2 4 6	Wash. Pierce with fork. Put on paper towel in circle 1 inch apart.	4-5 mins. 6-7 mins. 8-10 mins. 10-11 mins.	None None None None	3 mins. 3 mins. 3 mins. 3 mins.	Rotate once during cooking.
White Potatoes	1 2 3 4 5	Wash. Pierce with fork. Put on paper towel in circle 1 inch apart.	4-6 mins. 6-8 mins. 8-12 mins. 12-16 mins. 16-20 mins.	None None None None None	3 mins. 3 mins. 3 mins. 3 mins. 3 mins.	Rotate once during cooking.
Boiled Potatoes	3	Peel & cut in quarters.	12-16 mins.	1 cup	None	Stir once during cooking.
Spinach	1 pound	Wash. Remove tough stems. Drain.	6-7 mins.	None	2 mins.	Stir once during cooking.
Squash: Acorn or Butternut	1 - 1 1/2 lbs. whole	Wash. Pierce with fork. Put on paper towel in circle 1 inch apart.	10-12 mins.	None	2 mins.	Slice in half. Remove seeds.
Spaghetti Squash	2-3 pounds	Wash. Pierce with fork. Place on a paper towel.	6 mins. per pound	None	5 mins.	Serve with butter, Parmesan cheese or spag. sauce.
Turnips	4 cups cubed	Peel and cube.	9-11 mins.	1/4 cup	3 mins.	Stir after 5 mins.
Zucchini	3 cups sliced	Peel and slice.	7-8 mins.	1/4 cup	2 mins.	Stir after 4 mins.

COW PATTY NUT CLUSTERS

Fast and yummy.

12	ounces peanut butter chips	2	cups Spanish or other peanuts
6	ounces semi-sweet chocolate chips		

Put all chips in a microwaveable bowl. Microwave for 1 ½ to 2 minutes. Stir. Microwave another 1 ½ to 2 minutes. Stir. Add nuts and stir. Drop by teaspoons on wax paper. *Makes 24 clusters.*

Prep. Time: 10 minutes.

Hint: Try substituting pecans for peanuts.

MARTHA WASHINGTON BON BONS

¼	pound margarine or butter, softened	2	cups pecans, finely chopped
2	boxes powdered sugar (2 pounds)	1	7 ounce can coconut
1	14 ounce can sweetened condensed milk	1	12 ounce package semi-sweet chocolate chips
2	teaspoons vanilla	1	block paraffin (⅕ pound)

Mix together first six ingredients. Chill mixture. Form mixture into balls of desired size. Melt chocolate pieces and paraffin in double boiler. Pick up balls with toothpick and dip into melted chocolate and paraffin. Place on waxed paper to cool.

Prep. Time: 2 to 3 hours.

Hint: Works well if two people can do this together. It shortens your preparation time. Store in refrigerator.

DARK CHOCOLATE CARAMEL BARS

1	16 ounce bag light caramels	⅓	cup evaporated milk
⅓	cup evaporated milk	½	cup pecans, chopped
1	German chocolate cake mix	6	ounces semi-sweet chocolate chips
¾	cup margarine, melted		

Remove the wrappings from the caramel candies and place caramels in a double boiler. Add evaporated milk. Heat until melted. In a large mixing bowl, mix together the German chocolate cake mix, melted margarine, evaporated milk and pecans. Press half of this mixture into a greased and floured 9 x 13 inch cake pan. Bake in a preheated 350° oven for 6 to 8 minutes. Remove from oven. Sprinkle the bag of chocolate chips on top. Spread caramel mixture on top. Dot on the remaining cake mixture. Place back in the oven and continue to bake an additional 15 to 18 minutes. Allow to thoroughly cool before cutting into bars. *Makes 32 bars.*

Prep. Time: 45 minutes.

QUICK FUDGE

3 ²/₃ cups powdered sugar
½   cup cocoa
¼   cup milk
½   cup butter, melted

1   tablespoon vanilla
½   cup pecans
2   tablespoons peanut
     butter (optional)

Microwave first four ingredients on high for 3 minutes. Remove and stir until smooth. Add vanilla, peanut butter and nuts. Pour into greased 9 x 9 inch pan. Cool. *Makes 20 to 30 squares, depending on the size of the pieces you cut.*

Prep. Time: 15 minutes.

CHOCOLATE FUDGE SQUARES

This recipe won Division Champion at the Permian Basin Fair and Exposition.

3   eggs, beaten well
1   cup sugar
2   tablespoons cocoa
½   cup flour

½   cup vegetable oil
1   teaspoon vanilla
1   cup nuts

Beat eggs and add sugar mixed with cocoa. Add flour and oil. Add vanilla and nuts. Bake in a preheated 350° oven for 15 to 20 minutes in a 9 x 9 inch pan which has been greased and floured. Cut into squares. *Makes 1 dozen.*

Prep. Time: 10 minutes.

ROCKY ROAD FUDGE

Pop this in your microwave and zap it.

3   4 ounce bars milk
     chocolate, cut up
1 ½ cups tiny
     marshmallows

1   cup walnuts,
     coarsely chopped

Place milk chocolate in microwaveable 1 quart casserole dish. Microwave uncovered on 100% power for 1 ½ to 2 minutes or until chocolate is melted, stirring once. Stir in marshmallows and nuts. Drop by teaspoons onto waxed paper. Chill in refrigerator for 15 minutes or until firm. *Makes 24 to 28 pieces.*

Prep. Time: 10 minutes.

ROCKY ROAD CANDY

1	12 ounce package semi-sweet chocolate morsels	2	cups dry roasted peanuts
1	14 ounce can condensed milk	1	10.5 ounce package miniature white marshmallows
2	tablespoons butter or margarine		

In top of double boiler, over boiling water, melt morsels with condensed milk and butter. Remove from heat. In large bowl, combine nuts and marshmallows. Fold in chocolate mixture. Spread in wax paper lined 9 x 13 inch pan. Chill 2 hours or until firm. Remove from pan, peel off wax paper; cut into squares. Cover and store at room temperature. *Makes 40 pieces.*

Prep. Time: 30 minutes,
             plus 2 hours to chill.

Hint: May be dropped by spoonfuls onto wax paper.

TURTLES

Texans call 'em horny toads.

1	tablespoon margarine	1	large milk chocolate candy bar (4 to 5 ounces)
2	tablespoons evaporated milk		
1	14 ounce package caramel candies	⅓	bar paraffin
1	cup pecans, chopped (1 ½ cups if needed)		

In a double boiler, over a low heat, melt margarine. Add the evaporated milk and continue to heat. Add the caramels and heat until all the caramels are melted. Stir in the pecans. Drop by spoonfuls on a cookie sheet that has been greased with margarine. Allow to cool. Meanwhile, in a double boiler, melt together the candy bar and the paraffin. After the caramel mixture has cooled, dip nut clusters in the chocolate mixture until completely covered. Return to the cookie sheet and allow to cool completely. *Makes 20 to 24 turtles.*

Prep. Time: 1 hour.

HAZELNUT TRUFFLES

1 ¾	cups powdered sugar	½	cup toasted hazelnuts, chopped
⅓	cup unsweetened cocoa powder	6	1 ounce squares semi-sweet chocolate
¼	cup butter, softened	4	teaspoons vegetable oil
3	tablespoons liqueur (Frangelico, brandy, other)		whole toasted hazelnuts to garnish
⅛	teaspoon salt		

In medium bowl, beat sugar, cocoa and butter until well blended. Mixture will resemble coarse cornmeal. Blend in liqueur and salt. Stir in chopped nuts. Roll into 1 inch balls. Place on baking sheet lined with wax paper. Chill. In double boiler, heat semi-sweet chocolate and oil until chocolate is melted. Using a fork or toothpick, dip 1 ball at a time, turning to coat evenly. Scrape gently against side of pan to remove excess chocolate. Return truffles to wax paper. Top each with a whole nut if desired while chocolate is still warm. Store in air tight container, up to 2 weeks in refrigerator. *Makes 2 dozen.*

Prep. Time: 1 hour.

CHOCOLATE CHIP COOKIES

1	cup shortening	1 ½	teaspoons baking powder
1	cup sugar	2	cups pecans, chopped
¾	cup brown sugar, packed	4	cups chocolate chips
3	eggs, lightly beaten	1	teaspoon vanilla
3	cups flour		
2	teaspoons salt		

Cream shortening until light and fluffy. Add sugars and mix. Add eggs and mix well. In a separate bowl, combine flour, salt and baking powder. Add to creamed mixture. Stir in vanilla. Fold in pecans, then fold in chocolate chips. Place by tablespoonfuls on greased cookie sheets. Bake in a preheated 325° oven for 12 to 15 minutes. *Makes 5 dozen.*

Prep. Time: 30 minutes.

Hint: Depending on your taste, 4 cups of chocolate chips may be too many. Let the chips fall as they may.

CHOCOLATE DIPPED PEANUT BUTTER BALLS

1	cup peanut butter	12	ounces semi-sweet
1	cup butter		chocolate chips
1	teaspoon vanilla	2	inch square paraffin,
1 ½	pounds powdered		shaved
	sugar		

Cream peanut butter, butter and vanilla until smooth. Gradually beat in powdered sugar. Knead by hand if it gets too stiff to beat. Refrigerate until firm. Form into balls. Melt chocolate and paraffin in double boiler. Dip balls into chocolate. Place on waxed paper to harden.

Prep. Time: several hours.

Hint: Work with small amount of mixture at a time to form balls or it gets too soft to easily form balls.

CHOCOLATE SHORTBREAD COOKIES

4	tablespoons butter, softened	½	cup flour
2 ½	tablespoons sugar	2 ½	tablespoons cocoa, unsweetened
½	teaspoon almond extract		dash of salt

In a small bowl, cream butter. Add sugar and vanilla, beating until well blended. Sift together flour, cocoa and salt. Stir dry ingredients into butter mixture until smooth. Refrigerate for 15 minutes. On a lightly sugared surface, roll out dough until it is ³/₈ inch thick. Cut out cookies with your favorite cookie cutter. Place cookies on a lightly buttered cookie sheet. Prick cookies with tines of a fork. Bake in a preheated 275° oven for 40 to 45 minutes or until firm to touch. Let rest for 5 minutes on cookie sheet before removing to cool. *Makes 1 dozen cookies.*

Prep. Time: 30 minutes.

BUCK–A–ROO CAMP COOKIES

Bunches and bunches of cookies for hungry cowboys.

3	cups sugar	4	teaspoons baking
1	pound brown sugar		soda
2	pounds shortening	2	teaspoons salt
8	eggs	2	12 ounce packages
3	tablespoons vanilla		chocolate chips
8 ½	cups flour		

Mix in dishpan or HUGE bowl. Beat eggs, sugars, shortening and vanilla. Add flour, soda and salt. Stir in chips. Using ice cream scoop, drop 2 inches apart on ungreased baking sheet. Bake in a preheated 350° oven 15 to 18 minutes. *Makes 16 dozen cookies (regular cookies) or 100 4-inch cookies.*

Prep. Time: 25 minutes.

YUMMY BARS

½	cup margarine	1	pound box
1	box chocolate		powdered sugar
	cake mix	1	teaspoon vanilla
1	egg		chocolate chips
8	ounces cream cheese		pecans
2	eggs		

Melt margarine. Mix with cake mix and 1 egg. Press into bottom of 9 x 13 inch greased pan. Mix remaining ingredients together and pour over chocolate mixture. Sprinkle top liberally with chocolate chips and pecans. Bake in a preheated 350° oven for 40 to 50 minutes. Do not overbake, check after 40 minutes. It will still be soft in the middle. Cool and cut like brownies. *Makes 20 squares.*

Prep. Time: 15 minutes.

CHOCOLATE ROPE

To lasso in the compliments.

½	cup butter	6	ounces semi-sweet
¾	cup sugar		chocolate
2	eggs	¾	cup pecans,
1	teaspoon vanilla		finely chopped
2 ½	cups flour		
2	teaspoons baking		
	powder		

Cream butter and sugar until light and fluffy. Beat in eggs and vanilla. Add flour and baking powder, mixing until well blended. Wrap in plastic and refrigerate until well chilled. (1 to 2 hours) Meanwhile, melt chocolate over hot water. Roll dough into half inch rope. Cut into 3 inch pieces and place on baking sheet. Bake in a preheated 350° oven for 10 to 12 minutes until lightly browned. Remove from oven and let cool a few minutes. Dip one end of cookie in melted chocolate, then in chopped pecans. *Makes 5 dozen.*

Prep. Time: 30 minutes,
plus 1 hour to chill dough.

CHOCOLATE NUT PIE

¼	cup butter	1	teaspoon vanilla
1	cup sugar	½	cup pecans, chopped
3	eggs, beaten	2	tablespoons bourbon
½	cup chocolate bits	1	10 inch unbaked
¾	cup light corn syrup		pie shell
¼	teaspoon salt		

Cream butter; add sugar gradually and cream together. Add beaten eggs, syrup, salt and vanilla. Stir in chocolate bits, nuts and bourbon until well mixed. Pour into unbaked 10 inch pie shell. Bake in a preheated 375° oven for 40 to 45 minutes. Serve warm.

Prep. Time: 15 minutes.

RICH CHOCOLATE PIE

2	ounces German	½	cup flour
	sweet chocolate	1	cup sugar
½	cup butter	1	teaspoon vanilla
3	eggs	½	cup pecans, chopped

Melt chocolate and butter; cool. Beat eggs until thick. Add flour, sugar and vanilla. Add cooled chocolate to egg mixture. Stir in nuts. Grease and flour a 9 inch pie pan. Pour mixture into the pie pan. Bake in a preheated 350° oven for 25 minutes. Serve with whipped cream. *Makes 8 to 10 servings.*

Prep. Time: 10 minutes.

Hint: Add coconut for variation.

CHOCOLATE CREAM PIE

4	tablespoons flour	1	teaspoon vanilla
¾	cup sugar	1	tablespoon butter
½	teaspoon salt	1	10 inch baked
3	tablespoons cocoa		pie shell
2	cups evaporated milk	4	tablespoons sugar
2	eggs, separated		

In a saucepan, mix flour, sugar, salt and cocoa with a little of the milk. Add egg yolks. Beat well. Add remaining milk. Cook until mixture thickens, stirring constantly (20 minutes). Add butter and vanilla. Beat. Pour into baked pie shell. Beat egg whites in a mixing bowl until stiff. Add the 4 tablespoons sugar gradually. Spread meringue onto pie. Brown in 350° oven. Refrigerate any leftovers.

Prep. Time: 1 hour.

FROSTY MUD PIE

20	chocolate wafers	1½	cups (1 jar) fudge ice
¼	cup butter, melted		cream topping
2	pints (or 1 quart)		whipped cream
	coffee ice cream		slivered almonds

Crush wafers and add butter. Mix well. Press into 9 inch pie plate. Cover with softened ice cream. Put into freezer until ice cream is firm. Top with fudge sauce. Store in freezer at least 3 hours, until firm. To serve, slice pie and serve on chilled dessert plate with chilled fork. Top with whipped cream and slivered almonds.

Prep. Time: 15 minutes, plus at least 3 hours freezing time.

OLD-FASHIONED CHOCOLATE MERINGUE PIE

1 ¼	cups sugar	1 ½	teaspoons vanilla
½	cup cocoa	1	9 inch baked
⅓	cup cornstarch		pastry shell
¼	teaspoon salt	¼	teaspoon cream
3	cups milk		of tartar
3	eggs, separated	6	tablespoons sugar
3	tablespoons butter		

Combine first four ingredients in a heavy saucepan. Mix well to remove lumps. Gradually add milk, blending. Cook over medium heat, stirring constantly until mixture thickens and comes to a boil; boil 1 minute. Remove from heat. Beat egg yolks until thick and lemon colored. Stir in ¼ of hot mixture into yolks; add to remaining hot mixture, stirring constantly. Cook over medium heat 2 minutes. Remove from heat and stir in butter and vanilla. Pour into pastry shell.

Combine egg whites and cream of tartar. Beat until foamy. Gradually add remaining sugar, 1 tablespoon at a time, beating until stiff peaks form. Spread over filling, sealing to edge of pastry. Bake in a preheated 400° oven for 8 minutes or until lightly browned. Cool.

Prep. Time: 30 minutes.

BLACK BOTTOM PIE

Crust:

1 ¼	cup graham	2	cups milk
	cracker crumbs	4	eggs, separated
½	cup butter, softened	1	package chocolate
¼	cup sugar		chips
¼	teaspoon cinnamon	1	teaspoon vanilla
		¼	cup white rum
		¼	teaspoon cream

Filling:

1	tablespoon gelatin		of tartar
¼	cup cold water	½	cup sugar
½	cup sugar	½	cup whipping cream,
½	teaspoon salt		whipped
¼	cup cornstarch		

Combine graham cracker crumbs, butter, sugar and cinnamon. Press into 10 inch pie pan. Bake in a preheated 375° oven for 8 minutes. Cool.

For pie filling: Sprinkle gelatin over water to soften. Set aside. Combine sugar, salt and cornstarch. Stir in milk. Bring to boil. Stir until thickened. Beat egg yolks. Stir in half of hot mixture into beaten yolks. Pour back into hot mixture. Return to heat and cook 2 minutes. To 1 ½ cups custard removed from pan, add chocolate chips and vanilla. Stir until melted. Add gelatin to remaining custard. Add rum. Stir well. Beat egg whites with cream of tartar. Add remaining sugar slowly. Fold beaten egg whites into rum mixture. Pour chocolate mixture into pie crust. Let set for 10 minutes while mixing the rum mixture. Pour rum mixture over chocolate mixture. Garnish with whipped cream.

Prep. Time: 45 minutes.

HOT FUDGE SAUCE

6	ounces chocolate chips	1 ⅓	cups evaporated milk
½	cup butter	1	tablespoon vanilla
2	cups sifted powdered sugar		

Melt chocolate chips and butter. Sift in sugar. Add milk and boil for 10 minutes. (Not a hard boil.) Stir in vanilla.

Prep. Time: 10 minutes.

HOT FUDGE SUNDAE

1	cup flour	1	teaspoon vanilla
¾	cup sugar	1	cup pecans, chopped
2	tablespoons cocoa		
2	teaspoons baking powder		Mix together:
¼	teaspoon salt	1	cup brown sugar & ¼ cup cocoa
½	cup milk	1 ¼	cups hot tap water
2	tablespoons oil		vanilla ice cream

In an ungreased 9 x 9 inch pan, mix together first five ingredients. Add milk, oil and vanilla into pan. Mix with a fork until smooth. Stir in nuts and spread out evenly in pan. Sprinkle with brown sugar and cocoa mixture. Pour hot water over batter. Bake in a preheated 350° oven for 40 minutes. Let stand 15 minutes before serving. Spoon servings into bowl and top with a scoop of vanilla ice cream. Spoon some of remaining sauce in the pan over ice cream. *Makes 12 servings.*

Prep. Time: 15 minutes.

TRIPLE LAYERED DESSERT

Layer after layer of goodness.

1	stick margarine	3	cups milk
1 ½	cups graham cracker crumbs	1	cup non-dairy topping
¼	cup powdered sugar	1	1.5 ounces chocolate candy bar
8	ounces cream cheese		pecans (optional)
1	cup powdered sugar		
1	cup non-dairy topping		
2	4 ounce packages instant chocolate pudding		

Melt margarine in 9 x 13 inch pan. Add graham cracker crumbs and powdered sugar. Stir, press down slightly. Bake 7 minutes in a preheated 350° oven. Mix cream cheese and sugar. Fold in 1st cup of non-dairy topping. Spread on cooled crust. Mix pudding and milk. Let stand until thick. Spread on cream cheese layer. Top with 2nd cup of non-dairy topping. Grate chocolate candy bar on top. Refrigerate 1 hour. Pecans may be added to the crust, if desired. *Makes 12 to 16 servings.*

Prep. Time: 30 minutes.
Refrigerating Time: 1 hour.

FUDGESICLES

If you have a kid and a blender, you can do it.

1	4 ounce box instant chocolate pudding mix	½	cup sugar
		½	cup heavy cream
		2	cups milk

Mix all ingredients according to directions on back of pudding box. Pour into molds, ice trays or small paper cups. Insert popsicle sticks. Freeze. *Makes 10 to 12 fudgesicles.*

Prep. Time: 10 to 15 minutes.

Hint: May use any flavor of instant pudding.

DOUBLE CHOCOLATE COOKIES AND CREAM ICE CREAM

2	cups half-and-half	⅔	cup mini – chocolate chips
1 ½	cups sugar		
½	cup cocoa	11	chocolate, cream filled cookies, crushed
2	cups heavy cream		
1	teaspoon vanilla		

Blend the half-and-half, sugar and cocoa in a blender until sugar is dissolved. Pour into ice cream freezer. Add heavy cream and vanilla, stir. Freeze according to manufacturer's directions. Once frozen, stir in chocolate chips and cookies. Pour into container and freeze. *Makes 12 to 15 servings.*

Prep. Time: 45 minutes.

FUDGY CHOCOLATE ICE CREAM

5	1 ounce squares unsweetened chocolate, melted	2	cups half-and-half
		2	cups whipping cream, unwhipped
1	14 ounce can condensed milk, not evaporated milk	1	cup nuts, chopped (optional)
4	egg yolks	1	cup coconut (optional)
2	teaspoons vanilla		

In large mixer bowl, beat first four ingredients. Stir in half-and-half, whipping cream and nuts or coconut. Pour into ice cream freezer container. Freeze according to instructions. *Makes 1 ½ quarts.*

Prep. Time: 15 minutes.

CHOCOLATE ORANGE SOUFFLÉ

4	tablespoons cornstarch	3	tablespoons Grand Marnier
1	cup milk	1	teaspoon vanilla
4	egg yolks	7	egg whites
½	cup sugar	¼	teaspoon cream of tartar
4	ounces semi-sweet chocolate bits	⅓	teaspoon salt
zest of 1 orange		1	tablespoon sugar

Spray a 2 quart soufflé dish with a non-stick baking spray, preferably that includes flour. Make a collar with wax paper so it stands up several inches above the dish's rim. Either tie with string or use tape to hold in place. Not over heat, combine the cornstarch and ⅓ cup of milk in a medium-sized saucepan. Add the remaining milk, whisking until well blended. Cook the mixture over medium-high heat, stirring until the mixture thickens. Whisk rapidly until smooth, but very thick. Remove from heat. Mixture needs to cool for a minute so eggs won't cook when they are added. Whisk in the egg yolks, one at a time. Add the chocolate bits and stir until the chocolate melts. Gradually add the sugar and stir until well blended. Add the other flavorings. Set aside. In a separate bowl, beat the egg whites, salt and cream of tartar until soft peaks are formed. Gradually add sugar and continue beating until the mixture forms stiff, moist peaks. Now comes the scary part, but don't be afraid. Fold 1 cup of the whites into the warm base to lighten the mixture. Then pour the lightened mixture down the side of the beaten egg white bowl. Gently fold the mixtures together with a whisk. You only need to fold the mixtures a couple of times. Pour the mixture into the soufflé dish. Smooth the top of the soufflé with a spoon. Place it in the oven on the bottom rack. Bake in a preheated oven at 375° for exactly 35 minutes. Do not open while baking. Remove the collar once the soufflé is done. Serve immediately.

Prep. Time: 20 minutes.

Hint: *Substitute ¼ cup of almonds, 2 tablespoons amaretto and 1 teaspoon almond extract for the orange zest and Grand Marnier. Leave out all flavorings for a plain chocolate soufflé.*

CHOCOLATE CREPES

Cowboys call these thin pancakes.

Crepe mix:		*Hot chocolate sauce:*	
½	cup flour	½	cup cocoa
3	tablespoons cocoa	1	cup sugar
1	tablespoon sugar	1	cup corn syrup
½	cup milk	½	cup cream
4	eggs	3	tablespoons butter,
3	tablespoons unsalted		unsalted
	butter, melted		

coffee ice cream

Sift together flour, cocoa and sugar. Whisk the liquid ingredients into the dry until smooth. Set aside for 1 hour. Heat a crepe pan until water dances on the surface. Using a scant ¼ cup of the batter, swirl it in the pan. Cook about 1 minute on each side. Slide crepes onto a cooling rack and make more crepes. Fill the cooled crepes with coffee ice cream. Roll up and freeze.

For chocolate sauce: Combine all sauce ingredients in a saucepan and bring to a boil. Boil for 3 minutes. Sauce should be thick and fudgy. Top crepes with hot chocolate sauce. *Makes 12 crepes.*

Prep. Time: 15 minutes.

Hint: You can fill crepes with other ice cream flavors or with chocolate mousse. If using the mousse, re-frigerate instead of freeze.

FUDGE CAKE

Cake:		*Icing:*	
1	cup butter (not margarine), softened	2	cups sugar
		3	tablespoons cocoa
1	cup sugar	1	tablespoon white
4	eggs		corn syrup
1	cup flour	*pinch salt*	
1	16 ounce can chocolate syrup	1	5 ounce can evaporated milk
		½	cup butter (not margarine)
		1	teaspoon vanilla
		1	cup pecans, chopped

Mix all cake ingredients together. Pour into a greased and floured 9 x 13 inch pan. Bake in a preheated 325° oven for 30 to 35 minutes.

For icing: Mix all of the icing ingredients, but butter and vanilla, in large saucepan. Boil 3 minutes. Remove from heat. Add butter and vanilla and beat. Pour on cooled cake in pan. Top with chopped pecans. Put in refrigerator.

Prep. Time: 15 minutes.

BUTTERMILK FUDGE CAKE

3	eggs	2	teaspoons soda
1	cup vegetable	1/2	teaspoon salt
	shortening	1	cup buttermilk
2	cups sugar	1	cup boiling water
2 1/2	cups flour	1	teaspoon vanilla
1/3	cup cocoa		

Beat eggs, set aside. Cream shortening and sugar. Add eggs. Sift together dry ingredients 3 times. Add to creamed mixture, alternating with buttermilk. Add water and vanilla. Grease and flour 9 x 13 inch pan. Bake 1 hour in a preheated 350° oven. *Makes 12 servings.*

Prep. Time: 30 minutes.

FUDGE ICING

2	scant cups sugar	3/4	cup milk
1/3	scant cup cocoa	2	teaspoons vanilla
pinch salt		1/2	cup margarine

Mix sugar, cocoa and salt in heavy saucepan. Add milk, then bring to a boil. Reduce heat. Boil 2 minutes. Remove from heat and cool. Add vanilla and margarine. Beat until creamy and thickened. Then pour on warm cake. Add pecans to top if desired.

Prep. Time: 15 minutes.

DEEP DARK CHOCOLATE CAKE

1 3/4	cups flour	1	teaspoon salt
2	cups sugar	2	eggs
3/4	cup cocoa	1	cup milk
1 1/2	teaspoons baking	1/2	cup vegetable oil
	soda	2	teaspoons vanilla
1 1/2	teaspoons baking	1	cup boiling water
	powder		

Grease and flour 9 x 13 inch pan. Mix dry ingredients in large mixing bowl. Add next 4 ingredients. Beat 2 minutes on medium speed. Stir in boiling water. Spread batter in pan. Bake in a preheated 350° oven for 30 to 40 minutes. *Makes 12 to 15 servings.*

Prep. Time: 10 minutes.

FLAT AS THE PLAINS CHOCOLATE CAKE

Cake:
1   box chocolate fudge cake mix with pudding mix
1   cup evaporated milk
24   large marshmallows
14   ounces coconut

Icing:
1 ½   cups sugar
½   cup evaporated milk
½   cup margarine
1 ½   cups chocolate chips
1   teaspoon vanilla
⅔   cup almonds or pecans

Mix cake mix and spread (very thin) in a greased and floured 10 ½ x 15 ½ inch jelly roll pan. Cook 15 minutes in a preheated 350° oven. While cake is cooking, melt 1 cup of evaporated milk and marshmallows, but leave lumpy. Take off heat and add coconut. Pour over the hot cake.

For the icing: Bring sugar, milk and margarine to a rapid boil. Add chocolate chips, vanilla and nuts. Spread over the coconut mixture. Cool and eat.

Prep. Time: 30 minutes.

CHOCOLATE ZUCCHINI CAKE

2   cups sugar
¾   cup oil
3   eggs
2   teaspoons vanilla
2   cups zucchini, coarsely shredded
2 ½   cups flour
½   cup cocoa
1 ½   teaspoons baking soda
1   teaspoon salt
1   teaspoon cinnamon
½   cup milk
1   cup pecans, chopped

In a large bowl beat sugar, oil and eggs. Add vanilla and zucchini. Mix dry ingredients together. Add alternately with milk to zucchini mixture. Blend well. Pour into a 10 inch tube or bundt pan that has been sprayed with vegetable spray. Bake 50 to 60 minutes in a preheated 350° oven. Allow to stand 10 minutes in pan, then turn onto plate.

Prep. Time: 30 minutes.

Hint: *Could be made into muffins. To make "Heart Smart", use canola oil, skim milk, reduce sugar and use egg substitutes.*

CHOCOLATE CAKE

1	package either devil's food or chocolate cake mix	2	eggs
		1 ¾	cups milk
1	small package chocolate instant pudding mix	1	12 ounce package chocolate chips

Mix together all ingredients, except the chocolate chips. Mix with an electric mixer. Then by hand, add chocolate chips. Mix well. Bake in prepared bundt or tube pan. Spray pan with a non-stick cooking spray. Bake in a preheated 350˚ oven for 50 minutes.

Prep. Time: 30 minutes.

BLACK FOREST DESSERT

Easy and delicious.

1	chocolate cake mix (unmixed)	1	stick butter
		½	cup pecans, chopped
1	16 ounce can cherry pie filling		whipped cream (optional)

Spread cherry pie filling over bottom of medium-size oven dish. Pour cake mix over cherries. Do not mix cake mix. Pour melted butter over cake mix. Sprinkle pecans over entire cake. Bake in a preheated 350˚ oven for 20 minutes. Serve warm. Garnish with whipped cream. *Makes 8 to 12 servings.*

Prep. Time: 15 minutes.

GERMAN CHOCOLATE CAKE

Cake:

1	package German sweet chocolate
½	cup boiling water
1	cup butter
2	cups sugar
4	egg yolks, unbeaten
1	teaspoon vanilla
2 ½	cups cake flour, sifted
1	teaspoon baking soda
½	teaspoon salt
1	cup buttermilk
4	egg whites, stiffly beaten

Frosting:

1	cup evaporated milk
1	cup sugar
3	egg yolks
¼	pound butter
1	teaspoon vanilla
1 ⅓	cups flake coconut
1	cup pecans, chopped

For cake, melt chocolate in boiling water. Cool. Cream butter and sugar until light and fluffy. Add egg yolks, one at a time, beating after each. Add vanilla and chocolate, mix until blended. Sift flour with soda and salt together. Add sifted dry ingredients alternately with buttermilk and chocolate mixture, beating after each addition. Fold in stiffly beaten egg whites. Pour into three 8 or 9 inch layer pans. Bake in a preheated 350˚ oven for 30 to 40 minutes. Cool.

For frosting: Combine milk, sugar, egg yolks, butter and vanilla in saucepan. Cook over medium heat, stirring constantly until mixture thickens, about 12 minutes. Remove from heat. Add coconut and pecans. Beat until cooked and easy to spread. Only frost between layers and on top of cake.

Prep. Time: 1 hour.

CHOCOLATE POUND CAKE

This won the Division Champion at the Permian Fair and Exposition.

1	cup margarine, softened	3	cups flour
½	cup vegetable shortening	½	teaspoon baking powder
3	cups sugar	½	teaspoon salt
6	eggs	½	cup cocoa
1	cup milk	2	teaspoon vanilla

Cream margarine and shortening. Add sugar and eggs then beat. Sift flour, baking powder, salt and cocoa. Add dry ingredients alternately with milk. Fold in vanilla. Bake in greased and floured tube pan in a preheated 350° oven for 1 ½ hours. *Makes 12 to 16 servings.*

Prep. Time: 20 minutes.

Hint: Serve with fresh fruits or ice cream.

CREAM-FILLED CUPCAKES

1	package chocolate cake mix	1	egg
1	8 ounce cream cheese, softened	⅛	teaspoon salt
¼	cup sugar	6	ounces semi-sweet chocolate chips

Prepare cake mix according to directions on box. Fill baking cups two-thirds full. Beat cream cheese with sugar until well blended. Add egg and salt. Stir in chocolate pieces. Drop rounded teaspoons of cheese mixture into each cupcake. Bake 20 to 25 minutes in a preheated oven at 350°. *Makes 32 cupcakes.*

Prep. Time: 30 minutes.

EASY BROWNIE CUPCAKES

4	squares semi-sweet chocolate or 6 ounces of chocolate chips	1 ¾	cups sugar
		1	cup flour
		4	eggs (stir in one at a time)
1	stick butter	1	teaspoon vanilla
1	stick margarine	2	cups nuts, chopped

In a double boiler melt the chocolate, butter and margarine and set aside. In a large bowl mix the sugar, flour, four eggs, vanilla and nuts. Mix in the melted chocolate and butter mixture. Pour into muffin tins lined with paper. Bake in a preheated 325° oven for 30 minutes. Remove from oven and cool. *Makes 24 cupcakes.*

Prep. Time: 30 minutes.

CREAM CHEESE BROWNIES

4	ounces sweet chocolate squares	¾	cup sugar
5	tablespoons butter or margarine	½	teaspoon baking powder
3	ounces cream cheese, softened	¼	teaspoon salt
¼	cup sugar	½	cup all-purpose flour, unsifted
1	egg	½	cup nuts, coarsely chopped
1	tablespoon all-purpose flour	1	teaspoon vanilla
½	teaspoon vanilla	¼	teaspoon almond extract (optional)
2	eggs		

In a small saucepan, melt chocolate and 3 tablespoons of the butter over very low heat, stirring constantly. Cool. Blend remaining butter with cream cheese until softened. Gradually add sugar, beating well. Blend in egg, flour and vanilla. Set aside. Beat eggs until thick and light in color. Gradually add sugar, beating until thickened. Add baking powder, salt and flour. Blend in cooled chocolate mixture, nuts, remaining vanilla and the almond extract. Spread about half of the chocolate batter in greased 8 or 9 inch square pan. Add cheese mixture, spreading evenly. Top with tablespoonfuls of remaining chocolate batter. Zigzag a spatula through batter to marble. Bake in a preheated 350° oven for 35 to 40 minutes. Cool. Cut into bars or squares. *Makes 16 to 20.*

Prep. Time: 30 minutes.

CHOCOLATE BRICKLE BROWNIES

1	cup butter	1	teaspoon vanilla
½	cup cocoa	1	cup pecans, chopped
4	eggs	½	cup semi-sweet chocolate chips
2	cups sugar		
1 ½	cups unbleached flour	½	cup Heath Bits or Brickle chips or chopped Heath Bars
⅛	teaspoon salt		

Preheat oven to 350°. Melt butter and dissolve cocoa in the butter and set aside. Beat eggs and sugar together until fluffy. Beat in flour, salt and vanilla. Add cocoa and butter. Stirring well add pecans, chocolate and brickle chips. Bake in a greased and floured 9 x 13 inch metal pan for 30 minutes or until done. *Makes 2 dozen.*

Prep. Time: 15 minutes.

HOBO BROWNIES

1	stick margarine	2	eggs
¼	cup cocoa, rounded	½	teaspoon baking powder
1	cup sugar		
¾	cup flour	¼	teaspoon salt
½	teaspoon vanilla	½	cup nuts (optional)

Melt margarine in an 8 x 8 inch baking dish in microwave. Mix all ingredients with a fork until smooth. Bake in a preheated 350° oven for 20 to 25 minutes. *Makes 16 brownies.*

Prep. Time: 10 minutes.

CHOCOLATE CHIP BLONDE BROWNIES

½	cup flour	1	cup brown sugar,
½	teaspoon baking		packed
	powder	1	egg, beaten
⅛	teaspoon baking soda	1	teaspoon vanilla
½	teaspoon salt	½	6 ounce package
½	cup nuts, chopped		semi-sweet
⅓	cup butter or		chocolate chips
	margarine plus		
	1 tablespoon water		

Sift together flour, baking powder, baking soda and salt. Add nuts. Mix well and set aside. Melt butter in saucepan and remove from heat. If margarine is used, add 1 tablespoon water. Add brown sugar and beat well. Cool slightly. Add egg and vanilla and blend. Add flour mixture, a small amount at a time, mixing well after each addition. Spread in greased 8 x 8 inch pan. Sprinkle chocolate chips on top. Bake in a preheated 350° oven for 20 to 25 minutes.

Prep. Time: 15 minutes.

WHITE CHOCOLATE BROWNIES

8	ounces white	1 ½	cups sugar
	chocolate	4	eggs
2	teaspoons vanilla	1 ½	cups flour
½	cup butter		pinch of salt

Melt the white chocolate on low heat. Add the vanilla when melted. Combine the chocolate mixture with the remaining ingredients. Pour into a greased 9 x 13 inch pan. Bake in a preheated 350° oven for 30 minutes.

Prep. Time: 15 minutes.

CREAM CHEESE BLONDE BROWNIES

Crust:

2	cups all-purpose flour
1 ½	cups sugar
3 ½	teaspoons baking powder
1	teaspoon salt
1	egg
1	stick butter, melted

Filling:

1	8 ounce package cream cheese
1	pound powdered sugar
2	eggs
2	tablespoons vanilla

Mix all the crust ingredients together. Spread mixture in bottom of ungreased 9 x 12 inch pan.

For filling: Cream all the filling ingredients together. Pour mixture over crust layer. Bake 45 minutes in a preheated 350° oven.

Prep. Time: 20 minutes.

PECAN CHEESECAKE SQUARES

1	*cup all-purpose flour*	*1*	*egg*
⅓	*cup margarine or butter*	*2*	*teaspoons milk*
¼	*cup brown sugar, packed*	*½*	*teaspoon vanilla*
1	*8 ounce package cream cheese, softened*	*¼*	*cup pecans, finely chopped*

Mix first three ingredients. Press into ungreased square 8 x 8 inch pan. Bake 10 minutes in a preheated 350° oven. Beat next 4 ingredients in small bowl on low speed for 30 seconds, scraping bowl constantly. Beat on medium speed for 1 minute, scraping bowl occasionally. Spread over baked layer. Sprinkle with pecans. Bake in a preheated 350° oven for 25 minutes, until edges are light brown. Cool. Refrigerate at least 2 hours. Cut into 1¼ inch squares. Store in refrigerator.

Prep. Time: 30 minutes,
          plus two hours refrigeration.

Hint: For a variation, substitute ¼ cup granulated sugar for the brown sugar. Stir ⅓ cup chopped candied cherries into cheese mixture before pouring over baked layer.

HONEY BARS

¼	*cup honey*	*Glaze:*	
1	*cup sugar*	*1*	*cup powdered sugar*
¾	*cup oil*	*1*	*tablespoon mayonnaise*
1	*egg*		
2	*cups flour*	*1*	*teaspoon vanilla*
1	*teaspoon soda*	*1*	*tablespoon water*
1	*teaspoon salt*		
1	*cup nuts, chopped*		
1 ¼	*teaspoons cinnamon*		

Mix together honey, sugar, oil and egg. Mix together flour, soda, salt, cinnamon and nuts. Add to first mixture. It will be very thick. Spray 9 x 12 inch pan with a non-stick cooking spray. Spread dough into pan. Bake in a preheated 350° oven for 20 minutes.

For glaze: Combine all glaze ingredients and mix well. Drizzle over bars while they are still hot. Cut into bars.

Prep. Time: 20 minutes.

YUM YUM BARS

1	package yellow cake mix	8	ounces cream cheese
1	stick margarine, melted	1	egg
2	eggs	1	pound box powdered sugar

Mix cake mix, margarine and eggs together. Spread in greased and floured 9 x 12 inch pan. Batter will be thick. Mix cream cheese, egg and powdered sugar together. Spread on top of cake mixture. Bake in a preheated 350° oven 35 minutes or until golden brown. *Makes 20 squares.*

Prep. Time: 15 minutes.

TEXAROOS

1	6 ounce package butterscotch morsels	1	cup creamy peanut butter
1	6 ounce package semi-sweet morsels	6	cups Rice krispies cereal
1	cup corn syrup		
1	cup sugar		

Melt butterscotch morsels and semi-sweet morsels in double boiler. Combine corn syrup and sugar. Bring to a boil. Remove from heat and add peanut butter. Mix, then add cereal. Press into buttered 9 x 13 inch pan. Spread melted morsels over top. Chill until top is firm. Cut into bars. *Makes 24.*

Prep. Time: 20 minutes.

CHEESECAKE BARS

1	butter recipe cake mix (no substitutes)	1	pound box powdered sugar
4	eggs	1	teaspoon vanilla
1	stick butter, softened		
8	ounces cream cheese, softened		

Mix 1 egg with cake mix and butter. Press into 9 x 13 inch pan. Set aside. Mix softened cream cheese with remaining 3 eggs, powdered sugar and vanilla until smooth. Pour onto the cake and butter mixture. Bake in a preheated 350° oven for 10 minutes. Reduce heat to 325° for 30 to 35 minutes.

Prep. Time: 20 minutes.

FRESH FRUIT PIZZA

1   18 ounce package refrigerated sugar cookies
1   8 ounce package cream cheese
⅓   cup sugar
½   teaspoon vanilla assorted fruits
½   cup orange marmalade, peach or apricot preserves
2   tablespoons water

Cut cookie dough into ⅛ inch thick slices. Line ungreased 14 inch pizza pan with slices overlapping slightly. Bake in a preheated 375° oven for 12 minutes. Cool. Combine softened cream cheese, sugar and vanilla, mixing until well blended. Spread mixture over crust. Arrange fruit over cream cheese layer. Glaze with combined marmalade and water. Chill and cut into wedges. *Makes 10 to 12 servings.*

Prep. Time: 40 to 45 minutes.

LONESOME COWBOY BARS

1   cup sugar
1   cup corn syrup
1 ½ cups crunchy peanut butter
6   cups corn flakes
12   ounces butterscotch chips

Over a medium heat, bring the sugar and syrup to a boil. Stir in the peanut butter. Remove from heat and pour over the corn flakes. Mix well, then pack into a 9 x 13 inch cake pan that has been greased with margarine. In a double boiler over a low heat, melt the butterscotch chips. Spread evenly on top of the cereal mixture. Cool completely and cut into bars. *Makes 30 bars.*

Prep. Time: 30 minutes.

ALMOND SQUARES

2	cups graham cracker crumbs	Topping:	
2	tablespoons brown sugar	1	6 ounce package chocolate chips
½	cup butter, melted	1	6 ounce package butterscotch chips
1	14 ounce can sweetened condensed milk	4	tablespoons butter
		6	tablespoons chunky peanut butter
1	7 ounce package coconut	½	cup almonds, chopped
1	teaspoon vanilla		

Mix graham cracker crumbs, brown sugar and butter. Pat into a greased 9 x 13 inch pan. Bake in a preheated 325° oven for 10 minutes. Cool. Combine next 3 ingredients. Pour over baked crust. Bake at 325° for 25 minutes. Cool.

For topping: Melt topping ingredients in top of double boiler. Spread over baked ingredients. Cool and cut into squares. *Makes 3 dozen.*

Prep. Time: 30 minutes.

HELLO DOLLIES AND HOWDY PARDNERS

1	stick butter	1	cup chocolate chips
1	cup graham cracker crumbs	1	cup pecans, chopped
1	cup coconut	1	14 ounce can sweetened condensed milk
1	cup butterscotch chips		

Melt butter in casserole dish. Layer cracker crumbs, coconut, butterscotch chips, chocolate chips and pecans. Drizzle sweetened condensed milk over this mixture. Bake in a preheated 400° oven for 20 minutes. Cut into squares. *Makes 15 squares.*

Prep. Time: 10 minutes.

Hint: Just as good without the butterscotch.

PEANUT BUTTER BARS

For good ol' goobers.

⅔	cup sugar	3	cups corn flakes
⅔	cup light corn syrup	6	ounces semi-sweet chocolate
1 ½	cups chunky peanut butter	3	ounces butterscotch chips

Combine sugar and corn syrup in saucepan and bring to boil. Remove from heat. Stir in peanut butter. Pour over cereal in bowl and mix well. Spread in greased 9 inch square pan. Melt chocolate and butterscotch chips together. Spread over cereal mixture. Let stand until chocolate is firm. Cut into 2 x 1 inch bars. *Makes 32 candies.*

Prep. Time: 30 minutes.

RANCH SUGAR COOKIES

Cookie:
1 cup sweet butter
3 tablespoons confectioners' sugar
1 ¾ cups flour, divided
1 teaspoon cornstarch

Frosting:
2 tablespoons sweet butter
¾ cup confectioners' sugar
1 teaspoon vanilla
dash of salt
whipping cream

Cream butter thoroughly. Add confectioners' sugar. In a separate bowl, sift together ½ cup of flour and cornstarch. Add to butter mixture. Add remaining unsifted flour. Scoop out a heaping spoonful of dough. Roll into a ball with your hands. Place dough balls 1 inch apart on a lightly greased cookie sheet. Bake in a preheated 350° oven for 15 to 20 minutes until golden brown. Allow to cool.

For frosting: Cream butter, then add confectioners' sugar, vanilla and salt. Add enough whipping cream to make a nice smooth, thick consistency.

Prep. Time: 20 minutes.

MACADAMIA NUT COOKIES

½ cup shortening (butter flavored)
½ cup margarine
2 ½ cups flour
1 cup brown sugar, packed
½ cup sugar
2 eggs
1 teaspoon vanilla
½ teaspoon baking soda
1 package (2 cups) white chocolate chips
3 ½ ounce jar macadamia nuts

In mixing bowl, beat shortening and butter. Add half of flour and mix well. Add brown sugar, sugar, eggs, vanilla and baking soda. Beat until mixture is well combined. Add remaining flour. Mix well and stir in chocolate pieces and nuts. Drop dough by rounded teaspoons, 2 inches apart, onto ungreased cookie sheet. Bake in a preheated 375° oven for about 8 minutes. *Makes 36 to 48 cookies.*

Prep. Time: 20 to 30 minutes.

PEANUT BUTTER COOKIES

1	14 ounce can sweetened condensed milk	2	cups Bisquick
		1	teaspoon vanilla granulated sugar
³⁄₄	cup peanut butter		

Beat milk and peanut butter until smooth. Add Bisquick and vanilla, mix well. Shape into 1 inch balls. Roll in granulated sugar. Place 2 inches apart on ungreased cookie sheet. Flatten with fork. Bake in a preheated 375° oven for 6 to 8 minutes until lightly brown. *Makes 2 dozen.*

Prep. Time: 30 minutes.

PRETTY PARTY COOKIES

2	cups flour, unsifted	1	egg
1 ¹⁄₂	teaspoons baking powder	1	teaspoon almond extract
¹⁄₂	teaspoon salt		red or green food coloring
²⁄₃	cup butter, softened		multicolor nonpareils
1	cup sugar		

Sift flour with baking powder and salt. Set aside. In large bowl, combine butter, sugar, egg and almond extract. Beat until smooth. Add flour mixture, beating at low speed until combined. Turn 1 cup batter into small bowl. Add 2 or 3 drops of food coloring, mix well. On waxed paper, with hands, shape into a roll 10 inches long. Place in freezer for 10 minutes. Roll remaining dough between 2 sheets of waxed paper into a 10 x 6 inch rectangle. Place in freezer 10 minutes. To shape dough, place colored roll length-wise in center of rectangle-shaped dough. With hands, mold white dough around roll, covering completely. If dough is too cold, it will crack. Slightly moisten any cracks with water and work with fingers to close any gaps. Roll in nonpareils, thoroughly covering the roll. Wrap in waxed paper. Place in freezer another 20 minutes or until firm enough to easily slice. Cut into slices ¹⁄₈ inch thick. Place 2 inches apart on ungreased cookie sheets. Bake in a preheated 375° oven for 8 to 10 minutes. *Makes 6 dozen cookies.*

Prep. Time: 30 minutes.

GINGERBREAD COOKIES

One heck of a recipe.

2 cups all-purpose flour, sifted	1 ½ teaspoons cinnamon, ground
½ teaspoon salt	½ teaspoon nutmeg, ground
½ teaspoon baking soda	½ cup shortening, soft
1 teaspoon baking powder	1 cup sugar
1 teaspoon ginger, ground	1 egg yolk
1 teaspoon cloves, ground	½ cup dark molasses

Sift flour, salt, soda, baking powder, ginger, cloves, cinnamon and nutmeg together into a bowl. Work shortening in a bowl until creamy. Add sugar and beat until fluffy. Add egg yolk and molasses. Beat well. Gradually add sifted dry ingredients to molasses mixture. Mix until smooth. Cover and chill at least 1 hour. Divide dough in half. Roll out 1 portion at a time, leaving remainder in the refrigerator. Roll dough on a floured board or pastry cloth to a ¼ inch thickness. Cut with gingerbread man cutter. Place cookies 2 inches apart on a greased cookie sheet. Bake in a preheated 350° oven for 8 to 10 minutes. Remove from oven and cool slightly before removing cookies from cookie sheet. Use your favorite decorator frosting on cookies. *Makes 1 ½ dozen, 5 inch cookies.*

Prep. Time: 30 minutes,
plus 1 hour to refrigerate dough.

GINGER BALL COOKIES

Watch how fast these disappear.

¾ cup vegetable shortening	1 teaspoon cinnamon
1 cup sugar	½ teaspoon cloves, ground
1 egg	1 teaspoon ginger
6 tablespoons molasses	2 cups flour
2 teaspoons baking soda	¼-½ cup sugar

With a mixer on low speed, cream the shortening and sugar. Mix the egg and molasses together, then add to the above mixture and mix well. Mix in the next 4 ingredients and mix well. Slowly mix in the flour. After mixed, roll into 1 inch balls. Roll the balls in the remaining sugar and then place on an ungreased baking sheet. Bake in a 350° preheated oven for 10 to 15 minutes. Don't over bake. Remove from oven and allow to cool. *Makes 4 ½ dozen.*

Prep. Time: 20 minutes.

CHEESECAKE COOKIES

Crust:		Filling:	
⅓	cup butter	¼	cup sugar
⅓	cup brown sugar, packed	8	ounces cream cheese
1	cup flour	1	egg
½	cup pecans, chopped	1	tablespoon lemon juice
		2	tablespoons milk
		½	teaspoon vanilla

Mix all the crust ingredients, blend well. Reserve 1 cup. Pat the rest into a 9 inch square pan. Bake in a preheated 350˚ oven for 12 to 15 minutes.

For filling: Blend sugar and cream cheese until smooth. Add the rest of the ingredients. Pour over the crumb crust. Top with reserved crumbs. Bake at 350˚ for 25 minutes. Cool. Cut into 2 inch squares. *Makes 16 cookies.*

Prep. Time: 15 minutes.

TEXAS-SIZED COOKIES

1	cup brown sugar, packed	½	teaspoon nutmeg
1	cup white sugar	½	teaspoon salt
1 ½	cups flour	3	cups oats
2	teaspoons baking powder	1	cup oil
1	teaspoon soda	2	eggs
½	teaspoon cinnamon	5	tablespoons milk
		1	cup pecans

Mix sugars, flour, baking powder, soda and spices. Add oats. Mix oil, eggs and milk and add to dry ingredients. Stir in pecans. Drop by tablespoons onto ungreased cookie sheets. Bake in a preheated 375˚ oven for 10 to 12 minutes.

Prep. Time: 15 minutes.

OAT CRISPIES

1	cup vegetable shortening, melted	1	cup pecans, chopped
1	cup sugar	1	cup flour, sifted
1	cup brown sugar	1	teaspoon salt
2	eggs, well beaten	1	teaspoon soda
1	teaspoon vanilla	4	cups quick-cooking oats
1	cup coconut, shredded		

Combine shortening, sugar and brown sugar. Add eggs, vanilla, coconut and pecans. Mix together flour, salt, soda and oats. Add to other mixture. Mix well. Shape into 1 inch balls. Place on greased cookie sheet. Bake in a preheated 350˚ oven for 10 minutes. *Makes 9 dozen.*

Prep. Time: 30 minutes.

OATMEAL COOKIES

1	cup brown sugar	½	cup coconut
1	cup shortening	½	cup raisins
1	cup white sugar	1	teaspoon soda
2	eggs	1	teaspoon salt
1 ½	cups flour	2	teaspoons cinnamon
3	cups oats	2	teaspoons nutmeg
½	cup pecans, chopped	1	teaspoon vanilla

Cream together sugars and shortening. Add eggs, beat well. Add rest of ingredients. Blend with spoon. Roll into log, in waxed paper. Place in refrigerator to cool for 30 minutes. Cut in ¼ -inch slices. Bake in a preheated 350˚ oven for 5 to 10 minutes. Can be dropped by spoonfuls on greased pan rather than being rolled. *Makes 3 dozen.*

Prep. Time: 30 minutes.

PRALINE COOKIES

1	cup sugar	1	cup graham cracker crumbs
1	stick oleo		
½	cup evaporated milk	1	cup nuts
10	large marshmallows		

Combine sugar, oleo and evaporated milk in saucepan. Boil for 6 minutes. Remove from heat. Add marshmallows, graham cracker crumbs and nuts. Mix until marshmallows are melted. Quickly drop onto waxed paper to cool. *Makes 1 ½ dozen.*

Prep. Time: 10 minutes.

PECAN PIE COOKIE

1	cup flour	1 ½	cups brown sugar
1	stick margarine	2	tablespoons light corn syrup
3	tablespoons powdered sugar		
		1	teaspoon vanilla
⅓	cup pecans		dash of salt
2	eggs	1	cup pecans, chopped
1	tablespoon flour		

Combine flour, margarine, powdered sugar and pecans. Mix well. Pat into 9 x 9 inch greased and floured pan. Bake in a preheated 400˚ oven for 10 minutes. Remove from oven. Beat eggs. Add flour, sugar, light corn syrup, vanilla, salt and pecans. Pour over warm crust. Reduce the oven heat to 350˚. Return to oven and bake 20 minutes. Cool and cut into squares.

Prep. Time: 10 minutes.

MOLASSES COOKIES

¾	cup shortening, melted	2	teaspoons soda
1	cup sugar	2	cups flour
¼	cup molasses	½	teaspoon cloves
1	egg	½	teaspoon cinnamon
		½	teaspoon salt

Melt shortening and let cool. Add sugar, molasses and egg. Beat well. Sift together flour, spices, soda. Add to first mixture. Chill. Form into 1 inch balls. Roll in sugar and place on greased cookie sheet. Bake in a preheated 375° oven for 8 to 10 minutes. *Makes 4 dozen.*

Prep. Time: 20 minutes.

CRITTER COOKIES

The very best cut-out cookie recipe.

3	cups flour	2	eggs
4	teaspoons baking powder	½	teaspoon salt
½	cup sugar	3	tablespoons vanilla (yes, 3 tablespoons of vanilla)
2	sticks margarine, softened		

Mix flour and baking powder. Cream remaining ingredients together. Slowly stir in flour. Generously flour board, rolling pin and cookie cutter. Roll dough to ½ inch thickness. Cut with cookie cutter. Bake in a preheated 350° oven for 8 to 10 minutes.

Prep. Time: 30 minutes.

BROWN-EYED SUSANS

1	cup butter, softened	*Icing:*	
2	cups flour	1	cup powdered sugar
1	teaspoon almond extract	2	tablespoons cocoa
		2	tablespoons hot water
2	tablespoons sugar	1	teaspoons vanilla

Cream butter, flour, almond extract and sugar together. Roll small amounts of dough into balls. Flatten slightly with thumb or base of spoon. Bake in a preheated 350° oven for 8 to 10 minutes or until bottoms are golden brown.

For icing: Mix the icing somewhat thick. Ice each cookie. *Makes 3 dozen.*

Prep. Time: 45 minutes.

Hint: *Flour your hands before rolling the dough. Pour icing into a plastic storage bag. Poke a small hole in corner of bag. Squeeze icing onto cookies.*

WEST TEXAS SNOW BALLS

1	cup butter or margarine	2	cups flour
		1	teaspoon vanilla
3	tablespoons powdered sugar	1	teaspoon ice water
		2	cups pecans

Cream butter and sugar. Add flour. Stir in remaining ingredients. Shape in small balls. Bake in a preheated 375° oven for 10 minutes. Roll hot cookies in powdered sugar.

Prep. Time: 30 minutes.

SUGAR COOKIES AND ICING

2	cups flour	*Icing:*
1/4	teaspoon salt	1 cup powdered sugar
1/2	teaspoon baking	1 egg white
	powder	*few drops lemon juice*
1/2	cup butter	
1	cup sugar	
1	egg	
2	tablespoons brandy	
1/2	teaspoon vanilla	

Sift together dry ingredients. In separate bowl, cream butter and sugar. Add egg, brandy and vanilla. Beat well. Add dry ingredients a little at a time. Mix until well blended. Wrap and chill dough for 30 minutes before rolling. On a lightly floured surface, roll out 1/3 of the dough at a time. Place shapes on buttered sheets. Bake in a preheated 400° oven for 10 minutes. Do not allow to brown. Cool.

For icing: Mix icing ingredients until smooth. Coloring may be added. Spread on cooled cookies. *Makes 40 cookies.*

Prep. Time: 20 minutes,
              plus 20 minutes to chill the dough.

LEMONY CUT-OUT COOKIES

1	cup margarine	*Frostings:*
2	cups sugar	3 egg whites at room
3	eggs	temperature
2	tablespoons buttermilk	1/2 teaspoon cream
5	cups flour	of tartar
1	teaspoon soda	16 ounce package
1 1/2	teaspoons fresh lemon	powdered sugar
	rind	
1	teaspoon lemon	
	extract	

Cream margarine and sugar. Add eggs one at a time. Add buttermilk. Combine soda, flour and lemon rind. Stir in lemon extract. Refrigerate 4 hours. Roll to 1/8 inch thick. Bake on a greased cookie sheet 6 to 7 minutes in a preheated 400° oven. Cool on rack.

For frosting: Mix egg whites until frothy. Add cream of tartar. Slowly add sifted powdered sugar. Beat at least 5 minutes—7 minutes is preferable. Use pastry tubes and tips to decorate cookies. Keep covered. *Makes 4 to 5 dozen.*

Prep. Time: 30 minutes,
              plus 4 hours to chill the dough.

Hint: *Frosting will decorate 20 cookies.*

CAKE MIX COOKIES

1	18 ounce package cake mix, any flavor without pudding	4	ounces non-dairy whipped topping
1	egg	1	pound box powdered sugar
			jelly beans

Grease cookie sheets. Combine cake mix, egg and non-dairy topping. Mix well. The mixture will be very sticky and thick. Drop into the powdered sugar by the teaspoon. Roll in balls and coat well with the sugar. Place 1½ inches apart on the greased cookie sheet. Bake in a preheated 350° oven for 10 to 15 minutes, or until light brown. Decorate with jelly beans. *Makes 4 dozen.*

Prep. Time: 10 minutes.

COOKIES CAKE

2	cups flour	*Icing:*	
2	cups sugar	1	stick margarine
1	teaspoon soda	3 ½	tablespoons chocolate syrup
3 ½	tablespoons chocolate syrup	⅓	cup sweet milk
1	stick margarine	1	box powdered sugar, sifted (3 cups)
½	cup shortening		
1	cup water	1	cup nuts
⅓	cup buttermilk	1	teaspoon vanilla
2	eggs, beaten		
1	teaspoon vanilla		

Mix flour, sugar and soda. Set aside. Bring to boil the chocolate syrup and margarine. Then add shortening and water. Pour over dry ingredients. Then add buttermilk, eggs and vanilla. Mix well. Bake in greased and floured cookie sheet at 350° for 20 to 30 minutes.

For icing: Bring to boil the margarine, chocolate syrup and milk. Add rest of icing ingredients. Mix well. Pour over while cake is still hot.

Prep. Time: 30 minutes.

ANGEL FOOD CAKE ICING

3	cups whipping cream (1 ½ pints)	1	3 ounce package raspberry gelatin
½	cup sugar	1	angel food cake (can be store -bought)

Beat cream until almost stiff. Gradually add sugar, beat until stiff. Slowly add gelatin, beating until all is absorbed. Cut angel food cake horizontally into three layers. Put filling between layers and over cake. Serve immediately. Refrigerate any leftovers.

Prep. Time: 5 minutes.

PLUM CAKE

Cake:

2	cups sugar	½	teaspoon salt
1	cup vegetable oil	½	teaspoon soda
3	eggs	2	teaspoons red food color
1	pound can Oregon purple plums, drained, pitted & chopped	1	cup pecans, chopped
2	cups flour		*Glaze:*
1	teaspoon cinnamon	1	small can frozen orange juice
½	teaspoon cloves	1	cup sugar

Mix ingredients in order given. Pour into greased and floured bundt pan. Bake in a preheated 350° oven for 45 minutes. Meanwhile, bring the orange juice and sugar to boil. Punch holes in cake and pour glaze over it. Pour the glaze while it is still hot.

Prep. Time: 20 minutes.

Hint: 1 large jar red plum baby food can be used instead of chopped plums.

ANGEL FOOD CAKE

1 ¼	cups confectioners' sugar	1 ½	teaspoons cream of tartar
1	cup cake flour	¼	teaspoon salt
1 ½	cups egg whites (12 to 14 egg whites), at room temperature	¼	teaspoon almond extract
		1	cup sugar

In a small bowl, stir confectioners' sugar and cake flour. Set aside. Add egg whites, cream of tartar, vanilla extract, salt and almond extract to large bowl and beat until well mixed. Beating at high speed, sprinkle in sugar, 2 tablespoons at a time. Beat just until sugar dissolves and whites form stiff peaks. Do not scrape bowl during beating. With rubber spatula, fold in flour mixture, about ¼ at a time, just until flour disappears. Pour mixture into ungreased 10-inch tube pan. With spatula, cut through batter to break any large air bubbles. Bake in a preheated oven at 375° for 35 minutes or until top of cake springs back when lightly touched. Any cracks on the surface should look dry. Invert cake in pan on a funnel; cool completely. With spatula, loosen cake from pan and remove to plate.

Prep. Time: 20 to 30 minutes.

LUSCIOUS LEMON DESSERT

1st Layer:
2   sticks melted butter
2   cups flour
2   cups pecans, chopped

2nd Layer:
8   ounce package cream
     cheese
1   cup non-dairy
     whipped topping
1   cup powdered sugar,
     sifted

3rd Layer:
1   14 ounce can
     condensed milk
3   egg yolks
½   cup lemon juice

non-dairy topping
pecans, chopped

Mix 1st layer ingredients and place in bottom of 9 x 13 inch pan. Bake in a preheated 350° oven for 15 minutes. Cool completely. Mix together 2nd layer ingredients and place on cooled first layer. Mix together 3rd layer ingredients and put on top of second layer. Top with non-dairy topping and chopped pecans. Chill and serve. *Makes 12 servings.*

Prep. Time: 30 minutes.

APPLESAUCE CAKE

½   cup shortening
1   cup sugar
1   egg
1   can applesauce
2   cups flour
2   teaspoons soda

1   teaspoon cloves
1   teaspoon allspice
1   teaspoon cinnamon
½   cup pecans, chopped
     (optional)

Cream together shortening, sugar and egg. Add applesauce and mix. In separate bowl, sift together flour and soda. Add to mixture and mix well. Add spices and mix until well blended. Bake in a preheated 350° oven for 30 to 40 minutes.

Prep. Time: 10 minutes.

RING CAKE

2   cups sugar
1   stick butter or
     margarine
6   eggs, beaten
12   ounces vanilla wafers,
     crushed

2   cups pecans
7   ounces coconut
2   teaspoons vanilla

Cream sugar and butter. Add beaten eggs. Add vanilla wafers and mix well. Add pecans, coconut and vanilla. Bake in greased and floured tube pan in a preheated 350° oven for 1 ½ hours.

Prep. Time: 30 minutes.

BANANA SPLIT CAKE

Crust:
2   cups graham
    cracker crumbs
½   cup margarine,
    melted

Filling:
1   cup margarine,
    melted
2   cups powdered
    sugar
2   eggs

Topping:
4   bananas
1   20 ounce can
    crushed pineapple,
    well drained
1   12 ounce container
    non-dairy topping
¾   cup cherries, chopped
¾   cup pecans, chopped

Mix crust ingredients. Line a 9 x 13 inch cake pan. Bake in a preheated 350° oven for 5 minutes.

For filling: Cream margarine and powdered sugar. Add eggs and beat 15 minutes, no exceptions. Spread over crumb crust.   Refrigerate 15 minutes.

For topping: Slice bananas and place on top of custard. Spread crushed pineapple on top of bananas.   Spread with non-dairy topping, sealing edges.   Sprinkle with nuts and cherries. Keep refrigerated. Cut into squares to serve.

Prep. Time: 35 minutes.

STRAWBERRY CAKE

1   package white
    cake mix
1   small package
    strawberry gelatin
4   eggs, separated &
    beaten
½   cup vegetable oil
½   cup water
½   large package frozen
    strawberries, thawed

Icing:
1   package powdered
    sugar
1   stick margarine,
    melted & cooled
½   large package frozen
    strawberries, thawed

Combine all cake ingredients but egg whites. Beat 4 minutes. Fold in beaten egg whites. Pour into greased and floured jelly roll pan. Bake in a preheated 350° oven for 30 minutes.

For icing: Mix all icing ingredients. Do not allow to become too thin when adding strawberries. Ice cooled cake.

Prep. Time: 10 minutes.

CHERRY PUDDING CAKE

2	cups sugar	2	eggs
2	cups flour	1	cup pecans, chopped
¼	teaspoon salt	1	16 ounce box brown
1	16 ounce can dark		sugar
	red cherries & juice	2	tablespoons flour
2	teaspoons baking	2	cups plus 2
	soda (1 ½ teaspoons		tablespoons hot water
	in high altitudes)	2	teaspoons vanilla
2	tablespoons water	½	teaspoon salt
2	tablespoons		
	margarine, melted		

In a large bowl, combine sugar, flour and salt. Stir cherries in by hand. Combine baking soda and water until mixed and add to cake mixture. Add margarine, eggs and pecans and mix until smooth. Pour into a 9 x 13 x 2 inch cake pan that has been lightly greased and floured. Bake in a preheated 350° oven for 40 minutes. While cake is baking, in a large saucepan, combine brown sugar and flour mixing well. Stir in hot water, vanilla and salt. Bring to a boil over a medium-high heat, stirring constantly. Simmer for 2 minutes. Pour this mixture over hot cake.

Prep. Time: 20 minutes.

PINEAPPLE SHEET CAKE

Cake:		Icing:	
2	cups sugar	1	8 ounce package
2	cups flour		cream cheese
¼	teaspoon salt	¼	cup margarine,
2	teaspoons baking		melted
	soda	1	teaspoon vanilla
2	eggs	1 ¾	cup powdered sugar
1	16 ounce can crushed	¼	cup walnuts,
	pineapple & juice		finely chopped
1	teaspoon vanilla		
½	cup walnuts, finely		
	chopped		

In a large mixing bowl, combine sugar, flour, salt and baking soda. Stir in eggs. Add pineapple, pineapple juice and vanilla. Beat until thoroughly mixed. Stir in walnuts. Pour into a lightly greased and floured 11 x 17 x 1 inch sheet cake pan. Bake in a preheated 350° oven for 20 minutes.

For icing: Place cream cheese, margarine and vanilla in a mixer and beat until creamy. Add powdered sugar and continue to beat until smooth. Stir in walnuts. Spread on warm cake.

Prep. Time: 20 minutes.

BUTTER CAKE WITH BUTTER SAUCE

3	cups flour	2	teaspoons vanilla
1	teaspoon baking	1	cup nuts
	powder		
1	teaspoon salt		Butter Sauce:
½	teaspoon baking soda	1	cup sugar
1	cup butter	½	cup butter
2	cups sugar	¼	cup water
4	eggs	1	tablespoon vanilla
1	cup buttermilk		

Mix all cake ingredients thoroughly with electric mixer. Pour into greased and floured bundt or tube pan. Bake in a preheated 350° oven for 60 to 65 minutes.

For butter sauce: Melt all the butter sauce ingredients in saucepan and pour over cake while hot.

Prep. Time: 20 minutes.

COCONUT CAKE

1	package yellow cake		Topping:
	mix, without pudding	1	can cream of coconut
1	cup water	1	cup coconut
2	eggs		non-dairy topping
1	can crushed pineapple,		
	drained		
1	cup coconut		

Mix together cake ingredients. Bake in a 9 x 13 inch pan in a preheated 350° oven for 30 minutes or until cake leaves sides of pan. While cake is hot, punch holes in top of cake.

For topping: Cover with cream of coconut. Cool completely. Mix coconut and non-dairy topping and spread on cake. Refrigerate for 12 hours.

Prep. Time: 15 minutes,
plus 12 hours to refrigerate cake.

FRUIT COCKTAIL CAKE

2	cups flour	1	cup margarine
1 ½	cups sugar	1	12 ounce can
1 ½	teaspoons baking soda		evaporated milk
½	teaspoon salt	2	cups sugar
2	eggs	1	teaspoon vanilla
1	16 ounce can fruit	1	cup coconut
	cocktail	1	cup pecans, chopped

In a large bowl, combine flour, sugar, baking soda and salt. Stir in eggs by hand. Add fruit cocktail and mix until smooth. Pour into a 9 x 13 x 2 inch cake pan that has been lightly greased and floured. Bake in a preheated 325° oven for 45 minutes.

While cake is baking, in a large saucepan, melt margarine. Add evaporated milk and sugar. Bring to a boil over a medium-high heat, stirring constantly. Simmer for 8 minutes. Remove from heat and stir in vanilla, coconut and pecans. Pour this mixture over hot cake.

Prep. Time: 20 minutes.

CHRISTMAS COCONUT CAKE

Cake:
2	cups all-purpose flour
1 ½	cups granulated sugar
2 ½	teaspoons baking powder
1	teaspoon salt
½	cup shortening
1	cup milk
1	teaspoon vanilla
4	egg whites
⅔	cup coconut, flaked

Tutti-frutti filling:
2	egg yolks
⅔	cup sour cream
⅔	cup sugar
1	cup pecans, finely chopped
⅔	cup coconut, flaked
½	cup raisins, finely chopped
½	cup candied cherries, finely chopped

Frosting for top and sides of cake:
1	cup whipping cream, chilled
¼	cup powdered sugar
¾	teaspoon almond extract

B eat the first seven cake ingredients in large bowl on low speed for 30 seconds, scraping bowl constantly. Beat on high speed for 2 minutes, scraping bowl occasionally. On high speed, beat in egg whites for 2 minutes, scraping bowl occasionally. Stir in coconut. Pour into 2 greased and floured 9 inch round pans. Bake in a preheated 350° oven for 30 to 35 minutes. Cool 10 minutes. Remove from pans. Cool completely.

For filling: Mix egg yolks and sour cream, then stir in sugar. Cook over low heat until mixture begins to simmer, stirring constantly. Continue to stir and simmer until mixture begins to thicken. Remove from heat. Stir in remaining ingredients. Cool. Spread filling to within one inch of edge of bottom layer.

For frosting: Beat whipping cream, powdered sugar and almond extract in chilled bowl until stiff. Spread side of cake with whipped cream mixture. Using decorator's tube, pipe remaining whipped cream mixture around top edge of cake.

Prep. Time: 1 hour.

GOOEY COCONUT CAKE

This recipe has won at two Permian Basin Fairs.

Cake:
1	cup shortening
2	cups sugar
1	teaspoon vanilla
4	eggs
1	cup milk
3	cups flour
2	teaspoons baking powder

Coconut icing:
1	cup sugar
2	teaspoons flour
1 ½	cups milk
1	teaspoon vanilla
1	egg white
½	cup coconut

C ream shortening, sugar and vanilla. Add eggs, 1 at a time. Add milk alternately with dry ingredients. Bake in a 9 x 13 inch greased and floured pan, in a preheated 350° oven for 25 to 30 minutes.

For icing: Cook sugar, flour, milk and vanilla until it starts to thicken. Beat egg white and pour sauce over it. Add coconut. Punch holes into cake. Pour hot icing over it. Sprinkle with more coconut.

Prep. Time: 15 minutes.

SOUR CREAM CAKE

1	cup butter, softened	1	teaspoon baking
2	eggs		powder
2	cups sugar	1 ½	cups pecans, chopped
1	cup sour cream	½	teaspoon cinnamon
½	teaspoon vanilla	½	cup powdered sugar
2	cups cake flour		

Cream butter and eggs. Add vanilla, sour cream and dry ingredients. Combine pecans, cinnamon and powdered sugar in separate bowl. Grease and flour a tube pan. Pour half the batter in pan. Sprinkle half the pecan, powdered sugar and cinnamon mixture on top. Then add remaining batter. Sprinkle remaining pecan, powdered sugar and cinnamon mixture on top. Bake in a preheated 350° oven for 1 hour.

Prep. Time: 30 minutes.

WILD WEST DATE LOAF

1	pound dates, chopped & pitted	1	teaspoon cinnamon
		1	teaspoon cloves, ground
2	cups hot water		
1	cup shortening	1	teaspoon nutmeg
2	cups sugar	1	teaspoon baking powder
2	cups flour		
1	teaspoon soda	1	cup nuts, chopped

Place dates in saucepan, cover with hot water. Bring to boil and boil 3 minutes. Add shortening and sugar. Cool. Mix together flour, soda, cinnamon, cloves, nutmeg and baking powder. Add to date mixture. Add nuts. Grease and flour pan. Bake in a preheated 350° oven for 1 hour.

Prep. Time: 15 to 20 minutes.

DIRT CAKE

1	16 ounce package Oreo cookies	2	small packages (3.5 ounces each) vanilla instant pudding
1	8 ounce package cream cheese	3	cups milk
1	stick (½ cup) margarine or butter	1	teaspoon vanilla
1	cup confectioners' sugar		
8	ounces non-dairy whipped topping		

Crush cookies and put half of crumbs in 9 x 13 inch pan. In a separate bowl, mix cream cheese and margarine until smooth. Mix in confectioners' sugar. Fold in non-dairy topping. In separate bowl, mix together pudding, milk and vanilla. Fold cream cheese mixture into pudding mixture. Pour in pan on top of crumbs. Sprinkle remaining crumbs on top. Refrigerate to set.

Prep. Time: 30 to 40 minutes.

Hint: *Serve in a clean clay pot with flowers on top.*

CREAM CHEESE CAKE

1 box butter recipe golden cake mix	1 box powdered sugar
2 eggs	2 eggs
1 stick margarine, melted	1 8 ounce package cream cheese

Mix cake mix, eggs and margarine. Pour into a greased and floured 9 x 13 inch cake pan. In a separate bowl, mix powdered sugar, eggs and cream cheese. Drop by spoonfuls on the top of the cake mixture. Bake in a preheated 350° oven for 45 to 50 minutes. Do not over bake. The middle of the cake will be very soft until it cools. Cool completely and cut into squares. *Makes 36 small bars.*

Prep. Time: 30 minutes.

POPPY SEED CAKE

1 package yellow cake mix	1 box instant vanilla pudding
4 eggs	¼ cup poppy seeds
½ cup margarine	½ cup pecans, chopped (1 cup if needed)
1 cup water	whipped cream

Place all ingredients except the nuts, in a mixing bowl. Beat 3 to 4 minutes. Fold in the pecans. Bake in a preheated 350° oven for 50 to 60 minutes in a bundt pan. Cool 10 minutes before removing from the pan. Serve with fresh whipped cream.

Prep. Time: 15 minutes.

CHEESECAKE

4 eggs	½ cup whipping cream
1 ¾ cups sugar	½ package graham crackers (about 12)
2 pounds cream cheese	strawberries
1 tablespoon vanilla	

Beat all ingredients, except graham crackers, at medium speed until creamy. Dust a heavily buttered bundt cake pan with crushed graham crackers. Pour in mixture and shake down. Place pan within another pan filled with boiling water. Bake in a preheated 300° oven for 2 hours. Remove to serving place and let stand. Cake will settle. Serve chilled with strawberries.

Prep. Time: 45 minutes.

BLUEBERRY CREAM CHEESE COFFEECAKE

½	cup brown sugar	2	tablespoons milk
2	tablespoons cinnamon	1	3 ounce package
1	13 ounce blueberry		cream cheese
	muffin mix	3	tablespoons
¼	cup flour		margarine
2	eggs		

Mix cinnamon and brown sugar, set aside. Mix muffin mix, flour, eggs and milk. Pour ½ in pan. Cut cream cheese in cubes, dip in melted margarine, cinnamon mixture then margarine. Lay cubes on top of batter mixture in pan. Pour in rest of the batter to cover. Sprinkle on blueberries and remaining butter and cinnamon mixture. Bake in 8 inch square or 9 x 13 inch oblong pan. Bake in a preheated 350° oven for 20 to 24 minutes.

Prep. Time: 15 minutes.

Hint: Cream cheese does not melt, but stays lumpy.

BUTTER CAKE

Cake:		*Icing:*	
2	cups sugar	1	cup sugar
1	cup butter	¼	cup water
3	cups flour	½	cup butter
1	teaspoon baking	1	tablespoon vanilla
	powder		or rum flavoring
1	teaspoon salt		
½	teaspoon soda		
4	eggs		
1	cup buttermilk		
2	teaspoons vanilla		

Grease and flour tube pan. Combine sugar and butter, mix well. Add flour, baking powder, salt, soda, eggs, buttermilk and vanilla. Pour in tube pan. Bake in a preheated 325° oven for 1 hour or until top springs back when lightly touched.

For icing: Combine icing ingredients and bring to a boil. Pour over hot cake. Cool completely before removing from pan.

Prep. Time: 30 minutes.

CHERRIES IN THE SNOW

A rare Texas treat.

2	envelopes whipped	1	cup powdered sugar
	topping (1.3 ounces	1	baked angel
	each envelope)		food cake
1	cup cold milk	1	16 ounce can cherry
1	tablespoon vanilla		pie filling
8	ounces cream cheese		

Beat first three ingredients. Set aside. Beat cream cheese until soft and creamy. Add powdered sugar and whipped topping. Blend well. Spread half of mixture in 9 x 13 inch dish. Slice angel food cake ½ inch thick and lay on top. Add other half of mixture. Top with the pie filling. *Makes 10 servings.*

Prep. Time: 30 minutes.

BUTTER ICING

1 ½	cups sugar	1	teaspoon vanilla
½	stick margarine (¼ cup)		pinch of salt
1	small can evaporated milk		

Mix all ingredients into a saucepan and cook until thickened. Stir constantly and beat until it looks like icing, not glossy. *Makes icing for one bundt cake.*

Prep. Time: 5 minutes.

REAL BUTTER POUND CAKE

2	sticks butter	2	teaspoons baking powder
4	eggs, separate & beat whites	1 ¼	cup buttermilk
2	cups sugar	¼	teaspoon soda
3	cups flour	3	teaspoons vanilla
¼	teaspoon salt		

Cream butter and beat in yolks. Mix sugar, flour, salt and baking powder. Mix buttermilk, soda and vanilla and add alternately with flour mixture to butter mixture. Fold in beaten egg whites. Pour into greased and floured bundt pan. Bake in a preheated 325° oven for 1 hour.

Prep. Time: 20 minutes.

CARAMEL APPLE POUND CAKE

16	light caramels	3 ¼	cups flour, sifted
1 ½	cups butter or margarine, softened	2	teaspoons cinnamon
4 ½	cups confectioners' sugar, sifted	1	teaspoon allspice, ground
1	tablespoon vanilla	1 ½	cups cooking apples, peeled & coarsely chopped
6	eggs		

Using kitchen shears or sharp knife, cut each caramel into eight pieces, set aside. In large bowl, cream butter, sugar and vanilla until light and fluffy. Add eggs, one at a time, beating well after each. Sift together flour, cinnamon and allspice. Add gradually to creamed mixture, blend until thoroughly combined. By hand, stir in caramels and chopped apple. Bake in greased and lightly floured 12 cup bundt pan in a preheated 325° oven for 1 ¼ to 1 ½ hours or until cake tests done. Cool in pan 10 to 15 minutes. Turn out on a wire rack or serving plate to complete cooling. Serve warm or cool. If desired, top with ice cream and caramel ice cream topping.

Prep. Time: 30 minutes.

CREAM CHEESE FROSTING

1	large package cream cheese	1	teaspoon vanilla
1	16 ounce box powdered sugar	1	14 ounce can coconut

Cream together the cream cheese, powdered sugar and vanilla. Stir in the coconut. Spread evenly on a cooled cake.

Prep. Time: 10 minutes.

BUTTERMILK POUND CAKE

1	cup shortening	¹/₂	teaspoon soda	
2	cups sugar	1	cup buttermilk	
4	eggs	1	teaspoon vanilla	
2	cups flour	1	teaspoon lemon	
¹/₄	teaspoon salt		extract	

Cream shortening, sugar and eggs. Add next 3 ingredients. Add buttermilk and vanilla and lemon extract. Stir until batter is fairly smooth. Pour batter into well greased and floured tube or bundt pan. Bake in a preheated 325° oven for 45 minutes or until done.

Prep. Time: 15 minutes.

MOST WONDERFUL POUND CAKE

3	sticks unsalted butter	6	eggs	
1	8 ounce package cream cheese	¹/₂	teaspoon salt	
		3	cups flour	
3	cups sugar	1	teaspoon vanilla	

Cream butter and cream cheese together. Add sugar and beat until creamy. Add eggs 1 at a time. Add salt and flour, mix slowly. Add vanilla. Pour in greased and floured pan. A bundt pan works okay but this cake comes out wonderfully in an oblong 16 x 5 x 5 inch pan. Bake in a preheated 325° oven for 1 hour and 45 minutes. *Makes 12 to 16 servings.*

Prep. Time: 30 minutes.

TOASTED ALMOND CRUNCH

¹/₂	cup corn oil margarine (do not substitute anything else for this or the recipe will not set up correctly!!)	¹/₂	cup almonds, coarsely chopped (toasted & blanched if you can find them)	
²/₃	cup sugar	¹/₂	pound chocolate	
1 ¹/₂	tablespoons water	¹/₄	stick paraffin	
2	teaspoons light corn syrup	¹/₄	cup almonds, finely chopped	

In a heavy saucepan, melt the margarine. Stir in the sugar, water, corn syrup, and almonds. Over a medium-high heat, cook until it reaches a hard crack stage (290°). Stir only slightly to keep from burning. Mixture will turn to a golden color. Pour the mixture into a 8 x 8 inch pan that has been greased with corn oil. Allow to cool completely. Once cool, carefully turn the candy out onto waxed paper. In a double boiler, melt the chocolate and paraffin. Remove from heat and stir until nearly cool. Spread half of the chocolate on one side of the candy and sprinkle with ¹/₈ cup of the almonds. Lay another piece of waxed paper on top of the candy and turn it over. Spread the other half of the chocolate on candy and sprinkle the remaining almonds on top. Allow to cool completely then break into bite-sized pieces.

Prep. Time: 30 minutes.

GOOBER BRITTLE

3	cups sugar	2	tablespoons butter
1	cup white corn syrup	1	teaspoon salt
1	cup water	1	tablespoon soda
2 ½	cups raw Spanish peanuts		

Cook sugar, corn syrup and water until it forms a hard ball in cool water or candy thermometer registers 250° to 260° F. Add unblanched peanuts and continue to cook until the mixture turns a golden brown or candy thermometer registers 300°F. Remove from heat and stir in butter, salt and soda. Pour on a greased large area and pull out to a thin sheet. Break into pieces when cold.

Prep. Time: 30 to 40 minutes.

POPCORN BALLS

2	cups unpopped popcorn	1	cup margarine
2	cups sugar	1	teaspoon vanilla
1	cup white corn syrup	⅛	teaspoon salt
1	cup whipping cream, unwhipped		

Pop popcorn first. Combine sugar, syrup and whipping cream. Add margarine. Cook over medium heat so mixture is boiling. Stir constantly. Cook until syrup makes a soft ball in cold water. Add vanilla and salt. Combine syrup and popped corn. Place baggies on hands and form balls. Cool in single layer. *Makes 2 dozen popcorn balls.*

Prep. Time: 1 hour.

MICROWAVE PEANUT BRITTLE

1	cup sugar	1	teaspoon vanilla
½	cup white corn syrup	1	teaspoon baking soda
1	cup peanuts		
1	teaspoon margarine		

In a 1 ½ quart casserole dish, mix the sugar and corn syrup. Microwave on high for 3 to 5 minutes. Stir in peanuts. Microwave on high until the peanuts are lightly browned, about 3 to 5 minutes. Stir in the margarine and vanilla. Microwave on high 1 to 2 minutes. Stir in the baking soda and immediately pour onto a cookie sheet that has been greased with butter. Allow to cool completely. Break into small pieces.

Prep. Time: 15 minutes.

CINNAMON STICKS

1	cup butter	1	teaspoon cinnamon
1	cup sugar	1	teaspoon vanilla
2	cups flour	1	egg white
1	egg yolk	1	cup pecans

Mix first six ingredients. Press on cookie sheet ½ inch thick. Spread unbeaten egg white over top of mixture and press in pecans. Bake in a preheated 350° oven for 25 to 30 minutes. *Makes 36 bars.*

Prep. Time: 15 minutes.

PRALINES

¾	stick margarine	¼	cup corn syrup
1	cup brown sugar	1 ½	cups pecans, coarsely
1	cup granulated sugar		chopped
5	tablespoons milk	1	teaspoon vanilla

In a cast iron skillet, bring first five ingredients to a rolling boil. Boil 1 minute. Remove from heat, stir in vanilla and pecans. Beat candy until it looses its shine and starts to harden. With 2 teaspoons, drop on wax paper. If candy gets too hard to finish dropping, you may put it back on the stove on low heat to melt. *Makes 30 pieces.*

Prep. Time: 20 minutes.

BUTTERMILK PRALINES

2	cups sugar	2	cups pecans, large
1	cup buttermilk		broken pieces
1	teaspoon soda	2	tablespoons butter
⅛	teaspoon salt	1	teaspoon vanilla

Mix first four ingredients in large pan. Bring to rolling boil over medium-high heat. Turn to low heat immediately, and continue to boil until it becomes a light brown color. Stir and watch as this will boil over unattended. Add pecans and continue cooking to soft ball stage. Stir to keep from over-browning on bottom of pan. (Be sure to cook long enough here or candy will not harden; be sure of soft ball stage.) After adding pecans, turn to medium-high heat briefly, and then down to medium-low. Take from heat after reaching soft ball stage and add butter and vanilla. Beat until creamy and drop by spoonfuls onto wax paper or parchment paper. Use wooden spoon.

Prep. Time: 1 hour.

RUM RUM BALLS

36	vanilla wafers, finely crushed	1	tablespoon white corn syrup
1	cup powdered sugar	1	tablespoon cocoa powdered sugar
1	cup walnuts or pecans, chopped		
6	tablespoons rum (or to taste)		

Combine first six ingredients. Roll into balls approximately 1 inch in diameter. Dip into powdered sugar. Store in tightly covered tins.

Prep. Time: 30 minutes.

Hint: Crush vanilla wafers in plastic bag with rolling pin or in a blender. Shake rolled balls gently in plastic bag with powdered sugar. Do not store in refrigerator.

COCONUT MACAROONS

1	egg white	½	cup coconut, shredded
½	cup sugar		
¼	teaspoon salt	1	cup corn flakes
½	teaspoon vanilla		

Beat egg white until stiff. Gradually beat in sugar. Add salt and vanilla, and mix well. Fold in coconut and corn flakes. Drop heaping teaspoonfuls on oiled baking sheet. Bake in a preheated 350° oven for 20 minutes, until surface is dry. Do not allow to burn. Remove from pan while warm. *Makes 12 macaroons.*

Prep. Time: 15 minutes.

WHITE WALNUT CANDY

1	cup sugar	¼	teaspoon vanilla
⅓	cup sour cream	2	cups English walnuts, room temperature
⅛	teaspoon salt		
1	tablespoon white corn syrup		
1	tablespoon margarine		

Combine first four ingredients and heat to a soft ball stage. Continue to cook for 5 minutes at this stage. Stir constantly. Remove from heat. Add margarine and vanilla, stir well. Cool slightly and add walnuts. Drop by spoonfuls onto wax paper to cool.

Prep. Time: 30 minutes.

DIVINITY CANDY

So divine.

2	egg whites	2	cups sugar
pinch of baking powder		1	teaspoon vanilla
½	cup corn syrup	½	cup pecans, chopped
½	cup water		

In a big bowl, beat egg whites and baking powder until they stand in peaks. Cook corn syrup, water and sugar to threading, stirring frequently, on a medium-low heat. Pour half of syrup mixture slowly over egg whites, beating and moving constantly. Continue beating and replace remaining syrup on decreased heat until egg white mixture is thoroughly mixed. Pour remaining syrup into egg white mixture quickly as you continue to heat. As it cools down, add vanilla. When it is cool, add pecans and drop when it will drop onto paper without running.

Prep. Time: 15 to 20 minutes.

NO COOK DIVINITY

1	package fluffy white frosting mix	½	cup boiling water
⅓	cup light corn syrup	1	16 ounce package powdered sugar
1	teaspoon vanilla	1	cup nuts, chopped

Combine first four ingredients in large mixer bowl. Beat for 5 minutes on highest speed until stiff peaks form. On low speed, or by hand, gradually blend in powdered sugar. Stir in nuts. Drop mixture by teaspoonfuls, onto waxed paper. When outside of candy feels firm, turn over and allow to dry. Store candy in airtight container. *Makes 5 to 6 dozen pieces.*

Prep. Time: 20 to 30 minutes.

DATE LOAF CANDY

2	cups sugar	1	teaspoon vanilla
1/4	pound margarine	2	cups pecans,
1/2	cup milk		chopped
1	cup dates, chopped		

Cook sugar, margarine and milk with dates a little more than soft ball stage. Remove from heat. Add vanilla, pecans and beat. Put on 2 damp cloths. Roll into 2 rolls. Refrigerate 1 hour. Cut into slices. *Makes 2 dozen medium pieces.*

Prep. Time: 20 minutes,
            plus 1 hour to refrigerate dough.

COOKIE CANDY

1	stick margarine	2	teaspoons vanilla
4	tablespoons cocoa	1/2	cup peanut butter
2	cups sugar	3	cups oatmeal
1/2	cup milk		

Boil first four ingredients for 1 1/2 minutes. Remove from heat and add vanilla and peanut butter. Stir until smooth. Stir in oatmeal. Drop by spoonfuls onto wax paper. *Makes 3 dozen.*

Prep. Time: 10 minutes.

LEMON MOUSSE

5	eggs	2	cups heavy cream
1	cup sugar	1	tablespoon lemon
1	stick unsalted butter,		zest, freshly grated
	melted and cooled		fresh mint for garnish
3/4 -1	cup fresh lemon juice		
	(3 to 5 lemons)		

In large bowl, combine first two ingredients. Beat at medium speed on an electric mixer until pale, approximately 5 minutes. Beat in butter in a thin stream. Add lemon juice. Pour mixture into top of double boiler and cook over moderate heat, whisking constantly until mixture thickens, approximately 15 minutes. Transfer to medium bowl and refrigerate for 1 hour, stirring once or twice. At this point you have a luscious lemon curd. This is great on pound cake or in tart shells. Beat heavy cream until soft peaks form. Fold cream into chilled lemon mixture. Fold in zest and serve with mint sprigs as garnish. *Makes 8 to 12 servings.*

Prep. Time: 30 minutes,
            plus 1 hour to refrigerate.

MOM'S BANANA PUDDING

Banana Fofana Fe Fi Fo Fanalicious.

¾	cup sugar	1	teaspoon vanilla
4	tablespoons cornstarch	2	tablespoons butter
2 ½	cups half-and-half	3	bananas, sliced
	(or milk)		vanilla wafers
3	egg yolks		

Mix sugar and cornstarch. Add cold milk or half-and-half, and mix very well. Slightly beat egg yolks in a mixing bowl. Slowly add 1 cup of milk mixture. Pour remaining milk mixture into double boiler and heat slowly. Pour yolk mixture into warm milk in double boiler and cook on medium heat until thick. Allow to cool and stir in vanilla and butter. Layer vanilla wafers, pudding and bananas into 1 quart pan. *Makes 8 to 10 servings.*

Prep. Time: 45 minutes.

VERY RICH BANANA PUDDING

8	ounces cream cheese	1	8 ounce serving
12	ounces non-dairy		instant vanilla
	topping		pudding
1	14 ounce can	3	cups milk
	sweetened	1	12 ounce box
	condensed milk		vanilla wafers
		4	bananas, sliced

Combine the first three ingredients in a large mixing bowl. In separate bowl, mix next 2 ingredients. Fold 2 mixtures together. Crumble 1 box vanilla wafers. Alternate crumbs, sliced bananas and pudding mixture in 9 x 13 inch dish.

Prep. Time: 30 minutes.

QUICK AND EASY BANANA PUDDING

Yea! No cooking.

1	14 ounce can	3	medium bananas,
	sweetened		sliced
	condensed milk		lemon juice
1 ½	cups cold water	26	vanilla wafers
1	3 ounce package		(more if desired)
	instant vanilla		
	pudding (not mixed)		
1	8 ounce non-dairy		
	topping		

Blend together milk and water. Add pudding and mix well. Place mixture in refrigerator and cool well. Fold in non-dairy topping. Place ⅓ of pudding mixture in glass bowl. Add half of the bananas that have been dipped in lemon juice. Layer half of vanilla wafers. Repeat layers and top with remaining pudding mixture. Garnish with extra vanilla wafers if desired. *Makes 10 to 12 servings.*

Prep. Time: 30 minutes,
plus refrigeration time.

BREAD PUDDING WITH WHISKEY SAUCE

Custard:		Whiskey sauce:	
8	large eggs	8	ounces butter
1	teaspoon salt		(2 sticks), melted
2	cups sugar	2	cups powdered sugar
5 ½	cups milk	2	large eggs
1	teaspoon vanilla	1	ounce whiskey
½	pound French bread		
½	cup pecans, toasted		
4	ounces butter		
	(1 stick), melted		

Blend eggs, salt and sugar lightly with wire whisk. Add milk and vanilla. Blend and strain. Break French bread into medium pieces. Add pecans and melted butter. Arrange in 9 x 13 inch pan. Pour custard mix over bread pieces. Bake in a preheated 350° oven in pan of water for 45 minutes to 1 hour. Test with knife. For custard to bake properly, you must create this double boiler effect.

For sauce: Melt butter. Whip in powdered sugar. Fold in eggs. Add whiskey. Serve warm over bread pudding.

Prep. Time: 15 minutes.

BREAD PUDDING

1 ½	cups milk	butter
1	cup sugar	cinnamon
4	eggs	nutmeg
1	6 ounce can	
	pineapple juice	*Sauce:*
	(use ¾ of can)	½ cup sugar
2	slices bread	1 tablespoon flour
2	teaspoons clear	1 cup milk
	vanilla	2 teaspoons vanilla

Heat milk. Beat sugar and eggs. Add pineapple juice to egg mixture. Add egg mixture to milk. Remove milk/egg mixture from stove. Tear bread in small pieces and add to milk/egg mixture. Add vanilla. Pour into 8 x 8 inch pan. Drop small pieces of butter on top. Sprinkle cinnamon and nutmeg over top. Bake in a preheated 350° oven for 45 minutes, or until center becomes set. *For sauce:* Blend all sauce ingredients well. Cook over medium heat until thick. Serve over bread pudding. *Makes 6 servings.*

Prep. Time: 1 hour.

OLD–FASHIONED BOILED CUSTARD

4	eggs	1	teaspoon vanilla
⅓	cup sugar		dash of nutmeg
1	quart milk		

Beat eggs and sugar until thick and creamy. Add to milk. Stir until scalded. Do not boil. Add vanilla and nutmeg. Strain and cool. Keeps several days in refrigerator.

Prep. Time: 30 to 45 minutes.

EVERYONE'S FAVORITE VANILLA ICE CREAM

4	eggs	3	cups peaches or
1 ¾	cups sugar		strawberries
2	tablespoons vanilla		(optional)
	(more if desired)	1	pint half-and-half
⅛	teaspoon salt		(optional)
1	pint whipping cream		milk

In a large bowl, beat the eggs. Stir in the sugar and beat until mixed. Add the vanilla and salt and continue beating. Add the fruit (optional) and beat until mixed. Stir in the whipping cream and the half-and-half. Pour this mixture into a 1 gallon ice cream freezer. Fill to the fill line with milk and stir until mixed. Freeze. *Makes 1 gallon.*

Prep. Time: 20 minutes.

LEMONY VANILLA ICE CREAM

6	eggs, beaten well	1	tablespoon vanilla
3	cups sugar	1	tablespoon lemon
1	quart whipping		extract
	cream		pinch of salt
1	quart half-and-half		milk

Beat eggs well, 1 at a time until lemony colored and thick. Add sugar slowly, dissolve well by beating thoroughly. Add whipping cream and half-and-half. Add flavorings and salt. Pour into gallon ice cream freezer. If it does not come to within 2 inches from top, you may add more milk. Freeze as directed on your ice cream freezer. *Makes 1 gallon.*

Prep. Time: 30 minutes.

QUICK CUSTARD ICE CREAM

2 ½	cups sugar	1 ¼	teaspoons vanilla
1 ¼	tablespoons flour	½	pint whipping cream
2	quarts milk		
5	eggs, separated		

Mix 1¼ cups sugar and flour. Add 1 quart milk and egg yolks, well stirred. Cook over medium heat until mixture coats a wooden spoon. Do not boil. Beat egg whites until peaks form. Gradually add remaining sugar. Pour custard over egg white mixture and stir. Set aside to cool for 2 hours. This portion may be done days ahead. Store it in the ice cream freezer, in the refrigerator. Before freezing, add vanilla, whipping cream, and one quart milk. Freeze according to machine's instructions. *Makes 3 quarts.*

Prep. Time: 30 minutes.

SIX THREE'S ICE CREAM

Figure this one out!

3	cups milk		juice of three lemons
3	cups light cream		juice of three oranges
3	cups sugar	3	bananas, mashed

Combine first three ingredients, and stir until sugar dissolves. Freeze in ice cream freezer until mushy. Add fruit juices and bananas. Continue freezing until crank turns hard. Remove dasher; pack. *Makes 3 quarts.*

Prep. Time: 30 minutes.

BUTTER PECAN ICE CREAM

1	cup pecans, chopped	2	12 ounce cans evaporated milk
5	eggs		
1 ½	cups sugar	1	teaspoon butter flavor
2	14 ounce cans sweetened condensed milk	¼ - ½	teaspoon maple flavor

Roast pecans at 350° for 10 minutes. Mix eggs and sugar well. Add other ingredients and mix well. Fill ice cream freezer with above mixture and fill to the fill line with milk. *Makes 10 to 12 servings.*

Prep. Time: 20 minutes.

HOMEMADE SHERBET

6	10 ounce bottles orange soda pop	1	15.25 ounce can pineapple, crushed
2	14 ounce cans sweetened condensed milk		

Mix together and freeze in electric ice cream freezer according to instructions. *Makes ½ gallon.*

Prep. Time: 10 minutes.

STRAWBERRY ICE CREAM

4	eggs	1	10 ounce package
2	cups sugar		frozen strawberries
1	quart whipping cream		or 3 cups fresh
1	teaspoon vanilla		strawberries
1	12 ounce bottle		milk to fill
	strawberry soda pop		

Beat eggs until thick and creamy. Add sugar slowly. Beat until sugar dissolves. Add whipping cream and vanilla. Add strawberry soda pop and blend well. Add strawberries and stir well. Pour into ice cream freezer and finish filling to fill line with milk. Freeze as directed. *Makes 1 gallon.*

Prep. Time: 30 minutes.

BUTTERFINGER HUMDINGER

1	.25 ounce package	2	cups sugar
	unflavored gelatin	¼	teaspoon salt
1	cup boiling water	2	tablespoons vanilla
1	egg	8	ounces Butterfinger
3	quarts half-and-half		candy bar, chopped
	(or milk)		

Dissolve gelatin in boiling water, and set aside to cool. In electric mixer, beat egg. Add 1 quart half-and-half. Add sugar, salt, vanilla and gelatin mixture. Pour into 5 or 6 quart ice cream freezer. Add remaining 2 quarts half-and-half and candy bits. Freeze according to freezer's directions. *Makes 5 to 6 quarts.*

Prep. Time: 30 minutes.

COUNTRY PEACH ICE CREAM

1 ¾	cups sugar	½	teaspoon salt
4	eggs, beaten	5	cups fresh peaches,
4	cups milk		puréed (also may use
4	cups heavy cream		frozen)
1	teaspoon vanilla		
1	teaspoon almond		
	extract (1 ½ if needed)		

Add sugar gradually to beaten eggs. Continue to beat until mixture is very stiff. Add remaining ingredients and mix thoroughly. Pour into gallon freezer and freeze as directed. *Makes 1 gallon.*

Prep. Time: 30 minutes.

LEMON FREEZE

¾ cup corn flake crumbs
2   tablespoons sugar
¼ cup butter, melted
2   eggs, separated
1   14 ounce can
    sweetened condensed
    milk
⅓ cup lemon juice
½ teaspoon lemon peel,
    grated
3   tablespoons sugar

Combine corn flakes, sugar and butter in an 8 inch pie pan. Mix well. Remove 2 to 4 tablespoons crumb mixture and reserve for topping. Press remaining mixture evenly and firmly around sides and bottom of pie pan. Beat egg yolks until thick and lemon colored. Combine with canned milk. Add lemon juice and lemon peel. Stir until thickened. Beat egg whites until stiff. Gradually beat in sugar. Fold into lemon mixture. Pour into pan. Sprinkle with crumbs. Freeze until firm.

Prep. Time: 25 minutes,
              plus freezing time.

FROZEN LEMON DESSERT

3   eggs, separated
½ cup sugar
grated rind of 1 lemon
    (1 teaspoon)
¼ cup lemon juice
1   cup whipping cream
3   tablespoons sugar
pinch of salt
vanilla wafers
¼ cup butter, melted

Beat yolks of eggs. Add sugar, rind and lemon juice. Fold in whipping cream. Beat egg whites with sugar and a pinch of salt. Fold in. Prepare crust of crushed vanilla wafers mixed with melted butter. Place into 8 x 11 inch glass pan or 9 x 9 inch pan. Pour lemon mixture into crust and sprinkle a few crushed crumbs over top. Freeze.

Prep. Time: 45 minutes,
              plus freezing time.

FROZEN CHAMPAGNE DESSERT

Cheers to a non-alcoholic dessert.

8	ounces cream cheese	½	cup nuts (pecans or walnuts)
¾	cup sugar		
1	15.25 ounce can pineapple tidbits, drained	2	bananas, sliced
		1	12 ounce carton non-dairy topping
1	10 ounce package frozen strawberries with juice	12	coconut macaroons (see page 236)
		¼	cup butter, melted

In large bowl, mix cream cheese and sugar. In another bowl, mix pineapple, thawed strawberries, nuts, bananas and non-dairy topping. Mix gently, but thoroughly. Combine with cheese mixture. Use macaroons and butter for base in 9 x 13 inch glass dish. Pour cheese mixture on top and freeze. *Makes 15 servings.*

Prep. Time: 20 to 25 minutes, plus freezing time.

SIMPLE, BUT ELEGANT RASPBERRIES

1	cup heavy cream	½	pint raspberries, chilled (well drained, if frozen)
2	tablespoons brown sugar		
1 ½	ounces Drambuie		

Whip cream, gradually adding brown sugar. Fold in Drambuie. Fold in raspberries. Serve in iced champagne goblets.

Prep. Time: 20 minutes.

CLASSIC CHERRY COBBLER

Crust:		Filling:	
2	cups flour	2	cups sugar
²/₃	cup shortening	4	tablespoons flour
½	teaspoon salt	3	16 ounce cans sour
6	tablespoons water		pitted cherries
			butter
			sugar
			nutmeg

Mix crust ingredients well. Roll on floured surface. Cut into strips.

For filling: Mix the sugar and flour together. Add to the pitted sour cherries. Pour into 9 x 13 inch glass dish. Cover with strips of crust. Dot with butter and sprinkle with sugar and nutmeg, if desired. Bake at 400° for 30 minutes or until done. *Makes 12 servings.*

Prep. Time: 30 minutes.

EVERBEST FRUIT COBBLER
Microwave.

1	22 ounce can prepared pie filling	3	tablespoons pecans, finely chopped
½	9 ounce yellow cake mix	2	tablespoons brown sugar
¼	cup margarine, melted	1	teaspoon cinnamon

In an 8 inch round glass baking dish, spoon pie filling evenly. Sprinkle with cake mix. Pour margarine over mixture. Combine sugar, cinnamon and nuts. Sprinkle on top. Microwave on high for 9 to 11 minutes. Rotate a quarter turn halfway through cooking. Rest 10 minutes. *Makes 6 to 8 servings.*

Prep. Time: 30 minutes.

BLACKBERRY COBBLER

5	cups fresh blackberries (or other fresh fruit)	½	cup butter, softened
		½	cup sugar
		1	cup unbleached flour
¾	cup sugar	1	egg
¼	cup minute tapioca (optional)	1	teaspoon vanilla

Place fruit in a lightly greased 9 inch square baking dish. Sprinkle with sugar and tapioca. Cream butter and sugar. Beat well. Add flour and egg, mixing well. Stir in vanilla. Spoon mixture over fruit. Bake at 350° for 35 minutes or until browned.

Prep. Time: 35 minutes.

NO FAIL QUICK AND EASY PIE CRUST

1 ½   cups flour   ½   cup shortening
½   teaspoon salt   ¼   cup water

In a 10 inch pie pan, mix the flour and salt. Over a medium heat, bring to a boil the shortening and water. Pour over the flour mixture. Mix all of this well with a fork. Work with your hands and shape in the pie pan. This cannot be overworked. Be careful to press the crust out thinly in the pan. Prick and flute. Either fill and bake, or bake in a preheated 450° oven until golden brown for 10 to 12 minutes. Fill and serve.

Prep. Time: 15 minutes.

PIE CRUST

2   cups flour   pinch of salt
1   cup shortening   8   tablespoons milk

Combine flour and shortening with pastry blender (or fork) until coarse and crumbly. Add salt and milk. Stir just until blended. Do not handle more than necessary to prevent toughness. *Makes 2 pie crusts.*

Prep. Time: 30 minutes.

GRAHAM CRACKER CRUST

1   package graham   ¼   cup sugar
    crackers, crushed   ⅓   cup butter or
    (1 ⅔ cups crumbs)   margarine, softened

Crush graham crackers to a fine consistency. Combine crumbs, sugar and butter. Blend well with a fork or pastry blender. Using back of large spoon, press crumb mixture inside 10 inch pie plate to coat sides and bottom evenly. Bake at 375° for 8 minutes. Set on wire rack to cool. For no bake crust, chill in refrigerator 30 minutes before using. May freeze for ice cream pies. *Makes one 10 inch pie crust.*

Prep. Time: 15 to 20 minutes.

CREAM CHEESE PIE CRUST

| 1 | 8 ounce package cream cheese | 2 | cups flour |
| ½ | cup margarine | ½ | teaspoon salt |

Soften cream cheese and margarine. Blend together in food processor. Add flour and salt, blend. Shape into 2 balls and refrigerate overnight. Roll out next morning into a size adequate for a 10 inch pie pan. Bake in a preheated 400° oven for 10 minutes. *Makes 2 bottom pie crusts.*

Prep. Time: 15 minutes,
plus overnight refrigeration.

LEMON ICE BOX PIE

1	graham cracker crust	2	eggs, separated
½	cup lemon juice	2-3	tablespoons sugar
1	can condensed milk		

Mix lemon juice, condensed milk and egg yolks together. Pour into crust. Beat egg whites and add 2 to 3 tablespoons sugar. Beat until whites stand in a peak. Top pie with egg whites. Brown in a preheated 350° oven. *Makes 6 to 8 servings.*

Prep. Time: 15 minutes.

MAGIC LEMON MERINGUE PIE

1	baked 8 inch pastry shell, cooled or 8 inch crumb crust	Never Fail Meringue:	
		2	tablespoons sugar
1	14 ounce can sweetened condensed milk	1	tablespoon cornstarch
		½	cup water
		3	egg whites
½	cup lemon juice	⅛	teaspoon salt
1	teaspoon lemon rind, grated	½	teaspoon vanilla
		6	tablespoons sugar
2	egg yolks		

In medium size bowl combine milk, lemon juice and rind. Blend in egg yolks. Turn into cooled crust. Combine sugar and cornstarch in a small saucepan. Add water. Cook and stir over medium heat until mixture is thick and clear. Cool.

For meringue: Beat egg whites, salt and vanilla until soft peaks form. Gradually beat in sugar until stiff peaks form when beater is raised. Add cooled cornstarch mixture. Mix until blended. Spread on cooled filling. Seal to edge of crust. Bake in a preheated 325° oven for 12 to 15 minutes or until meringue is golden brown. *Makes 6 to 8 servings.*

Prep. Time: 1 hour.

CRACKER PECAN PIE

3	egg whites	1	teaspoon vanilla
1	cup sugar	1	foil pie pan, buttered
24	Ritz crackers, crushed		non-dairy topping
1	cup pecans, chopped		shaved semi-sweet chocolate for garnish

B eat egg whites; gradually add sugar. Stir in the crushed crackers, pecans and vanilla. Put in buttered pie pan and bake for 20 minutes at 325°. Do not brown or over cook. Cool. Add topping and garnish with shaved chocolate if desired.

Prep. Time: 30 minutes.

TEXAS PECAN PIE

$\frac{1}{2}$	stick butter (no margarine or blends)	3	eggs, well beaten
$1\frac{1}{4}$	cups light brown sugar	1	cup pecans, coarsely chopped
$\frac{1}{8}$	teaspoon salt	1	teaspoon vanilla
$\frac{1}{4}$	teaspoon cinnamon	1	9 inch pastry shell
$\frac{3}{4}$	cup light corn syrup		whipped cream

C ream butter and sugar. Add salt, cinnamon, corn syrup, eggs, pecans and vanilla, mixing well. Turn into pastry shell and bake at 350° for 45 minutes. Serve with whipped cream.

Prep. Time: 15 minutes.

CRUSTLESS PECAN PIE

6	egg whites	2	cups sugar
1	teaspoon baking powder	2	cups graham crackers, crushed
1	teaspoon salt	2	cups pecans

M ix the first three ingredients well. Add, at low speed, the sugar. Fold in graham crackers. Add pecans. Bake at 350° for 25 minutes in lightly greased pan. Top with whipping cream if desired.

Prep. Time: 15 minutes.

COCONUT CREAM PIE

2	baked pie crusts		Meringue:
²⁄₃	cup flour or ½ cup cornstarch	6	egg whites
1 ⅓	cups sugar	½	teaspoon cream of tartar
½	teaspoon salt	¾	teaspoon vanilla
4	cups scalded milk	12	tablespoons sugar
6	egg yolks, slightly beaten	½	cup coconut
4	tablespoons margarine		
1	teaspoon vanilla		
2	cups moist coconut		

Mix together flour (cornstarch), sugar and salt. Add milk gradually. Cook over moderate heat, stirring constantly until mixture thickens and boils. Boil 2 minutes. Remove from heat. Add ¼ of hot mix into egg yolks and mix well. Add remaining hot mixture. Cook 1 minute, stirring constantly. Add margarine, vanilla and coconut. Pour into pie crusts.

For meringue: Beat egg whites and cream of tartar. Add vanilla. Gradually add sugar. Beat until stiff peaks form. Spread over pies. Sprinkle coconut over meringue. Bake in a preheated 350° oven for 12 to 15 minutes. *Makes 2 pies.*

Prep. Time: 20 minutes.

IMPOSSIBLE PIE

¼	cup flour	2	cups milk
1 ½	cups sugar	4	eggs, beaten
½	teaspoon baking powder	½	teaspoon vanilla
½	stick margarine	1 ¼	cups coconut

Mix first three ingredients together. Add melted margarine, milk and beaten eggs. Add vanilla and coconut. Pour into a large pie plate, ungreased. Bake in a preheated 350° oven for 45 to 50 minutes.

Prep. Time: 20 minutes.

COCONUT CHESS PIE

½	cup milk	3	eggs
1 ¼	cups coconut	1	teaspoon vanilla or lemon extract
¼	cup butter	1	unbaked pie crust
1	cup sugar		

Pour milk over coconut and set aside. Meanwhile, cream butter and sugar. Add eggs to mixture and cream well, then add milk/coconut and vanilla. Pour into unbaked pie shell. Bake in a preheated 350° oven until set, approximately 45 minutes.

Prep. Time: 20 minutes.

SIMPLY DELICIOUS APPLE PIE

2	unbaked 9 inch pie shells	1	teaspoon cinnamon
¾ -1	cup sugar	1 ½	tablespoons flour
½	teaspoon salt	6	large firm tart apples
½	teaspoon nutmeg	2	tablespoons butter

Line a 9 inch pie pan with half the pastry pie shell. Mix the sugar, salt, nutmeg, cinnamon and flour in a large bowl. Peel, core and slice the apples and toss them in the sugar mixture, coating them well. Pile them into the lined pan and dot with the butter. Roll out the top crust and drape it over the pie. Crimp the edges and cut several vents in the top. Bake in a preheated 425° oven for 10 minutes, then lower the heat to 350° and bake 35 to 40 minutes more or until the apples are tender when pierced with a skewer and the crust is browned.

Prep. Time: 30 minutes.

PAPER BAG APPLE PIE

5-7	apples, peeled & sliced	1	10 ounce pie crust, unbaked
2	tablespoons lemon juice	1	stick butter
½	teaspoon cinnamon	½	cup sugar
½	teaspoon nutmeg	2	tablespoons flour

Mix first four ingredients and put in unbaked crust. Top with butter. Cut together flour and sugar, and put on top of apple mixture. Put pie in paper bag and fold up the end. On cookie sheet bake in a preheated 400° oven for 1 hour. *Makes 6 to 8 servings.*

Prep. Time: 20 minutes.

FRENCH APPLE PIE

¾	cup sugar	½	cup butter
1	teaspoon cinnamon	½	cup brown sugar
6-7	cups apples, sliced	1	cup flour
1	9 inch unbaked pie shell		

Mix sugar and cinnamon. Mix lightly through apples. Place apple mixture into unbaked pie shell. Cream the butter and brown sugar. Cut in the flour. Sprinkle this mixture over the apples in the crust. Bake in a preheated 400° oven for 50 to 60 minutes. *Makes 6 to 8 servings.*

Prep. Time: 30 minutes.

CHEESE-APPLE PIE

pastry for 2 crust pie		½	teaspoon nutmeg or cinnamon
5	cups apples, pared and thinly sliced	1	cup American cheese, grated
¾	cup sugar	3	tablespoons whipping cream
3	tablespoons flour		
⅛	teaspoon salt		

Toss together apples, sugar, flour, salt, nutmeg, or cinnamon and cheese. Put into pastry-lined pie pan. Pour cream over filling. Put top crust over filling. Bake in a preheated 425° oven for 40 to 45 minutes.

Prep. Time: 20 minutes.

CHERRY CREAM PIE

Pie:		Meringue:	
1	9 inch baked pie shell	3	egg whites
1	cup sugar	6	tablespoons sugar
1/3	cup cornstarch		
1/3	teaspoon salt		
2	cups scalded milk		
3	eggs		
1	teaspoon vanilla		
1	can (1 1/4 cups) sour pie cherries, drained		
2	tablespoons butter		

B lend sugar, cornstarch and salt. Stir in scalded milk. Cook in top of double boiler until mixture thickens. Add well-beaten egg yolks. Cook and stir for 2 minutes. Add cherries, vanilla and butter. Cool. Put in baked pie shell. Top with meringue. Bake in a preheated 350° oven for 12 to 18 minutes or until lightly browned.

For meringue: Beat egg whites and sugar until stiff peaks are formed.

Prep. Time: 1 hour.

CHERRY PIE

1	cup sugar	1/4	teaspoon almond extract
1/4	cup flour		
1/4	teaspoon salt	1	9 inch unbaked pie shell
1/4	teaspoon cinnamon		
1/2	cup milk	1/3	tablespoon margarine
juice from 16 ounce can of cherries (red, sour, pitted), reserve cherries			

O ver medium heat, mix first seven ingredients until thickened. Pour cherries into unbaked crust. Add sauce. Dot with margarine. Cover with top crust or lattice. Bake in a preheated 425° oven for 30 to 35 minutes. *Makes 6 to 8 servings.*

Prep. Time: 20 minutes.

PUMPKIN PIE

pastry for 2 pies		2	teaspoons cinnamon
6	eggs, beaten with fork	2	teaspoons ginger
		1/2	teaspoon cloves, ground
1	29 ounce can pumpkin		
		2	12 ounce cans evaporated milk
1 1/3	cup sugar		
2/3	cup brown sugar	2	teaspoons vanilla
1	teaspoon salt		

C ombine all ingredients in a large bowl. Pour into 2 deep dish pie pans. Bake in a preheated oven at 350° for 45 minutes.

Prep. Time: 10 minutes.

APRICOT PIE

1	17 ounce can		dot of butter
	apricot halves		unbaked pie shell and
½	cup sugar		top crust
1	tablespoon flour		

Put juice of fruit in saucepan. Heat to boil. Add sugar, flour and butter. Stir and cook until thickened. Pour into pie shell. Add cut-up apricots. Put top crust over pie. Bake in a preheated 350° oven for 50 to 60 minutes or until crust is lightly brown.

Prep. Time: 1 hour.

MOTHER'S CUSTARD PIE

1	9 inch unbaked pie shell	1	heaping tablespoon flour
2	large or extra-large eggs	2	cups whole milk
½	cup sugar	¼	teaspoon nutmeg, freshly grated

Beat eggs until lemon-colored. Add sugar and flour and beat well. Slowly add milk. Pour carefully into unbaked pie shell. Sprinkle with nutmeg. Bake in a preheated 450° oven for 10 minutes, then bake at 325° for 25 minutes until the filling is set and crust is done.

Prep. Time: 10 minutes.

HOMESTEAD BUTTERMILK PIE

1	10 inch pre-baked pie crust, chilled	3	tablespoons unsalted butter, melted
3	large eggs	3	tablespoons fresh lemon juice
1	cup sugar	1 ¼	cups buttermilk
⅛	teaspoon salt		
3	tablespoons flour		

In a large bowl, beat eggs until light and lemon-colored. Gradually add sugar, beating until thick. Blend in salt, flour, melted butter and lemon juice. With mixer at lowest speed, slowly add buttermilk. Pour filling into chilled crust. Bake in a preheated 350° oven for 40 to 45 minutes, or until the top is golden brown. Cool on a wire rack. Serve chilled or at room temperature. Refrigerate any leftovers.

Prep. Time: 1 hour.

BANANA SPLIT PIE

Crust:
1   stick butter
2   cups graham
      crackers, crushed

Filling:
2   cups powdered sugar
2   sticks butter
2   eggs

Topping:
1   15.25 ounce can
      crushed pineapple,
      drained
4   bananas, diced
strawberries
non-dairy topping
cherries
pecans

Melt butter and add graham crackers. Press into pie plate.

For filling: Mix powdered sugar, butter and eggs for 15 minutes. Spoon evenly into pie plate.

For topping: Spread pineapple, bananas, strawberries and non-dairy topping on top of filling. Garnish with cherries and pecans. Keep in refrigerator.

Prep. Time: 20 minutes.

WESTERN MOCHA PIE

18   Oreo cookies, crushed
1/3   cup butter, melted
1   quart coffee ice
      cream
2   squares bitter sweet
      chocolate

1/2   cup sugar
2/3   cup evaporated milk
1   tablespoon butter
whipped cream
nuts

Combine crushed cookies and melted butter. Press into 10 inch pie pan. Chill. Press coffee ice cream into pie shell. Freeze. Combine chocolate, sugar, milk and butter and cook until thick. Cool. Pour over ice cream. When ready to serve, top with whipped cream and nuts. Keep in freezer.

Prep. Time: 30 to 45 minutes.

BANANAS AND BLUEBERRIES CREAM PIE

½	cup sugar	2-3	sliced bananas
1	3 ounce package cream cheese	½	cup blueberry pie filling
1	package non-dairy whipped topping	1	prebaked pie shell, or graham cracker crust

Mix sugar with cream cheese until fluffy. Whip non-dairy topping according to package directions. Combine with cheese mixture. Cover bottom of crust with thinly sliced bananas. Pour cheese mixture over bananas. Add blueberry filling. Chill several hours before serving.

Prep. Time: 15 minutes,
          plus refrigeration time.

STRAWBERRY YOGURT PIE

1	prebaked pie shell, or graham cracker crust	½	cup strawberries, crushed
2	8 ounce strawberry yogurts	1	8 or 9 ounce container non-dairy topping

Mix yogurt, strawberries and non-dairy topping until smooth. Pour into pie shell. Refrigerate. Garnish with additional topping and whole berries.

Prep. Time: 10 minutes.

Hint: Match yogurt fruit flavor to fruit.
Follow instructions below.

Other fruits with matching yogurt:
½ *cup raspberries or blueberries, crushed*
1 *8.75 ounce can sliced peaches or apricot halves, drained & mashed*
1 *8.25 ounce can pineapple, drained & crushed*

FROZEN STRAWBERRY MARGARITA PIE

For adults only!

1 ⅓	cups graham cracker crumbs	3	tablespoons tequila
¼	cup sugar	3	tablespoons triple sec
¼	cup butter, melted	½	cup frozen strawberries with syrup, thawed
1	14 ounce can sweetened condensed milk	2	cups heavy cream, whipped
¼	cup freshly squeezed lime juice		

Combine crumbs, sugar and butter in a small bowl. Press into two 8 inch pie pan bottoms and sides. Beat milk, juice, tequila and Triple Sec in a large bowl with mixer at medium speed for 3 minutes or until smooth. Lower speed and beat in berries with syrup for 1 minute. Fold in whipped cream until no streaks of white remain. Pour into shells, mounding in center. Freeze overnight. Transfer to refrigerator 30 minutes before serving. Garnish with additional whipped cream around edge, strawberries and lime slices.

Prep. Time: 15 minutes,
        plus overnight freezing.

Hint: Might not be suitable for children.

STRAWBERRY DESSERT

6	egg whites		Pie filling:
¾	teaspoon cream of tartar	2	pints strawberries
1	teaspoon vanilla	1 ½	cups water
2	cups sugar	½	cup sugar
1	cup saltine crackers, crushed	2	tablespoons corn starch
1	cup walnuts, finely chopped		whipping cream

To make crust, beat egg whites, cream of tartar and vanilla until stiff. Gradually add 2 cups sugar. Fold in crushed crackers and chopped nuts. Bake in a preheated 350° oven for 25 minutes until cool.

For pie filling: Mash half of the berries. Mix with water, sugar and cornstarch in saucepan. Cool until thick. Let cool and add remaining berries (other half sliced). Top with fresh whipping cream. Blueberries can easily be substituted for strawberries.

Prep. Time: 30 minutes.

Good Ol' Hints

Hors D'Oeuvres

- Butter and Roquefort cheese sandwiched between pecan halves and chilled make wonderful party snacks.

- For a starter course, serve gazpacho in red or green pepper shells.

- To make Melba toast: Slice bread paper thin and place in preheated 300° oven and immediately turn the oven off. Leave until crisp.

- Large dill pickles with the center removed by an apple corer and then stuffed with cream cheese mixed with capers and parsley, is good for a cocktail snack.

- One-half pound of cheese shreds to about 2 cups of shredded cheese.

- Domestic Camembert cheese can look imported if you run it under the broiler until the cheese runs.

- When using ripe olives on a canapé tray, drain and pat dry with a paper towel. Roll in a bowl with salad oil and coat with toasted sesame seeds or instant onion.

- If you cannot find a convenient spot on your cocktail table for forks, stand them up in a goblet or vase.

- Roll slices of thin ham with cream cheese, chives and capers for a party.

- A pretty bowl of warm water and napkins are nice at the cocktail table for finger bowls.

- Cut the center out of a cabbage to serve caviar. It keeps it cool and looks pretty on the table.

- Serve snails in large pasta shells instead of their own.

- If you want your guests to spread toppings instead of dipping, place a butter knife by each bowl.

- $1/2$ to $3/4$ cups of canned fried onions and 1 cup sour cream make a fast delicious dip.

Soup

- Boiled soup is spoiled soup. Cook soup gently and evenly.

- If soup tastes too salty, a raw piece of potato placed in the pot will absorb it.

- Save leftover chicken stock for making soups, sauces and pasta. Freeze stock if to be kept longer than 3 to 4 days.

- One tablespoon of vinegar added to the cooking water will tenderize meat.

- To prevent sticking when sautéing, always add butter or oil to preheated pan.

- Salting food at the table instead of while cooking helps cut down on sodium intake.

Salad

- Lettuce and celery stay fresh longer when stored in paper rather than cellophane bags.

- Vegetables keep longer when stored on a paper towel to absorb moisture.

- To keep salad fresh for guests, wrap lettuce in paper towel and store in the refrigerator. Add dressing and tomatoes just before serving.

- Refrigerate onions before cutting to prevent teary eyes.

- Store tomatoes at room temperature for fullest flavor.

- Tomatoes cut over the bowl that they will be served in add extra flavor to a salad.

- To slice or chop an avocado: Cut avocado in half and remove seed. Using a sharp knife either slice or chop while still in shell ... without cutting the shell. Then turn the shell inside out to remove the avocado.

- Put avocado seed in guacamole to keep the dip from turning dark in color.

Eggs

- Beaten egg whites will be more stiff if one teaspoon cream of tartar is added to each cup of egg whites.

- Let egg whites reach room temperature in order to get maximum volume when beating.

- Hard-boiled eggs will peel easily when cracked if placed in cold water immediately after taking them out of the hot water.

- Do not wash eggs before storing. Washing will take away the coating that keeps bacteria out of the eggs.

- Store eggs, large end up, to maintain highest quality.

- To determine whether an egg is hard-boiled or raw, try the Cambridge Spin Test. The hard-boiled egg will spin quickly; the raw will only wobble.

Breads

- Always dissolve sugar and salt in warm water.

- Lightly-oiled hands make bread dough easier to knead.

- For quick rising bread, double amount of yeast used.

- All utensils should be room temperature for working with bread dough.

- Baking powder is still active only if it bubbles when mixed with hot water.

- Always slice quick breads when completely cool.

- Cut bread with a hot knife; it will keep its shape.

- To freshen or reheat bread, dampen with a few sprinkles of cold water, then warm in 350° oven for 10 to 15 minutes.

- For crusty breads, brush bread dough with egg whites diluted with water.

- To thaw frozen breads, wrap in foil and heat 5 minutes at 350°.

- Place a small dish of water in oven to keep crust from getting hard on bread.

Meat

- 1 ½ pounds raw shrimp makes 2 cups cooked (³/₄ pound)

- Quantity serving for 50:

Ground meat patties, purchase	14 pounds
Cold cuts, purchase	6½-8½ pounds
Hot dogs, purchase	8-10 pounds
Fried chicken, purchase	13-25 fryers

- Fresh herb bouquet for lamb consists of rosemary, parsley and celery.

- Fresh herb bouquet for veal consists of parsley, thyme and lemon rind.

- Fresh herb bouquet for beef consists of basil, parsley, bay leaf and clove.

- All meats freeze best when wrapped in heavy-duty moisture proof material to prevent drying and freezer burn.

- The primary rule of cooking pork is to cook it long enough to reach an internal temperature of 185° to ensure safety.

- To remove fish odor from hands, utensils and dish cloths, use one teaspoon baking soda to one quart of water mixture to soak or wash articles.

Oven Temperature Chart

Very slow	250-275°
Slow	275-325°
Moderate	325-375°
Hot	375-425°
Very hot	425-475°
Extremely hot	475-525°

Freezer Storage

Ground meat	2-3 months
Roasts and steaks	6-12 months
Stew	2-3 months
Hot dogs	2 months
Bacon	1 month
Pork chops	3-4 months
Ham	2 months
Pork roast	4-6 months
Chicken cooked	3-4 months
Chicken uncooked	4-9 months
Fish	2-3 months
Lobster, scallops or crab	1-2 months

Vegetables and Side Dishes

- For garnish, slice leeks, carrots and onions in several directions and place in cold water until they blossom.

- For fresher tasting frozen vegetables, do not boil them in water. Melt butter in a skillet and toss them for about 4 minutes.

- Green peppers and chilies are easier to peel if you roast the peppers in the oven until they blister. When blistered, put in a pot and cover for about 5 minutes. The steam will loosen the skins and they can be easily removed.

- When you sauté; add fresh basil to any green vegetables for a new taste treat.

- Horseradish creamed with sour cream goes wonderfully with spinach.

- Slice Brussels sprouts before cooking. They cook better and are prettier.

- When using canned vegetables, drain and remove the vegetables. Reduce the liquid by half by cooking it down. Return the vegetables and continue to cook with seasonings. They will taste better.

- To boil vegetables, use less water. One-half to 1 cup of water will take care of six servings of vegetables.

- One cup of uncooked dried beans makes 2 $\frac{1}{2}$ cups cooked beans.

- Anything that grows under the ground should begin cooking in cold water, i.e. potatoes, beets, carrots, etc. Anything that grows above the ground should begin cooking in boiling water, i.e. English peas, green beans, etc.

- To prevent water from boiling over when cooking noodles, add 1 teaspoon margarine to boiling water.

- Rice will be light and fluffy if a teaspoon of vinegar or lemon juice is added while cooking.

- To prevent a flourly taste in gravy or sauces, bake flour in a preheated 350° oven for 5 minutes.

Desserts

Chocolate:
- Bloom, the gray film that appears on chocolate, occurs when chocolate is exposed to varying temperatures. It does not affect the taste or quality of the chocolate.

- Beat hot chocolate beverages with a rotary beater until foamy to prevent formation of a skim and to enhance flavor.

- Chocolate absorbs odors from other foods. Therefore, wrap tightly and store in a cool, dry place.

- Chocolate deflates a stiffly beaten egg white mixture. So fold in carefully, just until blended.

Desserts (continued)

Chocolate:

- For chocolate curls, draw blade of vegetable parer over smooth side of a slightly warm block of baking chocolate or dark chocolate bar.

- Chocolate scorches easily. Therefore, melt chocolate in the top of a double boiler over simmering hot water, not boiling, or in a small saucepan set in a pan of hot water. High temperatures can cause milk chocolate to stiffen.

- When melting chocolate for coating and dipping candy, be sure all utensils are completely dry.

- When adding a shortening to the chocolate to make it more liquid, use only vegetable shortening, not butter or margarine.

- Add a tablespoon of brewed coffee to chocolate cakes or puddings to enhance the chocolate flavor.

- Hershey's cocoa may be used in place of baking chocolate. Three tablespoons of Hershey's cocoa plus one tablespoon of shortening or oil equals one ounce (1 square) of baking chocolate.

- Candy is best when made in a thick pan like that of a pressure cooker.

- When making chocolate cake, use cocoa instead of flour to prepare the pan.

- A potato peeler may be used to shave chocolate on ice cream, cakes or cookies.

Ice Cream:

- Use fine chunks of ice to make a smoother ice cream.

- To slow the melting of ice cream, add one tablespoon of dissolved unflavored gelatin in with milk.

Cookies:

- When freezing cookies with a frosting, place them in freezer unwrapped for about 2 hours. Then wrap without worrying about them sticking together.

- When rolling cookie dough, sprinkle board with powdered sugar instead of flour. Too much flour makes the dough heavy.

- Sponge icing cookies: Cover cookies with white icing made of a normal consistency. Make the remaining icing thinner by adding water and food coloring. Sponge onto cookies with a sponge.

- Add a piece of bread when packaging homemade cookies. The cookies will remain soft and fresh while the bread turns hard.

- Use a miniature ice cream scoop to ball cookie or candy.

- To decorate cookies with icing, cut a small hole on the top of a plastic baggie. Add icing and squeeze onto cookies like a professional.

Desserts (continued)

Cakes:

- Use dental floss to cut cheesecake neatly. Do not pull floss up through the cake, pull it out sideways.

- Slip your hand inside a waxed sandwich bag and you have a perfect mitt for greasing your baking pans and casserole dishes.

- To keep icings moist and to prevent cracking, add a pinch of baking soda to the icing mixture.

- Freeze cake before icing to prevent crust from mixing with icing.

- Occasionally check oven temperature for accuracy with a thermometer.

- Cake baking is a science. Success can be achieved by following the exact formula.

Pies:

- To prevent meringue from shrinking, make sure it touches the crust of the pie on all sides.

- Mix 1 tablespoon of cornstarch with sugar to prevent meringue for pie from weeping.

- Sprinkle pie crust with powdered sugar to keep crust from becoming soggy.

- For a flaky, light pastry, use half all-purpose flour and half cake flour.

Tips For Lowfat Southern Cooking

You can make healthy soul food. Here are tips on cutting fat and salt:

- Broil or bake instead of deep-frying. Use spiced crumb or cornmeal coating to mimic fried chicken.

- Use non-salt herb mixtures in place of salt; add onions to greens and other dishes.

- Use barbecued turkey pieces in place of ham hocks or salt pork when making greens.

- Use skim milk for corn bread.

- If you must have the pork flavor in greens, boil ham hocks or salt pork and discard meat. Refrigerate the water overnight, and skim off fat before boiling greens in the water.

- Trim all visible fat from meat.

- Use vegetable oil instead of lard for deep-frying.

- Consider barbecuing cuts of pork that are leaner than spare ribs: tenderloin (the leanest), loin chops, country-style or back ribs, loin roast.

- Don't boil all the nutrients out of greens. If you must have mushy greens, make sure to reuse the water for soup to recycle some nutrients.

Measurements

STANDARD MEASURES
(All measurements are level)

1 cup	=	8	fluid ounces	= 16 tablespoons
$^3/_4$ cup	=	6	fluid ounces	= 12 tablespoons
$^2/_3$ cup	=	$5^1/_3$	fluid ounces	= 10 tablespoons plus 2 teaspoons
$^1/_2$ cup	=	4	fluid ounces	= 8 tablespoons
$^1/_3$ cup	=	2	fluid ounces	= 5 tablespoons plus 1 teaspoon
$^1/_4$ cup	=	2	fluid ounces	= 4 tablespoons
$^1/_8$ cup	=	1	fluid ounce	= 2 tablespoons
1 tablespoon	=	$^1/_2$	fluid ounce	= 3 teaspoons
			Dash	= $^1/_8$ teaspoon

TABLE OF EQUIVALENTS

1 gallon	=	128 fluid ounces	=	4 quarts
1 quart	=	32 fluid ounces	=	4 cups
1 pint	=	16 fluid ounces	=	2 cups

Contributors

Dolores Abalos
Sharon Agnew
Mrs. Oscar Allbright
Catherine Alred
Elaine Anderson
Janet Anderson
Kim Arnold
Alissa Ashley
Letha Ashley
Barbara Atkins
Terilynn Babb
Nancy Barbour
Kim Barcena
Gaye Barclay
Amy Baker
Lynda Barker
Toni Baxter
Gerry Bearden
Angie Bell
Glenna Bell
Michelle Benish
Marcia Bennett
Diane Benson
Beverly Beranek
Eileen Sola Boehm
Lorraine Bonner
Mrs. Alfred Boudreaux
Carolyn Boyce

Frances Boyles
Bonnie Brannan
Joann Bridges
Connie Bridges
Belinda Brock
Martha Brock
Cynthia Brooke
Julie Brown
Patricia Brown
Shelly Brown
Susan Brown
Barbara Browning
Glenda Burks
Debby Casey
Eileen Carpenter
Mrs. F. Abe Caudle
Samantha Clack
Peggy Clark
Ruthann Clayton
Jamie Cleveland
Marcie Cole
Jeanette Compton
Doris Cooper
Lynn Correa
Jessica Crow
Barbara Crumrine
M. Cunningham
Carla Davis
Nadell Davis
Vicki Digby

Rachel Dobbs
Anne Doran
Denise Durell
Bobbye Durrett
Betty Stoker Elliott
Judy English
Laverne Etheredge
Debbie Fair
Chris Fannin
Anne Faulkner
Sue Faulkner
Helen Felker
Linda Felker
Jan Fisher
Carol Fleming
Lois Johns Fowler
Robert (Bob) Fox
Lydia Fox
Janet Gallogly
Shari Ganter
Jane Garza
Lyn Giesler
Rhonda Gilliam
Frances Goodall
Katy Graves
Evelyn Gray
Betty Green
Carol Gregg
June Griffith
Vicky Grimes

Pat Hankins
Elaine Hannon
Holly Hardin
Shonna Harper
Dana Harrington
Carol Harry
Lori Hart
Elizabeth Harvey
Alana Hawkins
Tammy Hawkins
Dayna Hayes
Margaret Hayes
Victor Hayes
Tammy C. Headley
Kathy Hendrick
Cathy Herzog
Karen Hildebrand
Olivia Hill
Gloria Holder
Jeanette Hollman
Paula Holloway
Narita Holmes
Janie Howell
Kendal Hudson
Susan Hunt
Kim Hunt
Kelly Hunter
Patti Hurt

Contributors

Nasreen Islam
Marta Johnson
Kimberly Johnson
Dee Ann Kauk
Georgia Kelly
Ann Kennedy
Betty Keyes
Vicki Kight
Sally Killman
Kathy King
Patty Kinnaird
Hugh Koenig
   (Odessa Fire Department,
   Central Station 'A' Shift)
Clare Kroh
Debbi Kuchinski
Cindy Kuykendall
Beverly Landgraf
Cari Langford
Renee Lanoue
Kerry Larson
Kathy Lisman
Vernon Logan
Susan Luskey
Rhonda Mareschal
Diana Massengale
Jan Maynard
Gerri Lu McAdams

Christa McClary
Margie McIlroy
Cindy McKeehan
Helen P. McMahon
Annette McMinn
Terri McWilliams
Marilynn Meek
Jerri Melton
J'Nevelyn Melton
Sharon Michie
Louise Milburn
Janet Miller
Denise Minyard
Audrey Montgomery
Jeanne Morales
Teri Morris
Carol Myrick
Norma Nagaty
June Naylor
Karen Nelson
Mary O'Hearn
Janet Oates
Teresa Owens
Diane Parker
Kim Passmore
Sue Payne
Nancy Perry
Ruth Perry
Ginny Pettey
Ruth Pickett

Lilly Plummer
Judy Potter
Velma Potter
Melinda Powell
Neysa Powell
Claudia Pratt
Reba Pritchard
Jeannie Pruett
Karilyn Pye
Margaret Rankin
Jennifer Rankin
Ethel Mae Ratliff
Sandra Reddell
Liz Roberson
Deborah Roberts
Terye Robertson
Johnna Rosson
Donna Salmon
Glenda Schneider
JoAnn Seefeldt
Katy Shelton
Suzie Sims
Edde C. Smith
Karen Snoddy
Holly Sorrells
Tracy Sterling
Cindy Stevens
Carole Stevens
Carole Stoker
Claudene Stoker

Bonnie Stubbs
Betsy Triplett
Kim Tucker
Sealy Vest
Cheryl Vickery
Joni Vincent
Aleesa Walker
Hope Walker
Regina Wehunt
Kristi White
Lori White
Marian White
Cindi Wiehle
Susie Williams
Myrna Woltz
Cathy Womack
Janet Wood
Jodie Woodward
Carolyn Yarbrough
Janice Yarbrough
Lindsay Zant

Special Thanks To:
Skaggs Alpha Beta
James Van Stavern
Gail Etheredge-
   Woods

Index

The Wild Wild West

P.O. Box 13675
Odessa, Texas 79768–3675

Please send me _____ copies of THE WILD WILD WEST!   @ $19.95 each $ _____
Texas residents add 8.25% sales tax   @ $ 1.65 each $ _____
Postage and handling   @ $ 3.50 each $ _____
Total enclosed $ _____

Mail THE WILD WILD WEST Cookbook to:

Name _____

Address _____

City _____   State _____   Zip _____

Make checks payable to: Junior League of Odessa, Inc.

- -

The Wild Wild West

P.O. Box 13675
Odessa, Texas 79768–3675

Please send me _____ copies of THE WILD WILD WEST!   @ $19.95 each $ _____
Texas residents add 8.25% sales tax   @ $ 1.65 each $ _____
Postage and handling   @ $ 3.50 each $ _____
Total enclosed $ _____

Mail THE WILD WILD WEST Cookbook to:

Name _____

Address _____

City _____   State _____   Zip _____

Make checks payable to: Junior League of Odessa, Inc.

The Wild Wild West

Please list any book or gift stores in your area that you would like to sell THE WILD WILD WEST.

Name _____
Address _____
City _____ State _____ Zip _____

Name _____
Address _____
City _____ State _____ Zip _____

Name _____
Address _____
City _____ State _____ Zip _____

Please list any book or gift stores in your area that you would like to sell THE WILD WILD WEST.

Name _____
Address _____
City _____ State _____ Zip _____

Name _____
Address _____
City _____ State _____ Zip _____

Name _____
Address _____
City _____ State _____ Zip _____